Praise for
THE ROAD *to* BURGUNDY

"Easy to read and engaging   er volume on life in Burgundy."   *Times*

"Wine lovers, Francophiles, and anyone who roots for dreamers will want to raise a glass to Ray Walker."   —USAToday.com

"An intoxicating tale. . . . Mr. Walker's story is sure to inspire a few more leaps of faith."   —*The Economist*

"*The Road to Burgundy* is an extraordinary story told by an extraordinary person set in the world's most extraordinary of wine regions. If Ray Walker's journey had been told in a work of fiction—or film—it would be, frankly, unbelievable. He set his mind to doing just about the stupidest, most difficult and unlikely thing an American could do. And emerged victorious. His story, like his wine, is a triumph of idealism, determination, and integrity. You will never drink Bordeaux again." —Anthony Bourdain

"*Salut, cin cin*, and cheers to Ray Walker, who followed his passion for wine to Burgundy. Pop a cork and enjoy this lively, brave, and absorbing story."

                —Frances Mayes, author of *Under the Tuscan Sun*

"Walker is a deft writer; as with the wines of his beloved destination, a light touch makes for a more engaging product. . . . Riveting reading. But the human side, especially the thoroughly French characters and Walker's saintly spouse, makes this an engaging account for anyone to savor on the patio or by the fireplace—a glass of wine optional but recommended."

                        —*Star Tribune* (Minneapolis)

RAY WALKER is a native Californian living in France. In 2009, Ray became the first non-French winemaker to produce a wine from Le Chambertin, generally considered throughout the past seven hundred years to be one of the best vineyards in the world. He has also been a pioneer in his use of ancient techniques in modern times and has been lauded in *The New York Times* and other publications. Ray and his wife, Christian, live in Burgundy, France, with their two daughters, Isabella and Siena.

Connect online: www.maisonilan.com

THE ROAD

to

BURGUNDY

THE UNLIKELY STORY OF

AN AMERICAN MAKING WINE *and*

A NEW LIFE IN FRANCE

RAY WALKER

GOTHAM BOOKS

GOTHAM BOOKS
Published by the Penguin Group
Penguin Group (USA) LLC
375 Hudson Street
New York, New York 10014

USA | Canada | UK | Ireland | Australia | New Zealand | India | South Africa | China

penguin.com
A Penguin Random House Company

Previously published as a Gotham Books hardcover

First trade paperback printing, June 2014

1   3   5   7   9   10   8   6   4   2

Gotham Books and the skyscraper logo are trademarks of Penguin Group (USA) LLC

The Library of Congress has cataloged the hardcover edition of this book as follows:

Walker, Ray, 1981–
The road to burgundy : the unlikely story of an American making wine and a new life in
France / Ray Walker.
pages cm
ISBN 978-1-59240-812-2 (hardback)   978-1-59240-878-8 (paperback)
1. Walker, Ray, 1981–   2. Vintners—United States—Biography.   3. Wine and wine
making—France.   I. Title.
TP547.W27A3 2013
663'.20944—dc23   2013007352

Printed in the United States of America
Set in ITC Galliard   ·   Designed by Elke Sigal

While the author has made every effort to provide accurate telephone numbers and Internet addresses at the time of publication, neither the publisher nor the author assumes any responsibility for errors, or for changes that occur after publication. Further, the publisher does not have any control over and does not assume any responsibility for author or third-party Web sites or their content.

Penguin is committed to publishing works of quality and integrity.
In that spirit, we are proud to offer this book to our readers;
however, the story, the experiences, and the words
are the author's alone.

To my Three Girls
Christian, thank you for giving to me
all that I truly Love in this world.
I always have and will forever Love you.

Isabella and Siena, I have Loved you both
since before seeing your beautiful faces
for the first time. You both fill me with such
Life, pride, energy, and laughter.

Everything you want in this world is possible.
Even your wildest Dreams may come true;
the proof is my being Loved by each of you.

THE ROAD
to
BURGUNDY

CHAPTER ONE

My bag was packed. One small black suitcase placed next to our front door. The house was still dark in the moments just before the sun would come up. There was a chill to the house, a briskness that kept me too alert for that time of morning. I tiptoed out, their trying not to awake my wife and my one-year-old daughter, Isabella. It was four in the morning, but they had just fallen asleep a short while ago. They wanted to see me off, but when their eyelids started getting heavy we had said our good-byes. Kissing my daughter's forehead and my wife's lips hours before made me realize that I would miss them the moment my hand touched my luggage. "Good luck, honey," said Christian. She'd said it a million times to me before that moment. She'd said it before my meetings with potential clients, before starting on a long drive, before any task that required strengthened resolve. But this time was different. I wouldn't hear her voice in person for another three months.

I shut the door quietly behind me and felt surprisingly calm. I knew my family was safe. And I knew that while I was entering into a situation filled with endless possible outcomes, I was undoubtedly walking toward a much brighter future.

Until now, every part of my life had been in the United States. Everyone I knew was here, the boundaries of my experiences were defined by this country. I only thought about *going* to France, not of *leaving* California. It was as if I had closed my eyes on the flight up to altitude only to notice how high we actually were above ground just as I was leaping from the airplane. Suddenly, I was feeling more excited than ever before. While planning everything leading up to this moment, I never gave into this feeling. I worried that it might jinx it. But the moment was finally here, and once I got into the car taking me to the airport, there would be no turning back. I would be calling Burgundy home.

As the driver pulled away from the curb I prattled manically about the turn of events that put me on this path—wine, history, movies, learning French, the possibility that every aspect of my family's life was changing during that car ride.

"You know, I'm from Brazil," he said. "I came here with a dream as well. I'm a musician but I also own this shuttle company. My friends at home were telling me that it would be tough on me and my family. But I believed that what I felt in my heart was the right thing. And that this feeling was best for my family. I'm sure it'll work out for you."

His words echoed the sort of mantra that had been playing on repeat in my brain for the past eight months. Hearing it spoken aloud by somebody else made me feel better about the giant leap of faith I was about to take.

Arriving at SFO, I found the Air France desk and queued behind a young French couple with their young daughter. I leaned in toward them, hoping to make out a bit of their conversation and hoping to validate my months of studying. I'd stayed up late every night watching old French movies and reading antiquated books about Burgundy. Now, eavesdropping as best I could, I celebrated a small victory every time I caught a word or phrase I understood.

This was the first time I'd be going on an international flight by myself. Gone was the fuss of getting Bella situated with toys and videos and other distractions, or helping Christian get her carry-on in the overhead bin. I was traveling light—just a few pairs of jeans, some T-shirts, and a wallet that had seen fuller days. Practical, yes, but perhaps more so if I'd also packed some formal winemaking training or experience beyond one brief harvest in California. Or maybe a location to produce wine. Or tools, equipment, the basics. Barring that, even having a place to live once I got to France would have been nice. That, or grapes. Or a visa. But this was my last chance. It was the only chip I had left. Failing in Burgundy would mean going back to a life that wasn't mine. It would mean working on someone else's time, for someone else's dream. There's no way I could go back to sitting at a desk hemmed in by monitors and memos and bad coffee, suits and ties, and central air; not after I'd gotten a taste of freedom.

I got comfortable and closed my eyes, but opened them again when I noticed the woman next to me needed help lifting her bag above our seats. Jumping up to help her I accidentally elbowed the headrest of the guy in front of me. "*Je m'excuse, pardon.*" It seemed like every passenger turned around to see who was recklessly destroying the grace of their language.

"You're American?" the woman's husband inquired. "You speak . . . lovely French."

"Really? It's not too bad?"

He offered an even wider smile, but saying nothing, glanced nervously at his wife as she sat down between us. "What are your plans in France?"

"I'm going to Burgundy," I answered, a bit relieved we were switching tracks from praising my clearly subpar mastery of his language.

"Burgundy?" he said. "Why not Paris?"

"Well, Paris is nice, but they don't have any wine."

"And what do you know about Burgundy?" the man and woman seemed to ask at the same time.

"I can't say that I know a lot, but I love Burgundy enough to change my life for it."

"We're from Champagne. It is quite close to—"

"Of course I know Champagne!" I explained that my wife and I had traveled there just months before with our baby girl. It was just over two hours away from Burgundy, but at the same time, they were worlds apart. To my mind, the fussy estate-riddled Champagne lacked the grounded, rich, agriculture-centric culture of Burgundy, but even I knew better than to say so.

"That's not a bad place to live!" I said, making my envy apparent to even those a few rows over from us. I might not have wanted to make wine there, but you couldn't beat the scenery.

"Burgundy is beautiful as well. Have you been?"

"Just once. I went there with my family earlier this year, in January."

"So, you will be living in France? In Burgundy?"

"Well, that's the plan. Well, actually, I don't really have a plan, but that's where I would like it all to end up."

"Oh, well, we must speak more French then. You need to practice right away. That is"—she looked at the *Wine Spectator* on my lap—"unless you are too busy."

"No, I'm not busy at all," I said, throwing my magazine under my seat as if I were in grade school and clearing the baseball cards off my desk before the teacher came back into the classroom.

For the rest of the flight we spoke in French. We exchanged thoughts about wine, food, their life in Champagne. I loved watching how alive they were when they spoke, so animated. Their eyes would open in excitement or for emphasis only to close narrowly to convey the gravity of a pronouncement. "You must visit the market on Saturday! [eyes wide] And then be sure you try the Époisses. [eyes narrow]" Their hands too said nearly as much as their lips did—opening, closing, widening, waving above them, or tightening down to a point with a finger pressed into their lap tray. I'd try to mimic the fluidity, repurposing their words in an attempt to learn more nuanced expressions. They were patient and kind, and seven hours later, we'd learned an incredible amount about one another, perhaps to the chagrin of those trying to sleep around us. The ease I felt in speaking with them erased much of my nervousness. They weren't "French" people waiting for me to slip up on a French word, they were just good people.

THE CUSTOMS OFFICER ASKED WHY I was visiting the country.

"*Monsieur, votre raison de visite?*"

"*Uh, pour le vin.*"

"*Le vin?*" He looked at me thinking I misunderstood his question. "*Monsieur*, why have you come to France?"

"For the wine. I want to make wine in Burgundy."

He looked at my passport.

"See, it says you are from California." He looked over his desk and saw my shorts. "They have wine in California, *non?*"

"Well, yeah," I said. "But it's different."

"Of course it's different, but there is good *terroir* in California too. Napa Valley."

Here I was, arguing on behalf of Burgundy terroir to a Frenchman, who was in turn defending the merits of California wines.

"Look, I understand that there is terroir in Napa and Sonoma, and everywhere else, but I feel connected to Burgundy." My fist was tight, pointer finger jabbing into the custom officer's desk.

He had a much more serious look on his face now and paused. I was beginning to worry that he wouldn't let me through when he grinned widely and said, "I'm just giving you a hard time. Good to see that you have your convictions. You will need them in Burgundy."

I was worried about missing my train, a TGV express that wouldn't stop until Dijon, a historically important city just twenty minutes outside of Beaune, the spiritual center of Burgundy. There were two trains waiting at the platform when I jogged up, both headed south, though neither was marked with the number that was on my ticket. A woman walking by could clearly see that I was lost, and when I told her my destination, she pointed me toward one of the trains.

I ran to where a station worker was collecting tickets.

"*Monsieur, c'est pas votre train. Votre train, il est là,*" he said, motioning to the other train across the platform.

"*Pardon?*" In my confusion I switched to English: "I was told—"

"*Monsieur, je ne parle pas anglais. Je suis français,*" he said with a bored calm, without taking the time to look at me. Instead he focused on a box of matches that he manipulated between his fingers as he spoke.

"*Est-ce que vous êtes sûr, c'est mon train là-bas?*"

"*Oui. C'est correct.*" He rolled his eyes before turning his back to me.

"*Merci, monsieur!*"

I climbed aboard, found a seat in a relatively empty car, and settled in for the brief one-and-a-half-hour ride that would take me straight to Dijon without any stops. At long last, I could get some sleep.

I moved around a bit in my seat, nearly contorting myself into a fetal position, with the immovable armrest digging into my ribs. It would have to do. I reached toward the window to pull down the shade, but an old woman sitting at the other end of the train car began snapping her fingers at me, gesturing to not touch the window. I could have pleaded with her, pointed to my painfully red eyes, but I was too tired to argue.

The train sped on, rushing through town after town. I tried squinting to catch a glimpse of one of the tiny white signs to see where we were, but it went by too quickly. There was a constant flash of green that shot past the frame of the window with churches, farmhouses, and picturesque villages huddled together on a stone-encrusted outcrop; horses lazily standing on hillsides; or bored cows watching the day pass. At times a jolt of yellow sunflowers would shoot by in a chaotic flash of color. Then the green would slam back into the frame.

Whoosh! There went another village. Stone buildings, bell tower of a church, post office. *Whoosh! Clank clank clank!* Curtains of darkness would sweep over the train as we tucked under overpasses, violently shooting out the other side, the whine whistling over the metal skin of the coach. It would be eerily serene for a few brief moments before *whoosh!* We came blasting out the other side like we were coming out of a rifle's barrel.

After what seemed like the fifteenth tunnel and thirtieth clank and after I'd made several attempts to pull the window blinds down only to be caught by the old lady and her snapping fingers, I decided again to get some sleep. Every so often, I would stir and see that we were in another tunnel, or over another bridge, but because there were no announcements about our impending stop, I'd go back to sleep. But then I realized: *Wait. Another bridge? Where the hell was I?* I didn't remember anything about several bridges. I sat up, dislodged the armrest from my spleen, and grabbed frantically for the bent-up tickets in my pocket. I rushed over to another passenger, but I couldn't find a single word in French to explain my problem.

"We *are* going to Dijon, right?"

"*Quoi?*"

"Dijon. *Nous sommes . . . allons . . . Dijon?*"

"*Ah, oui, Dijon,*" he said, nodding.

"We are going to Dijon?" I figured if I repeated it enough he might magically start understanding. Being from California, I had a choice in high school to learn either French or Spanish. I wish I had the choice to make again.

"*Ah, non.* We are going to Provence; it is beautiful there. Have you been?"

"Oh, no, I haven't been." I started to turn back to my seat. "Wait, did you say Provence? Like the south of France?"

"Yes."

"Um, look, I'm sorry, I think I made a mistake. I'm on the wrong train. When is the next stop?"

"This is a TGV. It doesn't stop until Provence."

Another village zipped by in a blur. He brought over a map.

"We are here," he said, pointing toward the bottom of the

map. And about halfway up the page, "this is Dijon." Beaune was now hours behind us.

With no scheduled stops until the very south of France, I had to let it go. It was just a part of the journey. And what would a journey be without a few sidesteps? The guy with the map excused himself to go to the dining car and came back with two of his friends and a few beers to cheer me up. We spent the rest of the ride to Provence laughing, talking about wine, and California—though they were a little disappointed that I didn't actually know anything about surfing.

By the time we'd reached our stop it was the afternoon, and the sun looked like a glowing orange floating above the rolling hills of the countryside. I had a few minutes to stretch my legs before the next train going to Dijon came roaring up from the other direction. I'd be in Burgundy just in time to see the sun set over the vineyards.

CHAPTER TWO

THE CEILING GAVE AWAY HOW OLD THE BUILDING WAS, ITS wooden beams coated in chipping varnish; light from the room above could be seen through the thin boards they supported. The floors were brick-colored marble, smoothed over by time and so much traffic in such a tiny place. The light from the candles on each table reflected off the yellowed imperfections of the stucco walls, casting dancing shadows on the signed black-and-white photos of famous Italian, French, and American entertainers. The room was ringing with the kind of laughter and chatter that can only follow a good meal, and whatever space wasn't filled by joy was made up for with 1950s Italian jazz.

Just days before, Christian and I had arrived in Venice under the guise of a simple vacation, but I had something more special in mind. She was twenty-six, taller than average, the portrait of exotic beauty. She had large honey-brown eyes, curly light-brown hair, and a hell of a sense of humor. And in spite of all that, she loved me enough to laugh at my jokes and didn't mind that my one plan in life was to be happy.

I'd met Christian at San Francisco State University. She was finishing up a degree in psychology just as I was dropping out as a junior. After finishing school she went on to work for nonprofits before becoming a probation officer. I was majoring in business but didn't see the point in delaying the inevitable, which was working for my parents' real estate business. Christian couldn't believe someone would throw away the opportunity for education, but I was adamant that studying business was a waste of time when I could actually be *doing* business. It wasn't that I particularly loved the idea of this line of work—I most likely would have been a liberal arts major had it sounded more impressive to my parents— but I appreciated the rational merits of putting your head down and making a living. I thought it was what it meant to be an adult, a man. I figured it was time to grow up and forget about dreaming and instead, learn how to make money.

But then again, I'd never been the one who was good at planning. I tended to get lost in the clouds with grand plans and "someday" schemes, while Christian kept me tethered to the ground and embraced a life that was neat and organized. Christian had seen enough turmoil in her life and now she wanted something steady and secure. And so on New Year's Eve, four years after we first met, standing in the cold under the bell tower of Venice's Piazza San Marco, I proposed. Her resounding yes filled me with a new desire to go after everything that I wanted in life. Whatever it took, I'd risk it if it meant the happiness of my new fiancée.

Christian and I were a study in opposites, and our opinions about wine were no exception. Growing up in the San Francisco Bay Area, I was well aware of the wine culture in my backyard. But it never really spoke to me. My parents didn't drink the stuff when I was younger—it was for rich people and snobbish wannabes. Come to think of it, they didn't drink much at all. If anything, they'd have a glass of Champagne on New Year's Eve or a random beer in the summer. They did start drinking wine when I was older, but I was already in my twenties and convinced that it was just an inefficient way to get drunk. Besides, how good could wine really be if it had the same ingredients as Welch's grape juice?

While Christian had taken trips to Napa Valley and tasted wines from Beaulieu Vineyard and Robert Mondavi Winery, my experience was limited to the four-dollar bottles you bought at the supermarket. And to me, there wasn't any difference between them.

Once when we were dating I cooked her a special meal for Valentine's Day. I'd made us a couple of beautiful steaks and couldn't have been more proud of the job I'd done. Wine wasn't my thing, but I knew the joys of a perfect steak.

"The food looks great," she'd beamed. "What are we having to drink with it?"

I thought it was a curious thing to ask, but I rushed over to the refrigerator.

"All right, we have orange juice, white cranberry, or apple."

"Is . . . that all?"

"Well, there is always water."

She'd opted for water but pointed out that wine would have gone great with the steaks and would make the meal even more special. All I could think was, *Why would you want to drink while you're eating?* I drank beer once in a while, never with food though. I ate because I was hungry, not because I wanted a buzz. But beer made sense to drink with a meal. It was refreshing, simple. Wine? Warm red wine sounded disgusting to me. And I didn't like that you had to drink it out of a fancy, breakable glass.

I hated watching people with their pinky shooting out, as though the more pretentious you looked holding your wine, the more you appreciated it. Nope, wasn't for me.

"I can grab a wine next time," was all I'd said. But I never did. And, when we would go to dinner parties, I would be the only one not drinking wine. I tried a few, but the whites were always freezing cold, bitter and watery, and the reds were too warm, bitter, and nauseatingly alcoholic. Embarrassed, sometimes I'd spend the whole night just holding a full glass or cup to stop anyone from trying to pour me more.

So when I chose Italy as the place we'd get engaged, I wasn't even thinking about the wine. Christian, on the other hand, couldn't have been more excited to drink in the pleasures of Italy's wine regions. She mooned over Chiantis, Barolos, and Barbarescos and even got me to try a couple of glasses, but I wasn't convinced that it was anything to get excited about. Spaghetti e vongole, pungent white truffles from Alba, carpaccio di manzo on the other hand—now *those* I could get behind. The food in Italy had such emotion and color, and one authentic Italian kitchen could spread its perfume across a whole neighborhood.

After Venice we went to Florence, where we'd spend the remainder of our trip. Our first night there we'd asked the hotel's concierge where the best place to eat was, and without hesitation he told us about a trattoria that wasn't to be missed. Each day that week, sometimes in the afternoon, and often in the evening, we'd walk by the corner where it stood, only to find a closed-up, lifeless restaurant. But on our last night, while taking a stroll around the neighborhood, we both smelled an aroma so seductive it could have been only home-cooked Italian cuisine. My mind shot to the image of an elderly grandma somewhere stirring the heavenly contents of an old family heirloom pot with a gnarled wooden spoon.

We turned the corner moments later to find the trattoria filled with people, all of the windows fogged up, and a small line dribbling out the front door and onto the abandoned street. We were hoping for a quick meal so we could get to bed early in preparation for our early flight, but no food that smelled like *that* could be worth missing. We hopped in line, hoping to get a last-minute table, and after forty-five minutes, we were seated at a tiny table crammed between two others. Two wineglasses were waiting for us, and before I could even take off my jacket, a waiter came by to fill them. He hadn't asked if we wanted any; it was simply understood that this was as essential to enjoying one's dinner as silverware and a plate. I figured it had to at least have been drinkable because everyone else in the restaurant looked to be ordering twice as much wine as they were food.

The wine had a pretty, strawberry-flesh color to it and it smelled intensely of fruit, herbs, and smoke. It didn't smell obnoxiously of alcohol, as I'd come to expect. Instead, it effortlessly blended in with the aromas of the restaurant. I took a sip. The taste was pretty straightforward—it was pleasant, fruity, and had a brightness to it that made it refreshing. Where was the great mystery? Surely this wasn't why men outfitted in smoking jackets, engraved gold pocket watches, and sterling-tipped walking canes huddled into small, cigar-scented, wood-paneled rooms studying wine while discussing life and politics. There wasn't anything overwhelming to dissect. The purpose—to my delight and surprise—was simply to enjoy it.

When the food came out, I was nervous that somehow my glass of wine would taint it. The dishes were simple Florentine staples that housewives had been preparing for their families as long as history could chart—handmade pastas; wine-braised meats; and local produce cooked down, drizzled in olive oil, and sprinkled with fresh herbs. I watched the other diners to try to understand the rhythms of their meals. They were talking, laughing, chewing, and sipping, all in fluid succession, and the wine was like a glue that held that entire experience together. I took a bite of my spaghetti, working the tender noodles and rich tomato, herb, and olive oil sauce around in my mouth, and then swished with a sip of wine. It was alchemy. The wine brightened the savory nuances of the food, and the food deepened the fruity flavor of the wine.

I waited for some smart-assed remark about wine-swilling snobs to come to mind, but it never came. I'd spent my entire life assuming that wine wasn't meant for people like me—that it was too exclusive, expensive, or just plain old bad tasting. But instead, something stirred inside of me. My brain went back to the time when I was growing up in Northern California and my family would go camping in the summers in Guerneville, in the Russian River Valley. One of my favorite memories had been driving there in my dad's old Toyota pickup truck, looking out at the huge expanse of vineyards. I'd crane my neck out of the window, balmy air bathing my face, and breathe in the smell of soil. I'd train my eyes on the horizon to try to spot the place where the never-ending rows ended, but I could never manage to see past the seam of sky and vines. I'd forgotten how happy that flickering image made me feel, and now suddenly I was back in the moment, as though time had held its breath for me.

"Are you Americans?" The man sitting next to us jerked me back into reality. "Yup," I said, figuring he had caught us doing something uncouth and was now calling us out on it. I had overheard them speaking French and assumed—as I'd never met anyone from that country—that they were sophisticated, well cultured, and potentially thought the opposite of us. But he looked genuinely interested in chatting.

"And you?" I asked. "Where are you guys from?"

"Paris," the woman sitting across from him responded, her eyes and lips smiling while she pouted out a billow of smoke. "I am Patricia, and this is my husband, Jean-Luc."

"Tell me, what do you think of the wine?" Jean-Luc asked, leaning ever farther across our tables, his hand clutching the base of his glass.

"Amazing," I said, looking at the glass. It *was* amazing wine. And really the best wine I had tasted during our entire trip to Italy. But was it really the best or was it just a neophyte's excitement?

"One of the best wines I've had," Jean-Luc said, Patricia agreeing. I relaxed a bit, then stiffened again—if the French guy was saying it was that good, then this was going to be an expensive night. Our trip was almost over, but our budget had taken a serious blow with my sudden, inexplicable addiction to the heavenly, soft as clouds creamy Italian pastries and densely flavored forest-green pistachio gelato. Whatever the price of the wine, though, I figured it had to be worth what they were charging.

Over the course of the next couple of hours we talked, laughed, ate, and sipped, our tables inching closer and closer together. More beautiful, soulful dishes appeared from the kitchen, and, magically, our glasses never emptied. Our conversation snaked from topic to topic, never allowing for dull or quiet moments. To our delight we disagreed about most things, which made the conversation that much better.

I'd never done anything like this before. Growing up on the east side of the San Francisco–Oakland Bay Bridge, there were just four of us—me; my mother, Linda; father, Dan; and my older brother, Richard. We moved a lot throughout my childhood. I was born in Berkeley but spent a lot of years moving between Oakland, Hayward, El Cerrito, San Pablo, Castro Valley, and Hayward yet again right before high school. My parents were kids of the 1950s. They were poor, but their lives were unbelievably rich in other ways. Growing up hearing of all the freedom and tight bonds they had in their small communities made me feel like I was somehow missing out on living in a real neighborhood, where kids got together and played and the neighbors would yell at you and tell your parents if you were acting up. While I was growing up, neighbors pretty much kept to themselves. Both of my parents had worked hard since before they were teenagers: my mother in sales, the same with my father, who eventually moved into finance. We weren't consistently middle class; we struggled quite a lot, but we didn't want for anything either. Working in real estate brought you feast or famine. It was instilled in me at an early age that if you want to have something of your own in life, you needed to put in the work to obtain it. My grandmother was known for saying, "You either rust out or wear out," and I wasn't going to live my life with rust on me.

Meals at my house were utilitarian. Food was simple and easy to prepare, quick. It was for sustenance. So long as nothing was burned, dried out, oversalted, or partially raw, we didn't think much more about it. At six years old, I remember using the world's sharpest steak knife to saw on a thin, dried piece of bison leather that supposedly had once been a rib eye of some sort. There was no such thing as eating for pleasure; you ate so you wouldn't be hungry—simple as that. But here I was, at the end of a nameless cul-de-sac in Florence, eating food good enough to make me feel just a bit guilty, drinking flashback-inducing wine, and laughing at jokes in a language I'd never heard before. And despite how unlikely it may have seemed, it felt like home.

Three hours later and we were the only ones left in the place. The waiter glided past, placing our bill on the table. I reached in for the check, fearing the worst. Flipping it over, I imagined the very real possibility that I'd have to wash dishes to work off this meal, leaning on an old sink while someone yelled at me, "Hurry up, you cheap American!" in Italian. I sobered up as best I could and squinted to make out the tiny black handwriting on the slip of paper:

2 Cena (dinner) 30€
3 Vino (wine) 12€

I couldn't believe it. *Twelve euros? For wine? For three bottles of wine?!* I considered messing with Christian, leading her on to think I'd have to spend the night scraping meat sauce out of pots while she found her own way back to the hotel. Then again, there was no sense in spoiling what had been, truly, the perfect evening in Florence.

We hugged Jean-Luc and Patricia good-bye, genuinely sad to be parting ways. Then we bought a bottle of the wine to take back with us to California. It wouldn't ever taste the same as it did that night, but I'd be able to remember every detail of it.

CHAPTER THREE

"WHAT'S THIS ONE CALLED?" ASKED CHRISTIAN. SHE WAS holding her bulbous glass to the light while swirling. Garnet flecks shimmered on her face.

"Château Lynch-Bages 1999. It was classified as a fifth growth in 1855, but it is known to be just as interesting as those classed at the second growth level," I smugly quipped, then made a show of burying my nose deeply inside of the glass. I anxiously swirled my glass too, hoping to encourage it a bit.

"Oh," she said, after taking a few sips. "Well, what do you think?" She was wearing her best poker face, but it still didn't do much to hide her verdict.

I shrugged. "Um, I guess it's all right. I don't know. I can't say I am enjoying it. But it's supposed to be a good wine from a historically successful château in Bordeaux."

"Do you like it or not?" I knew her answer.

". . . No, I can't say that I do."

Falling into laughter, she said, "It's pretty bad. I'm sorry, I know you wanted to like it."

AFTER WE GOT BACK FROM Italy, my interest in wine quickly became an obsession. I bought a tasting wheel that helped match grape types with the common aromas, colors, and flavors associated with them. It was supposed to be for beginners, but I couldn't make heads or tails of it. I splurged on expensive crystal glasses for every grape type, the philosophy being that the shape, size, even the curve of the lip affects how and where the wine hits your tongue. And you can't have crystal glasses without fine crystal decanters or decorative corkscrews or handy suction devices that can reseal the bottles, can you? What about a special funnel that spits wine out in a hundred directions to hyperaerate it? I had that too. I spent all my free time scouring the Internet, looking for other wine geeks like me. I eavesdropped on cyber conversations on wine bulletin boards about things like vineyards, classifications, and the characteristics of wines everyone enjoyed drinking, then shoehorned these phrases and tidbits into my own parlance when it came time to strike out on my own and choose what to buy.

The vocabulary of people who drank wine was so foreign to me. Attack, weight, presence, finish, extraction, depth, and palate all had new meaning. So many questions whizzed through my mind. Why was one vintage considered successful? How could you measure the length? How could a wine taste completely different after time, after doing nothing more than sitting in a bottle? Did wine basically go bad over time and some people liked the taste of spoilage more than others? What were natural wines? Why did some wines earn more points? Why didn't I like the wines that received glowing reports from professional critics? Did

I just not get it? What exactly did a wine of quality taste like? Absolutely none of it made any sense, so I just took all of it in.

I'd fallen hard in Italy, and once I got back to the States I searched in earnest for the Holy Grail. I figured if you were going to drink wine, then your goal should be to drink the best. And after weeks of research, every reference brought me to the same place: Bordeaux.

Bordeaux, France, is home to some of the most celebrated wines in the world. With names like Château Haut-Brion, Château Margaux, Château Latour, Château Lafite, and Château Mouton-Rothschild, it all smacks of prestige, excellence, and affluence. Pictures of the Bordeaux countryside reveal enormous, lavish estates, and you can just imagine the people inside—the men in ascots, the women in furs, all quaffing from their crystal goblets and congratulating one another on their latest acquisition of jets/yachts/small islands. But it's not all pomp; these wines are critics' darlings. The bottles can go for tens of thousands of dollars. And they've been celebrated for literally centuries. How could the wines not be amazing? Described as woody, supple, smoky, spicy, refined, chewy, truffled—and those were just the reds. And I read they can age for decades, whatever that meant. If you're a serious wine aficionado, you drink wine from Bordeaux.

Or so I thought. The only problem was I didn't like it. To be fair—namely because of the daunting price tag on most Bordeaux—I was doing more reading than I was drinking. But every time I'd bring one home, I hoped that this one, *this* one, would be *the* one, the wine that turned on the same switch that the one in Florence did. And it never was. I thought I was doing everything right—we tried older bottles, younger bottles, decanting, serving right after opening, serving under room temperature, and serving above room temperature. I would read countless articles and reviews on a given bottle, then deliver a thirty-minute dissertation to Christian about why it should be so great, starting off with "It's one of the most nuanced in this region" or "Everyone says this should be the most feminine," without a hint of irony. I'd go on to spout facts about the land it came from, which grapes went into the blend, details about its fermentation, the château's philosophy, and the weather patterns during growing season. I made sure we had the right glasses and, of course, the right food, like slow-roasted lamb or a huge, juicy rare steak, then we'd huddle around the bottle with anticipation, as I'd ceremoniously remove the cork. As the wine blossomed in the glasses, a concentrated aroma would fill the room. We would gently rotate our wrists just so as we swirled our glasses, which I'd read would aerate the wine after it sat in a bottle largely deprived of oxygen, so it would "open" and release all its fragrance and flavor. Then we'd lift the glasses to our noses. With closed eyes we'd inhale, then press the thin rim to our lips and allow the tiniest stream to trickle over our tongues. Moments would pass before I would ask, "So, honey, what do you think?" The answer was always the same: "Oh, it's nice." The remaining three-quarters of a bottle would find its way down the sink or, desperate to get our money's worth, we'd grudgingly drink the majority of it.

It didn't make sense. First of all, these wines were inky black, smelled of mildewed wood, over-ripened prunes, and rubbing alcohol, and tasted bitter. I couldn't see how drinking them was supposed to be even remotely pleasurable. Was a great wine taster someone who could hold a straight face for the longest amount of time before spitting the wine out all over his white silk ascot? Plus, weren't wines made from grapes? Shouldn't they taste more like, well, fruit? The older Bordeaux were easier to taste because some of the bitterness had aged away. But they still tasted like roasted fruit that had spices dumped on it. Some even tasted like ash from a cigar.

I had trouble reconciling that these wines are supposed to be the best in the world. The more I read about them, the more convinced I became that *I* was doing something wrong. Stellar Bordeaux reviews were splashed across almost every issue of *Wine Spectator* and just about every gentleman's magazine. These were wines that seemingly anyone could appreciate so long as they had a palate more evolved than a goat's. Maybe I was too young or just not refined enough to appreciate what was obvious greatness.

The solution hit me in a flash of inspiration: I didn't just need to try more Bordeaux; I needed to try more *expensive* Bordeaux! Up until now I'd been buying budget-friendly bottles of moderately priced Bordeaux, but according to my research, the expensive ones expressed more of the unique qualities of the region. I wasn't so sure I agreed, but if people were willing to shell out hundreds of dollars for just one bottle, then I figured there had to be more to it than what I'd tasted. Because Christian loved wine, I thought she'd be on board. Besides, most of the Californian wines that she had liked were from the Napa Valley, made from Cabernet Sauvignon and Merlot, and many Bordeaux were made with these same grapes. I felt certain we'd eventually find some that we liked.

"We should buy more expensive wines, and we should also put some away for a while so we can see how we feel about them in a few years."

Christian gave me a look similar to the time I told her I wanted to do all the roof repairs to our house myself.

"Put them away where? In our lavish cave under the mansion? Makes sense, but should we put them in the main house or the country house?" she said mockingly. "Seriously, why buy more only so we can hate them just as much in ten years?"

"Well, maybe by then we'll have learned to like them . . ." Even I could hear how ridiculous that sounded.

"All right. I'll make you a deal. Let's go to a wine tasting to get some experience with some of these expensive Bordeaux. If we find some we like, we can buy them."

But I didn't want to wait. I wanted to buy wines from the more famous producers now to see what the fuss was about. "These wines are some of the best in the world; if we wait too long there may not be any left at good prices!"

"Huh? Ray, how many bottles do they make in a regular year?"

"It can't be too many, one sec," I said, rushing to get my laptop to confirm just how quickly we needed to act. "I wouldn't be surprised if some of the recent vintages have already sold out locally—"

But there it was, the case productions of Bordeaux's top wines:

Château Haut-Brion—11,000 cases
Château Lafite—20,000 cases
Château Latour—18,000 cases
Château Margaux—12,000 cases
Château Mouton-Rothschild—17,000 cases

Christian crossed her arms, slowly rolling her eyes, the universal miming of "I told you so."

"OK," I said, defeated. "I'll go to the tasting."

I dragged my feet all the way to The Wine Club in San Francisco. Christian had done all the heavy lifting—sussing out a tasting nearby, driving us there—because I was petulantly resisting. In my mind, a wine tasting at a store was like drinking wine with training wheels on. By now I considered myself a wine geek, an aficionado. I could spout off any number of mind-numbing facts about vintages, soil types, fermentation techniques, and different grape characteristics. I didn't need someone walking me through how to like one of the undisputedly best wines in the world. I also supposed that part of me was somewhat worried. What if I just flat out didn't like Bordeaux wines? Would that mean I couldn't be a serious wine geek?

At first glance The Wine Club didn't look like much, much less a wine shop. It was housed in a small building with a nondescript painted brick exterior and didn't have a single window. It could just as easily have been a bait and tackle shop or a place to get bail bonds. Inside it was closed in and musty, like someone's cluttered garage. The inventory had bulged well beyond the few neat rows of shelves in the middle of the store, so whichever cases of wine weren't precariously stacked ceiling-high were strewn randomly around the space.

I didn't have much to compare it to; it was my first time in any wine shop. Until then I'd bought wine online, thinking I had a better shot of getting exactly what I wanted without having to go to an actual store to see what they had lying around. But I kind of liked the organized chaos of the cozy space. There was nothing pretentious or inaccessible about it. Inexpensive "staff picks" rubbed elbows with rare gems from some of the best producers in the world. Many of the boxes had handwritten notes taped on to them:

N.V. Billecart-Salmon Rosé

Fresh, lovely body, floral, beautiful red fruits and a persistent finish. This is one of our staff's favorites. Try one and you'll see why!

Calera Jensen
Pinot Noir 1996

California's slice of Burgundy, resting on an abundance of limestone typically only found in the French region. Lovers of precision, minerality and balance should look no further. Rocky, red and black fruits, floral. Drinking well, but can age if given the time.

Château Haut-Brion 2002

Long considered to be one of the finest estates in Bordeaux, this has proven to be one of the world's elite. Up-front fruit, juicy, deep, layered and elegant, nice refined tannins.

I moved toward the tidier rows in the center of the store, which were organized geographically. Get too engrossed in the Hermitage from the Rhône, and you'd find yourself wandering through the Riojas from Spain. Linger among the Mosel Rieslings from Germany, and you'd stumble upon the Australian Shirazes. There were wines from places I didn't even know made wine, like South Africa, Lebanon, and Chile.

I was sucked in farther and farther to the shop, until I reached the tasting table in the back. It wasn't anything fancy, but I supposed you didn't need much more than a mess of glasses, some bottles, and a knowledgeable guide with a corkscrew. *All right*, I thought, *this could be fun.*

I met Christian back up at the register where you purchased a glass for the tasting.

"How do we sign up for the Bordeaux thing?" she asked.

"Yeah, the Bordeaux tasting was last week," said the man behind the counter. "It was crazy—we had La Mission Haut-Brion, Lynch-Bages, Léoville Las Cases, Cos—"

I held my hand up to stop him. "We missed it?"

I looked at Christian in disbelief and asked again. "We missed it?" I was crushed. "I'm outta here."

Christian placed her hand on my back before I could walk out. "So, what are you guys tasting today?" she asked.

"Burgundy."

Burgundy. It was like having tickets to go see Led Zeppelin only to have the Backstreet Boys perform instead. I knew that Burgundy was respected by some wine lovers—it was occasionally talked about—but compared to the regal reputation of Bordeaux, Burgundy seemed like Little League wines, nothing to be taken too seriously. There was a mystique to it being so small and generally more difficult to understand than Bordeaux, but none of that was going to make the wine taste good.

He saw I was a bit disappointed, so continued. "You know, it should be a good tasting. If you don't like it, we can refund your tasting fee."

Christian nudged me. "Let's do it! You never know, we might like it."

"All right, we'll try it." I was already mentally calculating whether we'd have a shot of buying a bottle from one of the twenty thousand cases of Lafite that they produced each year.

While we waited for a group to finish up their tasting, we browsed through the wine garage. I recognized a few of the wines from reviews I'd read, good bargains and such. But I'd disregarded anything with a fifteen-dollar price tag as a waste of time because I figured it couldn't be much better than the swill I used to buy for parties at my dorm while in New Orleans during my freshman year in college. That stuff was cheap, but I'm not sure it could be called a bargain since you never wanted to drink or smell it ever again. Then again, the wine we'd had in Italy had been some of the most magical I'd ever tasted, and it was almost unbelievably inexpensive. Was that just a fluke? Or maybe I just liked cheap *Italian* wine? French wine, perhaps, needed a better pedigree.

"Hey, guys, you lookin' at wine bottles all day, or are you gonna taste some?" The young guy behind the tasting table had just finished up and was waving us over. In front of him were twelve bottles—six white, six red. They were slimmer in shape than the chiseled, broad-shouldered Bordeaux linebackers and had long, elegant necks leading to what looked like the graceful slope of a woman's shoulders.

"I'm Justin," he said, extending a hand to Christian and then me. He couldn't have been older than thirty and had a pile of blond hair that shook wildly like a bush with a cat stuck in it every time he laughed, which was often. He introduced himself as the wine buyer for the shop and the resident Burgundy expert. "Have you guys tasted Burgundies before?"

"We haven't," Christian said. "Ray was hoping for some Bordeaux. We just found out that we were going to be tasting Burgundy."

"Well," Justin said with a smirk on his face, "sounds like you guys just got really lucky then. The Bordeaux tasting wasn't the best, but we brought out some amazing wines for the Burgundy tasting. We sell a lot of Bordeaux, but Burgundy is—you'll see for yourself."

He filled our glasses about a quarter of the way. As strange a thought as it was, *This wine is pretty* was the first thing that popped in my head. It was a deep liquid gold that glowed brilliantly as though reflecting the sun that nurtured it. I tipped my glass to my nose and breathed in deeply. *Damn.* It smelled good. Almost familiar. I pulled it away from my face once more to take it in, then took another deep inhale. The perfume wrapped itself around my face and dug deep into the pathways of my nose. Lemons. The same lemons I'd picked off a neighbor's tree as a child. Honeysuckle. It was like those that I knew from walking past fields filled with bushes of the white flowers on my way home from school. The memory intensified by the smell made me smile. I used to love picking them off the stem and sucking the sappy sweetness through their petals. It wasn't just a moment of reflection, it was borderline time travel.

I couldn't believe it. "This doesn't taste like *wine*." I took another sip, held it in my mouth, and closed my eyes to be alone with it. There was an intimacy to drinking this wine, like it was revealing itself to me and only me. I was no longer in a cluttered, musty wine shop in San Francisco; every bit of my consciousness was being pulled back to the late 1980s. I looked over at Christian, who had closed her eyes. I could tell she was having a similar moment with her glass. Later, when I asked her what she'd experienced, she told me that it tasted like something living, undisturbed in nature: pure and unblemished. It was more special than anything she'd ever eaten or drank before, and she didn't think any of the other wines could match what she was experiencing. But in that moment, not knowing where her mind had wandered, or she mine, I just knew something in each of our worlds had been altered.

"What do you think?" I asked her when she opened her eyes.

She didn't say anything, only blinked and flashed a huge smile. "What about you?"

"I can't say, never had anything like that before." We both knew that we'd found something special together.

Justin just shook his head and laughed. "Trust me, it gets even better."

I shook my head in disbelief. "Justin, I don't even know what we're drinking. What is this? This is amazing."

"2002 Domaine des Comtes Lafon, from Meursault. It's a village-level wine, a small vineyard, Clos de la Barre. It's good, right?"

"Good? Uh, yeah, I'd say a lot better than good. What do you mean by 'village'?" Since I'd had my head so far up Bordeaux's backside, I hadn't bothered to learn much of anything about Burgundy from any of the many wine books I'd collected.

"That's gonna take a while. But, basically, you have the name of the producer here, the village, vineyard, classification level, and vintage."

"What's a classification level?"

"Man, we'll deal with that later. That would be a long one to answer. Remind me later; I'll go over it if we have time. But, yeah, it's kinda confusing unless you look at it a certain way. A wine label with 'Bourgogne' written on it is from a the lowest classification level. Moving up in quality you have 'village' and then 'premier cru.' Whatever village the grapes are from, it is mentioned on the label, doesn't matter if it is a village-level wine or premier cru. A premier cru generally shows the name of the specific vineyard though, since it makes more of a difference as you move up in potential quality. The top level is grand cru, and the vineyard is mentioned without bringing up the village it is located by."

"Like the wine."

"What?"

"Never mind."

"Oh, yeah. The wine. But, basically, the vineyards were classified a long time ago from Bourgogne to village to premier cru to grand cru."

"Grand cru is the top?"

"Exactly."

"So, how many grands crus are there?"

Justin stared at me, then looked at Christian while gesturing toward me. "Aw, man, he doesn't even know how bad he's got it." He yelled over to one of the guys putting away wines about four aisles over. "Jim, this guy's got it bad." He looked back at me. "Bro, you just got yourself an expensive hobby."

I shrugged it off. "Couldn't be that bad. I love nice cars, those aren't exactly cheap."

"Trust me, man, this can be much worse . . . you'll see."

Justin poured another white, this one from Chassagne-Montrachet from Domaine Leflaive, one of the most reputed white wine producers in all of Burgundy, I learned. This one looked paler than the first and had an almost tropical fragrance. Instead of the lacy sweetness of honeysuckle, there was a tangier, richer pineapple. Then there was a piercing familiar lemon, this time tinged with zestier lime. I'd always thought wine geeks were making it up when they said they smelled these things in their glasses. It was just fermented grape juice, right? So how could a liquid that was made of crushed grapes, aged in a wooden container for several years, and bottled for a few more years end up smelling and tasting like fresh fruit, flowers, and spices?

"Where do all of these smells and tastes come from?"

"That's the cool thing about Burgundy," Justin said. "Each vineyard produces wines that are completely different. They call it 'terroir.' Each place gives something different." My mind was spinning. Just how unique could each piece of land be? Vineyards are just dirt with vines planted in them, right? There had to be more to it for these wines to taste so dramatically different, but so distinct.

The delicate flavors lingered well after I swallowed. They seemed to somehow uncoil and expand, communicating with each and every one of my taste buds and filling them with an indescribably wonderful and unique sensation. Holding the slightly chilled wines in my mouth to warm them only intensified the more subtle flavors, or notes to wine geeks. White flowers turned honeyed, bright lemons deepened into ripe pineapples, and fresh almonds became magically toasted.

Justin poured wine after wine. He would speak, we'd listen, drink, and try to soak up every word, smell, and taste.

"So, these can't all be the same grape, right?"

"Each of these wines is Chardonnay based."

"I thought this one was a Saint-Aubin . . ." I was confused. Were we drinking the place or the grape? I was lost, but enjoying the game of trying to figure it all out. I was thankful that I didn't feel like I was asking too many questions.

"All right." Justin turned his palms up toward me. "Each of these are from the same grape type—Chardonnay for the whites and Pinot Noir for the reds. But because location is so crucial to the personality of a Burgundy wine, we call them by their place, not their grape. To illustrate this he grabbed a bottle of Saint-Aubin premier cru Dents de Chien, pointing at the label. "This one is from a vineyard with a bunch of decomposed sea-life fossils, oysters, and chunks of chalk, and the slopes are at a high elevation and are incredibly steep. Saint-Aubin is a beautiful area and the whole thing looks like one big fish bowl since it used to hold tons of water and sea life. This, on the other hand"—he held up a bottle of the village Meursault we tasted—"is from a vineyard that is pretty flat, with much more clay in the soil than limestone. It contributes a lot of the richness, we say fatness sometimes too."

In Bordeaux, reds are typically a blend of five grapes from different terroirs, so you don't taste place so much as you taste chemistry blended with design and a little bit of luck. What percentage of each grape type that actually makes it into the final wine in Bordeaux can change for a winery each year, so what a consumer experiences isn't just terroir but also a strong dose of what the winemaker thinks is the best expression of their château, including which grapes (at varying percentages) are included. This gives a lot of options to the winemaker, especially if a vintage is more or less kind to particular grapes.

In Burgundy, on the other hand, each wine is an expression of one single place. Learning more, I loved the idea that each parcel of land could produce a unique expression impossible to duplicate anywhere else. The idea of tailoring a wine like they did in Bordeaux began to seem like cheating to me. There was less of a spirit of history, an expression of one piece of land over centuries.

The wines change, but the name stays the same. It felt less special, and more like a product of manufacturing, a brand. But Burgundy? I didn't realize wine could be like this: a pure moment from one place and time encapsulated in a bottle. With just a few tastes of Burgundy, I had found something I instantly loved and was ready to defend.

With the last white Burgundy in my glass, reds were up next. I started to come down from the high of it all. Reds were generally trouble for me—they were either too tannic (that scratchy feeling on your tongue, roof of your mouth, and in your throat that makes you feel like you're chewing on sandpaper), too hot (had too much of an alcohol taste), or just didn't taste like fruit. Whites are easy. The worst of them doesn't taste like much, so you can spit them out and forget the experience quickly. Bad reds stay with you, wrapping themselves around your tongue and refusing to leave.

I didn't think these reds would stand up to the purity and freshness of the whites. Plus, I'd already started doing the math of just how many bottles of the whites I could afford to gift myself for Valentine's Day.

"How do the reds compare to the whites?" I asked Justin.

"C'mon, you've had Pinot before, right?"

I'd had only a few Italian Nebbiolos and fifty or so Bordeaux. I didn't know what the hell a Pinot was, but it sounded cool. "Are they any good?"

Justin shook his head, laughed, and said, "If you loved the whites, the reds are gonna ruin you for sure, man."

The sound drained from the room shortly after the pop of the cork rang out as he opened the first bottle of red. Something was different. A bouquet of roses, blackberries, and cherries wafted from the bottle. We swirled, inhaled, exhaled. It smelled like an exotic perfume. Though I braced myself for the wine to taste nothing like how it smelled, I wasn't ready for the let-down, so I paused, looking at it. It looked simple and common, like any other glass of red wine that I'd ever had, though it was a shade or two lighter. But as if it could hear my thoughts, another waft of its aroma hit me. It smelled like pressing your nose into a basket of the most intense sun-ripened berries, cherries, and plums.

"It's too pretty," I pronounced, shaking my head in disbelief. "I just need to look at it a little longer."

"Ray, just drink it," Christian said. "You look crazy."

But I couldn't be rushed. For once there were no meetings to go to, no clients waiting for me to call them or to pick up their calls. For the past six years, even during high school in Hayward and college at Dillard University in New Orleans and at San Francisco State University, I'd worked for my family's real estate business. I knew if I was going to make a good living, I'd have to hustle. So that's exactly what I did. I spent every day rushing from point A to point B. There was always a client to show a house to, a loan to construct and submit, a bank's phone call to return, a meeting I didn't want to be late for. Ten times out of ten I'd pick up the phone when someone called just to make sure I didn't miss the chance to bring in new business, close a deal, or just keep a current client happy. It didn't matter where I was when the phone rang, while I was in the shower, at dinner with Christian, in the dentist's chair, I'd pick up the phone. Living life in the moment? That wasn't going to happen for a guy like me. I didn't have the luxury to acknowledge the benefit of slowing down. Patience was for the guy who lost the deal.

But right now, in this shop, there wasn't a next moment to be in, to prepare for. It was only here, now. It wasn't about impressing someone either, or throwing around words like *notes, reputation, nose,* and *finish.* As Christian liked to say, "You either like it or you don't." It was just about the deeply intimate experience of enjoyment.

The wines kept coming, each one expressing something different, each more complex than the last.

> 1996 Gevrey-Chambertin Aux Echézeaux
> 1998 Corton Clos du Roi grand cru
> 2001 Volnay premier cru Taillepieds
> 2002 Vosne-Romanée premier cru Aux Brûlée

They didn't just show notes; they expressed their personalities. The Gevrey smelled of coffee grounds and mocha; the Corton, potting soil and warmed plums. The Volnay was all about dried flowers and lavender. Blackberries, chocolate, and cinnamon wafted from the Vosne. They ranged from bright and crisp to warmer and sultrier, sexy even. There was no having to rationalize these wines. They were so pure, effortless, and simply pleasurable to drink. I didn't need facts and stats to enjoy them, but I had to know more. I was hooked.

CHAPTER FOUR

Every morning seemed bleaker than the last. I'd get up before the sun had even begun its ascent, rising mechanically from bed and taking a steaming hot shower for some solace on cold, foggy mornings.

Wearing a navy-blue, thin-cut Italian-tailored suit, matching dress socks, and black leather wing tips, I would step out into the chill of the morning, my face often nicked from shaving and my tie nearly choking me. It would be four in the morning, and the neighborhood would still be dark. We lived in Fairfield, a city neighboring Napa, so in order to get to my office in San Francisco, I had to get on the highway for twenty minutes, wait at the train station for the five A.M., then spend another forty-five minutes staring blankly out the window to make it to my office by six. I'd arrive at the Embarcadero station, wipe the drool off my cheek, and put on my most convincing game face.

I didn't want to be miserable; I just wanted some stability and a healthy income. It was a good job—I was studying to become a securities representative at Merrill Lynch, and it offered me an opportunity to provide anything my family would one day need.

And that one day was going to be a lot sooner than I'd planned. Two months ago we had found out Christian was pregnant.

Since Christian and I had met, it was always feast or famine. When times were good, we felt like we were on the top of the world. But too often we'd put a big check in our account when it was close to bottoming out. We were making good money, but investing in rental property when we were in our early twenties had run a hole through our finances, making it close to impossible to make any headway.

I'd spent seven years working in the family business, but I was too drained to continue on that path—too many clients to please and too many appointments to keep. There wasn't anything physical to the work, really, but the mental aspects of it ran me ragged. I couldn't sleep at night, the buzzing of the day still fresh in my head. I had started out when I was only twelve years old, along with my brother, who was fourteen, cleaning up abandoned houses that my parents bought and sold. Once they started their mortgage business, I helped out, and by the time I was eighteen, I was meeting with clients, processing loans, and making deals. But even when the money was good, I felt like I was trying to be someone I wasn't. The money was great at first, but I quickly learned how unstable my income could be. And I wanted to be part of something bigger than just having a nice paycheck.

As a twenty-six-year-old with no experience to speak of and no college degree, I was willing to work for it. I had to. So when I got the job at Merrill, it seemed like something stable. Something smart. I could use my networking skills to build a client base. Unlike in real estate, when you'd run yourself into the ground for a single check only to have to start again from scratch, I'd be working with people long term. Sure, it wasn't what I wanted to do with the rest of my life, but that's what guys do, right? They make a good amount of money in finance, maybe get a free pass from dad duty during the daytime for a few years while they run themselves brain dead, build a nest egg, and then get the hell out. Except, I wasn't too interested in the first part and I didn't want to miss a second of our baby's life. I was starting to feel like I needed to find a way out. I had my eyes on something else, and it didn't involve an office and stiff clothes.

It had been three years since we'd gone to that Burgundy wine tasting, and I had become more and more consumed by wine. I bought Gevrey-Chambertins, Chambolle-Musignys, Volnays, those from Morey-Saint-Denis, and pretty much any red Burgundy I could find. The whites were nice to drink, but the reds drove me insane, pushing me to stay up late after drinking them to learn more about what I had just tasted. I'd take the thousand-page-plus wine tome *Côte d'Or* by Clive Coates on the BART train every morning. I'd spend my entire commute learning about the scattered patchwork of vineyards that made up the region. While the other passengers had their faces buried in market trend reports or *The Wall Street Journal*, I was learning about the history of Gevrey-Chambertin. I was enchanted by what I was discovering.

The concept of terroir was fascinating to me, and while it is embraced all over the world as an important element in wine, I learned that in Burgundy, it is more than a philosophy; it's a way of life. The tiny region has grown wine grapes for more than two thousand years, and over time, its vineyards split into microscopic parcels under the principal of terroir. I read stories of its early history, when the monks of Burgundy made the cultivation of wine grapes an intellectual pursuit of the highest order. Believing that each piece of land was a part of God, and that the produce from any given piece of land was his voice, they pursued clarity in this message by planting the same grapes in various locations. The clearer and stronger the voice, the better the land. "Gifted" land was often too meager for other plantings because other crops prefer an easy life. The monks found that the best wine comes from the poorest soil, which forces the vine's roots to dig deep into the substrata, across a patchwork of geological formations in search of food and water. Left with just the rudimentary processes, a wine from Burgundy can display an endless amount of complexity and above all, a sense of place.

It was as though I could taste all of this choreography, this dance between God and man and earth, in the reds. I'd track down bottles with interesting stories. I'd sip a bottle of 1959 Domaine Lamarche La Grande Rue grand cru in the evening, thinking of the grapes growing in the vineyard at a time when my parents were just seven years old. To me, each bottle was more than a way to impress others, or to feel a buzz, it was an expression caught in a moment and stored in a time capsule waiting to be opened and shared with others. I'd imagine the centuries of experience and wisdom that shaped these wines as I savored the bright plums, succulent cherries, and delicious raspberries of their bouquet. It was like a meditation.

My days at Merrill were anything but. Entering through the heavy glass doors of 101 California Street felt less like going to work and more like walking through the curtains of a theater. I'd have to pump myself up in the elevator so I could actually look like I wanted to be there. Then I'd settle into my three-walled cubbyhole, whose only contents were constant reminders of my current dilemma. I had two pictures from vacations with Christian pinned to the wall, one of the many cups of coffee I'd force down to keep me going until seven at night, a notepad where I'd scribble the names of my most recent Burgundy vineyard crushes and sketch vineyard rows, and two large flat-screen monitors running my Series 7 exam preparation software. I did my best to focus on the tests since I had to pass in order to keep collecting a paycheck. And while I didn't exactly like my job, I didn't want to lose it either. On top of that, in the middle of everything else we decided to move to Rohnert Park, thirty miles away from Napa, with Sonoma right in between the two. We had to move: We'd be closer to family and to our jobs. Besides, the area offered a beautiful environment for us as a new family. It just took a weekend, and we had shifted from next door to the Cabernet Sauvignon of Napa County to being surrounded by the Pinot Noir and Chardonnay of Sonoma County. It was going to be a lot harder to focus on work, but with our baby coming, I knew I needed to keep it all together, to be a man and look past my personal dreams.

There were five others that were hired around the same time I was, and each day, our job was simple: Learn the products that Merrill Lynch sold and run your practice exam program. I figured out quickly that the average new hire was running through the practice exams four to five times a day. Among our group, the average score was ranging between 50 and 75 percent per test. But with the countdown to baby hanging over my head, that wasn't going to cut it. I was plowing through eight tests a day, and after a month was averaging a score of 84 percent. I didn't consider myself smarter than the other guys, but the questions didn't seem that hard. What wasn't related to the same principles I'd already known from real estate was just common sense.

To everyone around me, I must have looked the part. I tried hard enough. But when I wasn't staring like a zombie at my monitors, I was dreaming about wine. What had started out as a hobby—OK fine, an obsession—now seemed like a lifeline. I hadn't worked with my hands since I was a teenager renovating those houses, duplexes, and apartments with my parents. Now I found myself craving that kind of all-consuming labor that gave me a sense of pride that pushing paper just couldn't provide. I missed collapsing into bed utterly exhausted, falling asleep the second my head hit the pillow. I missed the dirt, the sweat, the fresh air, and the soreness that came after a hard day's work. I missed being a part of something real, of literally building something that would endure.

The responsible thing to do would be to spend ten, fifteen, maybe even twenty years going through the motions at Merrill. In the end I would do right by my family, and it was the safe bet. But every night my mind would race while Christian slept beside me. To continue down this path would give me a career, but I would lose something. And I was worried that I wouldn't know how to get it back.

I knew I couldn't even wait the twenty-four weeks for my final review before making the transition to the official "team." I started visualizing how I would tell my boss that I was leaving, the satisfaction of telling him that I would go on to do something meaningful with my life while he sat in a glass box and pushed papers around. Leaving wouldn't be difficult. Telling Christian, on the other hand, would. I'd done too good a job of convincing her that the Merrill Lynch job would give us the financial foundation that we needed. And with my new salary providing consistency, it was a welcomed change for both of us from the usual cycle of lean and fat months. Now, just months later, I would be robbing her of that security. In two months she'd be giving birth to our first child, and I was about to voluntarily dry up our biggest source of income.

Christian had always stuck by me, even defended my screwups, but this would be the true test—could she see past the man I was for the man that I could be?

CHRISTIAN WAS ALREADY IN BED when I opened our bedroom door. I had raced home from the office, not wanting to give myself too much time with my thoughts and also hoping that I might make it home before she fell asleep. She'd been so exhausted lately, working more shifts to make up for the time she'd be off, and of course carrying our growing baby.

"Chris. . . . Chris, are you asleep?" Brushing her hair back to see her face, I immediately felt a surge of guilt. When she didn't stir, I got up slowly, feeling at once relieved as well as pathetic for not feeling enough conviction to say what had coursed through my mind nearly each waking moment for the past two years. I crept away from the bed. But I had already woken her up anyway.

"Honey, when did you get in?" As soon as she saw the look on my face she knew something was amiss. "What's wrong? Come sit down by me." She patted the bed.

I struggled to find the right words, speaking tentatively and abstractly about our future and its stability.

"I just can't see that I'm getting much out of this job," I finally mustered. "At best I'd make great money, but I'm just not happy. I'm going through the motions, and I don't know if it's worth it anymore." There it was. There was no unsaying the truth. I looked at the floor, too ashamed to make eye contact with Christian. I was being selfish, small. I waited for the yelling I deserved, the exasperation, maybe even the tears.

"Honey," Christian said softly. "What use is the money if you're so broken up about it?" Her eyes searched mine. She saw my pain was real. "Tell me. What would make you happy?"

"I can't say that it is a fix-all for what I'm feeling, and I know it wouldn't allow us the same type of livelihood, but I'd love to do something with wine."

"You want to own a vineyard?" She smiled and half laughed at the absurdity of the prospect.

I let out a nervous laugh. "No, well, not now. But I'd like to learn how everything is done."

"You mean you want to work in a winery?"

"Yeah . . ." I could see that she was starting to worry. "I mean, I don't know that I'd be able to get a job anyhow. But I'd like to try."

"Do . . . do they even make much money?"

"Vineyard owners? Uh, not really . . ."

"No, the people that work at the wineries."

I laughed a bit. "Oh, no. They don't really either." She didn't think the joke was funny. Then again, I wasn't making a joke.

"I don't think they make much, but I think we would be fine."

"You know I'm almost seven months pregnant, right?" Her voice softened, her eyes focused on mine. "So, you'd work in a winery and at Merrill? How would that even work?"

"I'd only be able to do one. Look, I don't even know why I brought it up—" I went to stand up.

"Wait. Sit down." I obeyed, and she put her hand on mine. "If you can get a job at a winery, I'd support you in it."

And then she said the four most beautiful words that would give me the strength to follow through with what I'd been dreaming about for the past three years.

"I believe in you."

CHAPTER FIVE

Harvest position needed in Sonoma Valley. Boutique winery, pinot noir and chardonnay, must be able to lift 45 pounds. Long hours during harvest, need committed, physical person with great attitude. No experience necessary.

It seemed like the perfect opportunity—especially the part about no experience being necessary. It'd been tough for me to catch a break, with not one nibble of interest in the past month I'd been feverishly looking for a position. Harvest was right around the corner and so it was going to take a lot of luck to find anything, since many wineries had filled their positions in February. Plus it was a total catch-22—most vineyards needed to hire someone in an entry-level position for pennies on the hour, and yet they wanted someone who had a working knowledge of the process. I didn't know anything and needed to be paid more than the going rate to make it work for us financially. So far six interviewers had turned me down, and jumping ship five weeks earlier from Merrill was starting to look like one of my dumber ideas.

After Christian had said she supported me, the next day I put my usual costume on and walked into my manager's office. I had visions of slamming down a cup of coffee on his desk, yelling a few obscenities, and throwing my tie on the ground, but all I managed was, "I appreciate the opportunity, but I have to go." He sat there blinking at me through his thousand-dollar reading glasses.

"You're leaving? Like that?"

"Do I need to give notice? Would you *prefer* if I gave notice?"

"No, it's fine. But what are you gonna do? Make wine?" He was alluding to the running joke all of the finance guys shared. If only we could be free of the rat race, we'd all be sitting in an old rocking chair overlooking our vineyards, making wine. If only he knew. I just nodded and shared in the laugh, then shook his hand and left.

I spent the next few weeks scouring the Internet for job openings. I wasn't qualified for any of them, but I figured I could talk my way into a position and, I hoped, make an impression with my work ethic and ability to learn.

Week after week went by. I was called back a few times on some of the listings I'd applied to. Some of them went as far as an interview, but nothing stuck. Then I interviewed with a woman and a man from the winery that had placed the first listing I'd seen. It was a winery that I knew well. I hadn't tried many of their wines, but I knew their Pinot Noir was considered one of the best in the country. We sat at a picnic bench in the picturesque back roads of the Russian River Valley. It was so peaceful, with vineyards lining rolling hills everywhere I looked. While I didn't know much about the wines grown in the area, I wanted so badly to be a part of it. But we'd barely been there ten minutes and I was already trying to extricate my foot from my mouth.

"... And that's what is so great about Burgundy—the land

there is so complex, so unique that they don't *need* to rely on 'wine-making' techniques to show large differences in their wines—er, I mean, what we have here is exciting too . . . but it can't compare to a place with over two thousand years of history, right guys?"

They weren't impressed.

"Do you know much about other wineries in the area?"

"Which area?"

"The one where you are currently located."

"I've been to a few tastings, but I don't drink much California wine." It was like I'd developed the first case of wine Tourette's ever recorded.

The blank stares from the other side of the table cued me to wrap things up and leave.

"You know, I think we are just looking for someone a bit more qualified. We like your passion, but what we need is someone who really gets it." I wanted to tell them how much I did get it, but I knew I should walk away with whatever dignity I had left.

By the time I got into my car I was more defeated than ever. No one was going to hire me. The only way I could hope to impress one of these wineries was if I had already worked at a good winery. But I couldn't get my shot because no one wanted to take a gamble on an ex-finance guy who wouldn't shut up about Burgundy. Someone was going to have to take a leap of faith.

"Hey, buddy," the guy I'd just interviewed with called as he waved his arms, trying to get my attention before I pulled away. My pulse quickened. *This is it*, I thought. *They'd had a change of heart. This is my shot!*

"Hey, buddy," he called again. "You forgot your résumé."

"Thanks."

"Yeah, we don't need it."

"Um, I get your point."

I drove back home on the pretty vineyard-lined highway through Guerneville toward Santa Rosa. The same expanse of vineyard plantings that once looked so large to me now seemed so small, far away, and out of reach.

When I came home Christian was sitting at the table sorting through a book of baby names.

"Did you get it?" She looked proud of me before I said a word. But I had to let her down, just as I'd done six other times in the same number of weeks. She looked more beautiful than ever, her belly a constant reminder of the special addition on the way to our family. We'd just found out we were having a little girl. Ever since we had gotten married we'd talked about having children, and in my daydreams I'd envisioned a little girl to spoil and watch over. Now that was coming true, and I had no plan in place for taking care of her.

I couldn't look Christian in the eyes, but I had to. She needed to see that I was trying, that there was still a fight inside of me worth her support, even if I kept coming up empty.

"No. I didn't."

"Was it, you know . . . close?"

"Nope. They want somebody qualified to do the work. And they—"

"But the listing said 'no experience necessary.'"

"I don't know." I did know. I knew that I'd blown the interview singing the praises of Burgundy. I knew the right answers but had chosen to be honest. Now I was at home being dishonest.

"Well, you'll get the next one!" She looked even more proud of me. I managed a tired smile and sat down with Matt Kramer's *Making Sense of Burgundy*.

"You know, you could probably get some help on the forum."

She'd seen me ask for advice on the online wine community's list several times before. I'd use it to ask for insight about particularly interesting vintages or whether a more expensive bottle was worth the investment. Lately, I had asked for advice on decorating and baby proofing Bella's nursery. The community had been helpful in guiding my education of Burgundy, so why not in finding me a job?

After we ate dinner, Christian went upstairs to read while I sat at the kitchen table with my laptop. I logged in and started composing a post about my search so far. I poured my heart out—detailing the stressful decision I'd made to leave finance in pursuit of a job in the vineyards, my dream of finally working with my hands again, and my frustrations at not being able to find a single winery that would take me. It was less a solicitation for advice than a personal post about my frustration, but I found some solace in thinking that there was a pretty good chance no one would even see it since the site was well trafficked and new posts were constantly going up.

I went to sleep just like I did most nights, thinking of the vineyards, letting my memory wander back to the times that I'd driven to Napa and Sonoma when I was in real estate. If I didn't have a lot of appointments, I'd get in my car, put the top down, and head toward wine country. I felt so drained being inside an office, and the drives revived something inside of me. The perfume of the vines and the flowers in the breeze was like a kind of smelling salt that jarred me back into my skin. I'd feel alive again. Stepping out of the car and onto the rocky earth was like being in a different world, a different time, a different life. I'd pick up the soil in my hands and clutch it tightly, then open my fist and let the pebbled bits fall away again, dust blowing in the wind. I'd wonder if I was made of soil or wind.

My alarm pulled me back into reality. I dragged myself out of bed, plodded down to the kitchen, and opened my laptop to log on to the wine forum like I'd done a thousand times before. This time a window popped up:

Thirty-eight new private messages.

It had to be a mistake. I went to my inbox to see what the issue was.

"Congratulations" read one subject line.

"Wish I could do it!" read another.

"Don't screw it up! Kidding. But really, don't screw it up"

"Rooting for you"

"Possible lead on winery position in Sonoma"

"What took you so long?"

"Intern tips"

The post that I had written just eight hours earlier had been opened more than two thousand times. Over the next two days my post would be opened more than six thousand times and receive six pages of responses. There was plenty of well-wishing, but sprinkled among the praise and "go get 'ems" were actual leads. Literally everyone was encouraging. I'd heard no so many times that I'd begun to question my own faith in my ability to succeed. But if my wife and all of these people were there to support me, why shouldn't I keep going?

One name kept coming up again and again: Ed Kurtzman. People made him out to be some kind of wine whisperer: knowledgeable, generous with his time, and willing to teach. A few people wrote lengthy e-mails about how if they could do it all over again, they'd kill to work for Ed. I did a quick search online, found his number, and gave him a call.

"Hi, is this Ed *Kersman*?"

"Yeah, it's Ed *Kurtzman*," he said, laughing a bit.

"This is Ray Walker."

"Oh, Ray! I saw the post. I figured you might be calling, so I saved you a spot for harvest."

My heart went to my throat.

"A position? I don't have any experience."

"I know. Doesn't matter. You will, though." Listening to his voice, I could sense a huge smile on his face. "Everyone has to start somewhere, right? You can start over here with me."

A day earlier, I couldn't get a single winery to keep my résumé, let alone hire me. Now I was talking to the man who held my future in his hands. I'd never met him, and already I owed him everything.

"Tomorrow you can come to San Francisco to help clean some tanks."

"I'll be there."

After we hung up, I rushed over to Christian, wrapped my arms around her, and kissed her.

"I got it!"

"Got what? A wine job? When did you go on an interview?"

"Well, I didn't. I just called the guy up, and he—"

"What guy?"

"The Ed guy a few people told me about."

"And then what?"

"I called, introduced myself, and he gave me a job."

"Just like that?"

"Just like that."

"Remember," she said, "I'm the one who believed in you first."

ED'S WAS ONE OF A handful of urban wineries in San Francisco. Excited as I was to start work, though, I still hated driving into the city. The traffic, the smog, the noise—it was all at odds with how I envisioned winery life. But I knew a good opportunity when I saw one, and I was grateful.

I pulled up to the enormous building, which could just as easily have been a meatpacking plant or sweatshop outpost. Ed walked out the front door with a mask on.

"I'm spraying ozone and you need a mask," he said, forgoing usual pleasantries.

"You mean, like ozone ozone?"

"Yes, there's only one."

"And why are you doing that?"

"Man, you *are* green. You'll get it though, don't worry."

Ed was in his early forties with a mess of curly light brown hair. He was wearing shorts, a T-shirt, and tube socks pulled up to below his knees. Clearly he wasn't trying to make a fashion statement, but he had a firm handshake and warm personality, which mattered much more, in my opinion.

As he showed me around the winery, I didn't have a lot to compare it to, but I knew enough to gauge that it was tiny. Equipment that would normally take up a fraction of an operation's space filled the warehouse's raw slab concrete floor to capacity. There were enormous stainless-steel tanks, plus what looked like hundreds of barrels stacked on racks of two, six levels high. In order for each level to be balanced, it had to be perfectly aligned with the one below. At seven hundred pounds apiece, plus the thousands of dollars' worth of wine inside, it seemed like a very expensive accident begging to happen. And seeing that one of my responsibilities would be to move the barrels from time to time, while Ed continued the tour I did mental calculations on how long it would take to pay him back once I knocked one of them over.

We stopped in front of a baker's rack lined with neatly arranged tools.

"This," Ed said, "is your new office."

Instead of hammers or screwdrivers, there were tools like C-shaped wrenches, oscillating tips for barrel washers, and an assortment of valves and clamps, all set up like a surgeon's tray in an OR, only cleaner. Ed may have been a nearly middle-aged hippie whose winery's namesake August West was an homage to the Grateful Dead, but when it came to doing things with precision and accuracy, he was a stickler for details. It would be just the two of us in the winery, so I not only needed to learn the ropes quickly, I needed to learn them *right*. Ed had two months to show me everything I needed to know before harvest.

Every day I reported to the winery and did whatever Ed asked. I cleaned out the tanks and barrels so they'd be ready to receive the grapes by the middle of August; swept the floors; rolled and rerolled the hoses; and brushed, scrubbed, and sanitized every last inch of reflective surface in the place, because if any surface touched wine, you needed to be able to eat off of it. The job wasn't glamorous, but I got to slowly piece together how all these chores, all these seemingly insignificant details, ultimately added up to making a winery successful.

"Ray, did you clean those clasps well enough?" Ed asked the first time he had me give some of the tank's parts a good wash.

"Uh, yeah. I think they're good."

"OK. Whatever you think. If you're happy, I'm happy." But I realized I wasn't sure, so I dug into the old paint bucket and pulled out a clasp and started cleaning them all again.

The lesson was simple: Do it right or do it twice. Each step is necessary and important. How well a tank was cleaned or how thoroughly the floor was swept or how neatly the barrels were lined up in their racks—it all affected the wine. If something wasn't cleaned properly or tended to efficiently, it could show up years later in the bottles customers brought home. I learned quickly that wine production isn't just about artistry and tradition; it is about preparation, precision, and patience.

It is also about having a good dose of common sense. If I complained that the citric acid I washed the tanks with burned the hell out of my eyes, Ed would shrug and say, "Try taking the taller ladder next time and climbing above your work space. Cleaning above your head gives things a chance to fall down on you . . . citric acid likes to spray into eyes though." When I almost flooded the warehouse while dumping some wine left in barrels and cleaning them out, Ed only coolly offered, "Maybe next time pull them next to the drain."

Despite my frequent gaffes, Ed was patient and kind. And best of all, asking him questions was like taking a one-on-one master class on how not to screw it up. One of the most important things that I learned was why one puts wine in the barrels to "top them up." As Ed explained, there is an oxygen exchange between the air outside of the barrel and the wine inside, which creates some evaporation. Over time, the barrel isn't so full, so it needs to be topped up. If the wine isn't topped up, bacterial spoilage can occur and turn the wine to vinegar, so it's always important to keep an eye on just how full the barrel is. We generally put more wine into the barrels every two weeks or so. I liked learning things like that, and soon, the process and work I was doing in the winery started making sense.

Each day, I came home thinking about how much more valuable this wisdom was than the fifteen dollars an hour I was being paid. I didn't even really deserve the money—I only slowed Ed down, but he was generous in overlooking this.

One morning, my phone rang at seven.

"Hey, do you want to bottle the '07s with us?" It was Ed.

"Sure, when?"

"In an hour. The bottling guy blew it and came a couple of days early."

"I'll be right there."

I'd gotten used to Ed calling at odd hours asking if I was interested in doing things at the last minute. That's how he was. He didn't tell you what to do; he'd just ask if you were interested. It was a small distinction, but it made a big difference in how we worked together. It didn't matter what I had planned for the day; if he needed me there, I'd be there.

Up until now it'd just been the two of us. But today Ed had assembled a crew from all over California to help get his wines bottled. Some were former interns who now had their own wineries. Others were friends. All of them were there to chip in free of charge, just to be able to be there with Ed. Once you met or worked with Ed, his easygoing nature was infectious. It just felt good to be around him.

The "bottling guys" are a service that wineries around the world use instead of equipping their small, relatively low-production facilities with expensive bottling machinery. It's basically a truck whose trailer is outfitted with a miniature-bottling factory. One such truck now sat idling in front of Ed's place, and as soon as the team was assembled, we got to work running sulfured water through the equipment before connecting our pumps and sending through Ed's wine. The two-man bottling crew adjusted the pressures, timing, and fill levels of the system and established a good pace for the machines that would apply the corks and labels as well. Then we hooked up the hoses to the four large stainless-steel tanks that I'd washed a hundred times before, which were now filled with the 2007 vintage wines. Just days before, Ed had pumped it into the tanks from the barrels, and now it would be funneled into bottles, packed into cartons, and shipped to his customers around the country.

Through the clear hoses you could see the wine make its way through the labyrinth of the trailer, snaking its way past the conveyor belts that flipped the empty bottles upside-down and ran them over the machine that sprayed them with water and then shot in some argon gas to get rid of any oxygen before they rotated upright again. At that point, precisely enough wine would fill each bottle to a regulated level. A hopper would release a cork and punch it in with a *pfft* of compressed air. Then a foil capsule would drop into position and a hair dryer–looking device would seal it around the bottle's neck as a label was applied and two heavy rubber rollers spun the bottle to secure it. Each bottle would continue down the conveyor belt until eleven more just like it were collected. Then we would drop them all into the slots of a cardboard wine box, tape it shut, and send it rolling down an aluminum rack, where it would later be stacked, wrapped in plastic, and shipped around the world. It was like *Charlie and the Chocolate Factory* for wine geeks.

Every so often we'd switch jobs. I might tape boxes closed for two hours or load and wrap them shut for a few more, but then someone somewhere else on the production line might ask for a trade.

The guy placing bottles in cases at the end of the bottling line shouted out over the maddening *click . . . clank clank clank clink*, "Hey, man, you want to switch it up for a minute?"

My hands were badly beaten from four hours of lifting full

cases and taping up all the cardboard boxes. I'd managed to clean my blood off of a few of them, but I was pretty sure I'd missed some. A change couldn't have come early enough.

"So, what do I do?"

"All right, the bottles come off hella fast. Just grab 'em and toss 'em in the case."

"That's it?"

We switched, and he looked way too happy about it. But I was just relieved to relax the same muscles I'd been using since eight that morning.

"All right," I called out, "I'm ready, turn it—"

The bottles that were halfway around the bend on the conveyor belt twelve feet away from me were now in front of me, with twenty bottles following closely behind. I panicked, looking around for the boxes. He'd told me where they were, but I forgot after seeing the black blur of freshly filled bottles charging at me at thirty miles per hour. If too many piled up at the end of the line, they could topple over. Scrambling to pull bottles off of the line, I knocked over the neat stack of open boxes sitting behind me. I grabbed the bottles by their necks, two in each hand. I needed to work quickly to keep up with the speed of the line, so I crammed the bottles in, the bases of the bottles slamming into the stainless-steel table beneath the case, then turned around just as quickly to grab another set of four, and then another, and then slapped the box down the ramp so it could be taped shut. My trade mate was waiting for the box with his thumb up. "Yup, that's it."

Bottle after bottle came racing down Satan's little bottling machine. The repetition shredded my obliques, having a nearly constant tight grip around bottlenecks for what felt like the past five hours had left the tendons in my arms feeling like they were tearing away from my bones, and I'd lost all mobility in my wrists. I looked at my watch to see how long it'd been, hoping it would be at least three hours. It had been one. I figured I had half an hour more of work left in me at best.

After looking on for a bit, Ed came up to check in. "You really impress me, Ray. But, man, you know you can switch it up. This one is a bear after an hour."

"I'm good."

"You're gonna be feeling it tomorrow."

As much pain as I was feeling, I felt like I needed to move quicker than the next guy, and seeing someone else breezing through their station pushed me even more. I knew I needed to be able to do all of these tasks well myself if I was going to have my own setup one day. There wasn't any room for complaining. I pushed on, leaning into the pain, hoping for numbness to set in. I might feel horrible later, but now wasn't the time to worry about tomorrow.

CHAPTER SIX

"OH, YOU FINALLY MADE IT."

"But I'm early today."

"You're not early if I'm here first."

It was a classic Eric move, and if he weren't my boss, I'd probably have thrown him into a headlock and told him just how big an asshole he was. Being just a few years older than I, he was more like an older brother than an actual supervisor, but he had seven years of wine experience on me, and I respected my place.

"What are we doing today? Cleaning more barrels?"

After working with Ed for two months, he'd offered me a full-time position helping out at Freeman Winery, a boutique operation nestled in a wooded area, just miles from the coast, in Sebastopol, north of San Francisco. Ed was the head winemaker, and he and his assistant, Eric, needed an extra pair of hands to keep up general maintenance before harvest. Even though the job promised many more days filled with skin-stinging cleaning solution, standing inside of tanks with freezing cold water up to my knees, and scrubbing grime out of tanks and barrels, it sounded like absolute freedom.

I'd been working there for a few weeks, showing up at seven every morning to help Eric keep the winery and cellar in order. Like Ed and his tie-dyed T-shirts, Eric could be deceiving with his laid-back attitude and thick muttonchops. But he too took precision seriously. When I'd shown up three minutes late on my first day, he'd ribbed me about it, and he hadn't let up since. He clearly wasn't too crazy about taking on someone with just two months of experience, but I'd worked hard and proven to him that I could handle anything he threw my way.

This morning I showed up ready for another day of labor. I looked forward to our time together—we'd worked out a rhythm where I didn't need as much supervising and he could be free to do what else needed to be done, like analyzing reports on malic and lactic acid levels of the wines from the lab, tasting barrels to assemble final blends, or organizing barrel placement in anticipation of the newest vintage. We'd wordlessly move through our tasks to the blaring soundtrack of Led Zeppelin's *IV*, both lost in what we were doing. Occasionally we'd even yell out the lyrics. And while we'd never, ever dare to sit around a campfire singing about it, I could tell that both of us found a spirituality to the work. I usually had my head in the clouds, imagining myself doing the same tasks in Burgundy.

"You know what?" Eric said. "Let's scratch the barrels today. You want to see some vineyards?"

The ecstatic look on my face gave him my answer. This was it. *The grapes!* Ever since falling in love with Burgundy wine I pictured myself spending entire days getting lost in the rows of a vineyard. While I had grown to enjoy the time I was spending inside dark stainless-steel tanks, scrubbing everything with citric acid, it certainly wasn't the stuff of my dreams.

We climbed into Eric's truck and pulled out of the winding driveway and headed out onto a road carved out of the towering redwoods. As we climbed higher in elevation, the mist trailed off the towering hillsides dotted with vineyards. It was still early enough that the sun was a sherbet orange backdrop, but soon it would be reddening our necks and scorching our shoulders. The air grew cooler, though it still held the salty fragrance of the ocean as it passed.

When we arrived at one of the vineyards where the Freemans sourced their fruit, Eric parked his truck and grabbed a few Ziploc bags, scissors, and a refractometer, a device that looked like a mini telescope and was used to measure the amount of sugar in grape juice. I paused for a moment to take in the unreal panoramic landscape that unfurled before me. Rising above us was a tremendous slope bursting with large, lush green rows of neatly manicured vines, each dotted with clusters of purple berries. The space in between each row was just six feet wide—just enough for the tractors to fit between to turn over the earth a few times during the season. The grapes apparently like being crammed in like that; it forces the vines to seek out food at lower depths in the soil, which makes for more complex wine as well as consistency, even in drought years.

It was one of the most beautiful things I'd ever seen.

I trailed Eric as he marched, his war-torn Timberlands leaving massive tracks in the wet earth between the rows of vines. I watched as he would grab a berry off a cluster and pop it in his mouth, then figured I could do the same. At first I picked just one, but then I got caught up in how surreal the moment was that I started grazing as I walked.

"You done yet? Damn, take you to a vineyard and you act like you're in a buffet."

I popped a handful of grapes in my mouth and chewed through their thick and crunchy skins and sweet, succulent flesh, through to the bitter seeds. "Yup, I'm done."

Eric passed me a bag. "Take this and head into a row. Randomly cut a cluster off of one side, and then the other side. Stop once you have around nine or ten clusters." He tossed a handful of grape berries into his mouth. "And remember, put more in the bag than you do in your stomach."

Scissors in hand, I went for the prettiest cluster I could find at the start of the row.

"And don't go looking for only the pretty ones; we need a good sample of average grapes." I placed a cluster into the bag. It had smaller berries than the other clusters around it, no mold or mildew, and it was heavier and denser than the other, larger clusters. I tasted a few berries, and the juice was a lot sweeter than the others I'd tried.

"Hey, Eric, why are the small ones so sweet?"

Eric was a few rows over, much farther down the slope than I was. He spit out a mouthful of seeds. "There's less juice in there, so the sugar is a higher percentage of the volume."

"So, if you used only the small grapes for the wine, what would happen?"

"Well, because sugar is what ferments into alcohol, you'd have some seriously high-alcohol wine, and maybe more concentration of flavor too since the tannins coming from the skin would be in larger ratio to the juice as well. Actually, it'd be pretty damned good. But everything gets put in together either way."

All that I knew about the growing season was that the grapes start out green and acidic. Over the course of the summer, they ripen, the amount of sugar rises and the acidity drops. You want to pick at the right moment to keep the best balance of acidity and sugar. The longer the fruit hangs, the generally darker the fruit character. Grapes that taste like red cherries can later taste of black cherries, those that remind one of bright strawberries can end up tasting like dark plums. Ripeness plays a strong role in the resulting wine.

I started noticing some clusters that looked bloated and were a paler shade of purple.

"Are we tossing in the pale ones too?"

"Toss in a good mix so we have an idea of what the vineyard is like."

The larger berries were tart and bitter, and the skins were tougher, not yielding much when I bit into them. The seeds weren't crunchy, just hard. I spit the whole thing out and kept walking.

"So, what do you think about the grapes?" I yelled over to Eric.

"Pretty damned good actually. It'll get us around twenty-two brix."

"Bricks?"

"*Brix*. It's the sugar in the juice. I'll show you in a sec."

"When are these going to be ready to be picked?"

"Can't say. We need to check the numbers in the lab, but I'd guess we're at least a month away."

"A month?"

"Could be a month, maybe two. Could be a few weeks if we got a heat spike, but it's been cool lately so I'd say a month."

"But you said they tasted good."

"Right, I said 'good.' I didn't wait a year just to harvest good grapes. They'll be great if we're patient."

"Here." He handed me a few grapes. "Chew the seeds."

They tasted green, like unripened peas. "We need these to taste more like nuts than vegetables. If the seeds taste green, the wine will too."

When I got home Christian was holding Isabella in one arm, feeding her with the other. Bella was just a little more than a month old, but I could already see so much of Christian in her expressive eyes. She had a little bit of Christian's beautiful hair too. I'd taken a couple of days off when Bella was born. Each day that I'd gone back to work since then, it'd filled me with an unexplainable pride that I hadn't felt before. But I loved coming home to them, kissing them both on their foreheads, and greeting Christian with another kiss on her lips.

"Hey, how was it?" I'd never seen her smile that way before; it warmed me. "I just ate, but your plate is in the oven."

"Everything worked out. I don't really know exactly what I'm doing, but it feels amazing."

"So, you'll be happy? Come here and sit by us."

She put her arm around me while I caressed one of Bella's feet. My hands and fingernail beds were dyed deep purple, all the cracks in the palms of my hands were stained grooves, my fingertips bloodied from sliding against the rough edges of the barrels and tanks.

"More than I can say."

THE PHONE COULDN'T POSSIBLY BE ringing; the sun wasn't up yet. The dim blue glow of the early morning was all I could make out as I blindly swept my hand along the side of the bed looking for my cell. The rings finally stopped because I'd missed the call. I squinted at the screen and saw that it had been Eric.

Christian and Isabella had miraculously been able to sleep through the noise, so I figured calling him back wouldn't wake them either.

When he picked up all I could hear was loud machinery, yelling, and Jimi Hendrix's "Purple Haze" blaring in the background.

"You coming or what?!" It had been two weeks since I last saw him. I'd gone on break until harvest in late September. Why the hell was he calling me in mid-August? And why was he calling at 5:20 in the morning?

"Coming where?"

"Here. Harvest. I said I'd call you. Remember?"

"Are you serious? You said September."

"Well, the grapes don't care what I told you. We had a heat spike; they're ready to roll."

"How much time do I have?"

"You aren't in the car yet?"

I wasn't sure if I should wake Christian. I gave her a kiss and started to creep out of bed. Without turning toward me, she reached for my hand.

"Good luck, babe. Be safe." I squeezed her hand to respond, but she'd already drifted back to sleep.

Pulling into the winery, I could already feel the change in energy. It was electric. People were scattered everywhere, and every machine that I'd washed over the past two months was alive with groaning gears, spinning tumblers, and swooshing with escaping compressed air. *Eeeerrrrr, weeeeeeerrrrrrrr, pfft!* Eric spotted me right as I came in, grabbed me by the shoulder with one hand, and used the other to vigorously shake my hand.

"Great to have you here. You ready?"

Before I had a chance to speak, a heavy plastic container filled to the top with a little over a ton of Pinot Noir fruit came rolling past us on a forklift. Eric quickly reached in and grabbed a few clusters, nudging me to take a bite. I pulled off a single berry and savored it, trying to sense any subtleties that it had. I felt the texture of the skin as I moved it around on my tongue, then bit down on the sweet and slightly firm flesh, biting through to the seed.

"Why'd you do that?"

"Do what?" I had no idea what he was on about. I grabbed another berry.

He gestured toward my face, almost like he was shooing it away. "That! Just eat the damn thing. Look."

He took the full grape cluster and shoehorned it into his face, barely managing to find his mouth.

"See. Just go for it. Tastes a whole lot better that way."

I took a larger bite out of my cluster, eating nearly everything in one go. The grapes exploded as I broke their skins, their sappy, sugar-rich juices coating the insides of my mouth with intense blackberries and Bing cherries. Their texture bathed my entire mouth—I could *feel* the grapes on my tongue. And the more I chewed, the sweeter and more intense the flavor grew.

I smacked Eric on his back. "Yup, you're right."

He smacked me even harder, his hand feeling like a baseball mitt filled with concrete landing square on my chest. "I know."

We walked over to the sorting table, which wasn't much more than an elevated conveyor belt. A forklift would lift the plastic containers (or T-bins) holding a ton of fruit about fifteen feet in the air, then tilt its load onto the belt. The grapes would then make their way down the length of the table, then fall into the hopper of the destemmer, which would separate the individual grapes.

Before the grapes could reach the destemmer though, they had to be sorted. All kinds of things could be, and most likely will be, in a vineyard. Snakes are fine enough. They don't bother the wine and wouldn't make it into the fruit bin to begin with. What you worry about are deer, birds, and other cute animals that wait just as we do for the perfect ripeness before they take their first bite of the year. Even that's fine. You count on there being a bit of competition for a prized cluster. What you don't always know about until it is on the sorting table is how much mold, mildew, hail damage, or *Botrytis*, might be in a given lot of grapes. The guys in the vineyard do the best they can to spot these things as they're picking, but you can do only so much while you are sorting through thousands upon thousands of tiny pieces of fruit with a small pair of clippers.

I took my place at the sorting table as the forklift brought over the first grapes of the day. I wasn't experienced like everyone else at the table, but it was a job most folks could pick up on the fly. The pile of Pinot Noir fruit hit the table with a wet thud, tinting the white conveyor belt a brownish-pink. The destemmer started up with a *whirrrr* and the table began to hum, slowly moving the grapes on their way. There were four of us, two on each side of the table, with a large bucket next to us for collecting moldy, Botrytised, rotted, or otherwise subpar grapes. It was a great setup; I even managed to get some into the bucket while tossing rejected clusters and leaves at my feet.

Out of the four of us, I was the least experienced, the oldest, and most out of shape. Megan, the twenty-four-year-old student from Australia who was stationed to my right, was tasked with showing me the sorting ropes. She was one of seven others that had come to the winery from Australia and New Zealand, having already worked harvest there months earlier. Like a few others, she traveled around the globe a harvest at a time. She loved the work, the freedom, and reason to travel. I admired her willingness to be in a constant state of transition just for the love of wine.

"No, no. Look at me," she said. "You can't just grab a few clusters at a time and try to catch everything. You just need to get in there, yeah. Turn over as many as you can, see. Watch me, my hands, yeah. They keep moving, you see. Don't stop until the grapes stop."

In any given lot, she explained, you could have clusters with *Botrytis* that look dried out, all of the life sucked out of them, and stiff as hardened clay. Mold is also a problem, especially with Pinot Noir because the moisture can get in between the berries, but without strong winds to dry it back up, things start to grow. You can't just toss out one of the berries that look bad; you have to look in between the berry's crevices to see if anything's growing in there too.

You didn't want leaves either, brown or green. They gave off a vegetal flavor. The best thing to do, Megan reiterated, was to get out everything that didn't look edible.

"If you wouldn't want to put it in your mouth, yeah, toss 'er out!" she said. "Don't put it in the wine."

"What about the caterpillars and pincer bugs? Toss 'em?"

"No, leave those in; they're good luck, those."

"Spiders?"

"I leave 'em in. I can't stand touching 'em. But have a go if you like."

Each time I tossed out a cluster I felt bad about it. A lot of time, sacrifice, and energy went into these grapes, not to mention money. I started letting some of them go—even the grapes that looked a little bloated, but in general seemed fine. That is, until Megan stopped the machine.

She handed me a cluster that I'd let slide. It was pretty, but translucent. "Give this one a try," she said. I took a big bite and my mouth immediately puckered from the unbearable sourness. I immediately spit everything out.

"Got it." Nothing was going to jar that experience from my mind.

After the bins were filled up with individual berries, the forklift would move the bin into the barn. The grapes were then poured into the tanks, along with the growing amount of juice that came from the weight of the grapes pressing on one another. The smell was heavenly. A thousand blackberry pies baking couldn't have come close to matching the concentrated perfume coming from the tanks.

Once a tank was filled, measurements were taken: level of sugar content, temperature, and pH, or acidity. We then placed long wooden planks across the tops of the tanks, which we used as balance beams while we pushed the grapes down using long rods with disks at one end, punch-down tools. The first day we only spread the grapes around to even everything out, but every time after, the idea was to resubmerge the grapes that had floated to the top of the tank to keep everything nice and moist. If grapes dried out on top, the wine could spoil.

"You sure this is safe?" The particularly old, brittle board under me wobbled with my every movement. I had to try to focus on balancing and not hitting my head on the ceiling beams—or getting caught in all the spiderwebs—at the same time.

"It's plenty safe unless you fall in. Mine feels good though," Eric said from his wooden perch, which looked like it had been milled that morning.

Over the next three days, we had somewhat of a set schedule. We knew that we'd have grapes every day, but we had no clue when they'd come in: six A.M., noon, after we started cleaning up to end the day—no one knew. If there was fruit, everything else stopped. When there were no grapes, we'd clean a tank, clean the sorting table, clean fruit bins, and wait. Somewhere in there a bottle of wine would be poured, maybe two, but we never sat down to drink if we had fruit to get to. I always waited to try the wines during food break, since to me, nothing was worth missing out on a second of working with the fruit. It was a manic pace, but the feeling of fatigue that came with it felt amazing, fulfilling. I felt like I was in control of the current of my life. Though, what I liked most about it was the not knowing where it would take me next.

"HEY, YOU WANT TO SEE something cool?" Whenever Eric asked me this, he'd usually surprise me by playfully throwing something at me. Not this time, though. Eric had made his own wine from the 2007 vintage and he said it was finally "tasting right." I didn't understand how it could taste right in one moment and not another, but I couldn't wait to see what he had done. I figured the wine had to be a bit of an oddball, knowing his character. But as much as we joked around, Eric knew what he was doing, and I respected him for it. I knew whatever he had in those barrels would be special to be worthy of his time.

He didn't own a spare-no-expense winery like the Freemans,

but he didn't need to—they let him make his wine using all of their equipment and even let him keep his barrels in their cave while the wines aged. Eric and his barrels made me feel like there really was a future for me in all of this, that normal guys like us could end up really producing something on our own. But the question remained: Would I need his experience to do it? I wasn't as patient as he was. He'd worked seven harvests, and I'd be on the road to forty years old if I waited that long.

We walked into the only area of the cave that wasn't filled with stacked-up barrels. There were just two barrels sitting there, and they were the oldest in the winery.

"This is it?"

Eric stood there with his arms folded across his chest. "That's it." It was the proudest I'd seen him.

"Try it." He handed me what looked like a long, slightly curved glass turkey baster, which I'd come to know as a "wine thief." I plunged the thief into the barrel, drawing a small amount of the wine into the glass tube from the top. Before pulling the thief out, I used my thumb to cap the hole at the end so no wine would spill as I pulled the thief out of the barrel. I'd watched Ed and Eric do this countless times, and it was strange how natural it now felt. Raising the thief over a wineglass, I removed my thumb. A deeply colored, almost ink-black stream shot into the glass. It smelled like maple syrup, chocolate, and blackberries.

"What is this?"

"Just taste it." I did. It was fruity, soft in my mouth, and sensationally ripe. The amount of fruit knocked me back, but it was utterly impressive to drink. It was so different from what I usually drank, but it didn't matter. This was an excellent wine.

"Zin."

"Well, yeah." I tried to get the words out of my mouth to compliment his efforts but that's all I could come up with.

". . . And you don't like Zinfandel."

"I never said I didn't like it. I said I don't drink it. Not that I wouldn't."

"Well, good to see you haven't turned into a complete Euro wine snob."

Eric knew all about my preference for Burgundy, and that for me, grapes from the United States tend to be too simple in their aromas: either overly intense like a metal rock concert or all but mute. Not many of them deepen when they matured or become more interesting; they pretty much just seem to hold on. Of course, there were more than a handful of exceptions, but I still couldn't find an emotional or intellectual connection to these wines. I tried my share of older Californian wines going back to the late 1950s thanks to many generous friends who were as passionate about those wines as I was about Burgundy. Some of them were quite good, but I didn't *feel* much in them. They generally give their best right out of the gate. If you don't want to wait for something to mature, this quality is actually a benefit. Wines from the Old World countries like Italy, Germany, and France, on the other hand, aren't so upfront with revealing the best they have to offer. It can take some time. And New World wines just didn't have the history, the language, and the culture that I'd learned to love. There was something larger at play in Burgundy. The way Burgundians honor the land is the most important aspect of the resulting wine's quality. It is religion, the *grapes* gospel, and their dearest principle.

Eric didn't see wine that way. To him, all good wine was the result of time, effort, and dedication. The wine was in his hands when they bled from turning valves and fixing tools, in the part of his back that never recovered from lifting barrels. What produced great wine wasn't just the land or the grapes, it was the right person *making* it. Anything else was myth. "You can have the best grapes in the world, outstanding terroir and all," he'd say, "but if you don't know what to do to 'em, you don't have nothin' but some site-specific vinegar."

While I didn't risk saying as much, with barely a harvest under my belt I had to respectfully disagree. I already felt deep down that the right grapes need only shepherding, and much less manipulation. I had a hunch that the smartest person in the winery is one who knows how to simply get out of the way.

CHAPTER SEVEN

"I just tasted Eric's wine."

"And . . ."

"It was good. Really good actually."

"Not surprised. How long has he been at it?"

"Since he was twenty-five." She knew the look on my face; I knew the one on hers too. This wasn't going to be easy. I looked at her like that only when I really wanted something and she could see it from six miles off through the fog.

"What, you want a wine now?" Now it was out.

"What . . . what do you mean *now*?" I asked with a growing smile. She knew as well as I did that this is what I wanted from the very beginning.

Unfortunately, I had no idea what to do. On one hand, I needed more experience. I could continue interning, learning more about what I should probably know before trying to find grapes of my own. I didn't know anything about Californian wine, and I sure as hell didn't have any connections to people who could sell me grapes. But I also couldn't picture scrubbing out tanks for seven more years, or however long it would take for fate to take its course.

"But where would you make the wine, the garage?"

"I don't know." Didn't sound like a bad idea actually.

"Do you think you know enough about wine to do it?"

"I mean, yeah."

"Not just drinking it, making it."

"Oh. Well, probably not. But I could learn." I shrugged and started to think about just how crazy I must have sounded.

"I know you learn quickly, but couldn't something go wrong?"

"Sure, but things go wrong all the time anyhow, even to experienced winemakers." Judging by the look on her face, I wasn't helping my case.

"So, do people just jump right into it like this?" Before I could think of a way to answer her, she started back as she thought it through. "Wait, no they don't. Isn't there wine school or something?"

"Well . . ."

"Is there?"

"Yes, but . . ."

"You left university in your junior year. Wouldn't you need to lump a bunch of classes together to get a degree?"

"I wouldn't *need* a degree."

"Does Ed have a degree?"

"Um, yeah. He does."

"I don't know. Sounds like a lot."

She was right. If I wanted to be hired for doing anything besides cleaning tanks I'd need a lot of years under my belt or a degree in my hands, preferably both. With anything less than that I wouldn't be taken seriously by winery owners, let alone vineyard owners. They worked hard to grow their grapes, and the wine business was an expensive one to get into anyhow. They wouldn't entrust a know-nothing with nothing to show but naive enthusiasm. Who didn't have passion? You needed to have dirt under your nails, scars on your hands. A neatly typed résumé with years of sales experience was useless in this culture. And saying you were successful in a distant career only made winery owners think that maybe you'd be better off back where you'd come from.

THE NEXT DAY AT WORK, I asked Eric about getting fruit.

"I wish I knew myself. I wanted some Pinot and wound up with Zin. Happy I did, but it wasn't my first choice." Then he looked at me as if he had forgotten who had asked him the question. "Wait, *you* want grapes?"

"Why wouldn't I?"

"What would you do with 'em? You don't even know how to wrap up a hose the right way." Those hoses did always give me a tough time. "Nah, I'm just breaking your balls. You could do it." He shrugged. "Anyone could." Was that a compliment?

I asked the winery's owner, Ken, if he knew anyone that would be interested in selling a ton of fruit to me. That would get me a couple of barrels or so.

"For something that small, I'd say to just ask some of the growers we deal with. See if they are willing to do it." I wasn't expecting such a simple solution.

A few growers came by that day to drop off fruit, but no one wanted to sell me anything. Each time the conversation would quickly change to concerns about how much experience I had, or where I would produce the wine—Ken and his wife, Akiko, had made it clear that they were out of room. Even Eric was going to have to look for a new home for his barrels soon because the Freemans had planted their own vines and were expecting a large increase in their own production.

What had started as an innocent thought quickly became a full-blown fixation. I needed those grapes, but with the next harvest only ten months away, I was already running out of time. There was a good chance that a lot of next year's fruit was already spoken for. So I was desperate. I tried calling a few of the local growers whom I knew only from tasting their wines. But weeks went by and nothing happened. Each time I'd check back with a winery, I was told to call another time. I'd usually do five callbacks before I'd get the hint. I didn't mind looking like a fool, but I was losing traction and in serious need of some inspiration.

I didn't have to look too far. Isabella was just learning to sit up on her own, starting to make sounds that hinted at her voice, smiling at me when I walked into a room and would cry whenever I'd head out of one. She looked exactly like Christian when she was her age. Big, deep dimples on her cheeks, huge beautiful brown eyes, and long brown curly hair. I enjoyed all of the things that my friends had warned me about, like staying up late, burping her, or having to pick her up to hold her in the middle of the night when she was scared or lonely. I had been the little brother, the youngest son that had grown up being looked after, now I was happily protecting and comforting my little angel. I knew that those moments would be fleeting and refused to let any of them pass me by.

Christian had taken some time off from being a probation officer in Novato. She missed the work, yet seeing her at home watching our girl was something that made the importance of being a father and a husband hit home. Watching how Christian nurtured life during those nine months had brought new meaning to every aspect of my life—it drove me, focused me, and forced me to face the reality that life is too brief to feel that "things were just meant to be a certain way."

We were happy. Living in the North San Francisco Bay Area, everything we had ever wanted was available at arm's length. Watersports like Jet Skiing, snowboarding in Lake Tahoe, trips to Los Angeles and Las Vegas, seafood at the Fisherman's Wharf, San Francisco nightlife, amazing restaurants that hosted unforgettable wine dinners, an unbelievable wine culture where you could always find a wine shop pouring interesting wines, and one of my favorite things about the States, driving on the Pacific Coast Highway. By spending just a few hours in the car, you could see the ocean, snow, forest, or any number of big cities. Los Angeles, San Francisco, Sacramento, they were all in my extended backyard.

The weather was generally comfortable, which made it easy to enjoy the beautiful landscape around us. We were surrounded by lush forests, thriving gardens, and of course the bay, which was only fifteen minutes away. We lived in a nice, modest suburban town in a respectable house filled with every gadget, device, and thing we could possibly want. We had the beginnings of the family we'd always wanted. But I couldn't get out of my head that we were living a life that had no real foundation. Soon we'd be caught up in what everyone else around us was—always wanting bigger, better, more. I wanted something more lasting for Bella. Every time the little voice in my head said, "You gotta go get those grapes," I knew exactly where the voice was coming from and I had no choice but to listen.

THREE WEEKS HAD PASSED SINCE the first time I'd asked Eric about getting grapes, and we were now moving all of the 2008 wines from the steel tanks and into their barrels inside of the cave. Harvest was long over, but a lot of the growers would still come by the winery to check on us, their boots muddied, their clothes showing that they worked for everything they had and didn't give a damn about how they looked doing it.

I admired them. They worked, sacrificed, and cared for their land. And they couldn't have been more fulfilled doing it. It would be impossible to untangle their struggle from their dedication and love for what they did.

"Eric, man, I need some grapes," I said, unable to stop pestering him.

"I told you before, if I could find some Pinot, I'd be buying it myself."

"Look, it doesn't have to be Pinot." Eric pushed his mouth to one side of his face as he thought about the different growers.

"Petite Sirah?"

"What about it?"

"You said anything, right?"

"I didn't say anything. I said I needed to make it happen."

Eric shrugged his shoulders and smiled. "Well . . . same difference."

"I dunno." I didn't know the first thing about Petite Sirah. I'd never even tasted it before. But I did know there may still be fruit hanging on the vines because Petite Sirah got picked later in the year.

"Well, I know a guy. Could be worth checking it out, even for a Euro snob in training. I have his number if you want."

"I'll take it."

"Listen, I didn't say that it was a sure thing. You still need to call him."

"Aw, man, really?"

"What? First you weren't interested and now you're pissed 'cuz it isn't a sure thing? Just call the guy." Eric scribbled the number on a piece of paper for me. For the rest of the day I thought about the grapes, *my* grapes. I dug into my pants pocket for the paper, folding it between my fingers in anticipation. As soon as we were done, I hopped into my car, pulled the worn paper from my pocket, and made the call.

"Yeah?" Eric's guy didn't sound too interested in speaking.

"Hi, I was just given your number by Eric at—"

"This is Eric *who*?"

"No, I was given your number by Eric at Freeman Winery."

All of a sudden his voice was more welcoming. "Oh, Eric. Yeah. Funny little bastard, that one." He let out a coughing laugh. "So, what can I do you for?"

"I'm just hoping I can get some grapes—"

"Ah, you're a winemaker?"

"Not really. I mean, I'd like to—"

"Wait, if you aren't a winemaker, what do you want grapes for?"

"I'm actually learning to do everything. Well, I will. I'm at the winery doing the basics."

"So, ferments, add backs, sulfur levels, volatile acidity, and topping up, you learnin' all that at Freeman?"

"Right now I'm just scrubbing tanks. But I'll get there."

"And just how do you aim to get there?" He sounded amused.

"That's the thing. I was going to ask if I could buy some grapes . . ."

"From who, me?" I listened as he took a drag from his cigarette and laughed out all of his smoke.

I laughed too. Well, it was funny. "Yeah. Do you still have grapes?"

He recovered from his laugh, working his way into a creaking wheeze. "I do. I do. You know what, let me talk to my son and see if we want to sell 'em. We will be picking in a couple of weeks or so."

"Thanks, I really appreciate it!"

"Oh no, son. Don't thank me yet. I ain't said you could have 'em just yet. But you never know, right?"

I rushed home to Christian. I had called her minutes before telling her that I had great news, and she'd sounded worried. Nervous maybe. At this point it was clear that my idea of great news could mean taking gambles without much in the way of guarantees.

I didn't even bother with hello when I flung open the door. "All right, you know how we were talking about getting grapes?"

"I remember *you* talking about grapes."

"Well, I found some." She looked genuinely excited, which surprised me.

"But isn't harvest over? Where'd you find the grapes?"

"Eric gave me a number today of a grower. He has some Petite Sirah for sale that is still hanging."

"Petite Sirah?" I couldn't tell if she was upset or if I had finally convinced her that I was crazy. "You don't know anything about Petite Sirah." Her face finally settled on the convinced-I-was-crazy look.

"That's just it. Does it really even matter that I don't know anything about the grape? I mean, aside from drinking a lot of it,

I don't know that much about Pinot Noir either! I'm willing to bet it doesn't make a difference what the grape is, you just do the basics and the rest comes down to where the vineyard is and how good the grapes are."

"Honey, no. It makes a difference. How would you think the grape wouldn't matter?"

"I mean, it does. Of course it does. But I need to start somewhere."

"And you are still young. You have time."

"Who says?"

"Honey. You still have time." She rested her hand on my shoulder.

"Don't you want to have our own wine?"

"Yeah. But not like this. I want us to have something we love. We don't even know what a mature Petite Sirah tastes like. What if it gets messed up?"

"Then at least I mess up on something that isn't too expensive."

"So, you are proposing spending money on something because it won't really matter if it gets ruined?" Her arms crossed tightly in front of her chest.

"Well, yeah. No. Not exactly. Maybe. Yeah, that's about it. Yup."

"Honey." Oh no, not again. "Why don't you wait for what you really want. If you are patient I know you will get exactly what you want. Think about it for a while. What do you *really* want?"

It was a valid question. And it was one I'd asked myself repeatedly since walking out of Merrill Lynch. It was time for me to put everything on the line and be honest with myself. I realized what I wanted most couldn't have been farther away from the place I'd called home my entire life. No matter the question, my answer would always lead me to Burgundy.

"If I *really* had a choice," I said softly, the tenor of my voice dropping with the gravity of what I feared could follow, "it would be Burgundy."

"Burgundy. Are you serious?" At first I thought I wasn't, that maybe when the words left my mouth they would seem comical, ridiculous even to me. But just like that, she had turned the unfathomable into something that seemed like it could actually work. She didn't intend it, but I heard something in her voice that sounded like she thought I could actually do it.

She began counting on her fingers, teasing me with each thought:

"We don't have much money."

"True."

"You have no experience."

"Hey, what about the harvest I just did?" I thought it over. "OK, I'll give you that one."

"What else? Oh, we don't have grapes. Would French people even sell grapes to us?"

"I don't know. They might." I was sure they wouldn't.

"Even if they did, how would they get here from France?" I knew she meant it as a final blow that would crumple the conversation, balling it up and throwing it into the trash, never to be retrieved again.

I thought for a second and then quipped, "We'd have to go there."

"We've never even *been* to France."

"This could work. . . ."

"How? How could it work when the most we know about France is the one French couple we met in Italy?"

"I guess, but what if . . ." But the conversation was already over in her mind. We both went to our separate corners— Christian still patting herself on her own back for averting disaster; me smiling as I thought seriously about how the puzzle could fit together. No one could hear it, but the starting gun had fired.

CHAPTER EIGHT

"*Bone jor. Jeswee oon American kee shersha por da ray-sone.*"

"*Vous êtes qui, monsieur?*"

Shit. I frantically scrambled to find my response list.

"Uh, I don't actually know what that means. I'm sorry. Can I call you back?"

The line went dead. This wasn't working out as I thought it would.

I should have been asleep by now. Christian and Bella had gone to bed hours ago, and were now resting soundly despite my attempts to make phone calls to grape brokers, *courtiers* in Burgundy. Using the light from the television, I could read my notes that I had scattered all over the bed. Littered among them were maps, documents, and scripts with a few keywords that I thought would be helpful in these conversations. Unfortunately, I couldn't easily make a connection between the sounds and how they were written, so I jotted everything down phonetically. Well, not phonetically, but pretty much how I imagined it might sound based on a free text translating service that I'd found online. What else could I do? I didn't actually know what French sounded like. The closest I had gotten was from hearing that French couple in Florence years earlier, but I heard just as much Italian, laughter, and old pans banging away in the kitchen at the same time to have taken anything from it.

In my mind, the plan was simple: I didn't need the best grapes from the highest classification level—all I wanted was village-level grapes, the third rank of potential quality. These wines weren't blockbusters, they didn't display terribly unique terroir, but what they did was show characteristics of the place they came from. The next qualitative level down, Bourgogne-level, would taste like a generic Burgundy because the grapes could come from anywhere, usually just outside the areas classified as village level or the plains somewhere. As you descended the classification tiers, the distinctiveness of a vineyard from the land next to it decreased significantly. The closer to Bourgogne-level land, the more the vineyards trended together. I wanted to see firsthand the magic, how grapes from a specific patch of dirt could express themselves with a clear and direct voice, distinct from that of its neighbor. Having a Bourgogne-level wine wouldn't get me much more than mumbling. I'd been offered Bourgogne grapes during my cold calls, but I was holding out for village level.

Village-level wines offered a general sense of the expression of grapes from the vineyards around each village. A Chambolle-Musigny village wine had amazing finesse; a Nuits-Saint-Georges usually had either supple fruit or austere meatiness; a Gevrey-Chambertin could display tons of wild dark fruits while being gentle, rarely tannic. That's what I wanted, the cheap seats to the terroir exhibition. Most important, I'd be able to experience the magic of holding grapes in my hand that could tell the story of where they came from. They were connected to the soil, to a place, and they already had a strong personality. Reading old passages about the character of these wines in modern books, known well by people who loved the wines centuries ago, made me appreciate how fleeting life is but how timeless the land is.

I called another of the more than three hundred grape brokers I'd found from googling "grape broker Burgundy."

"*Je sherch por raysan village.*" I was getting better, or maybe it was just that my increasing desperation did wonders in doing away with any hesitation or embarrassment about how awful I sounded.

"Ah." The guy laughed. "Your French is *horrible*."

"I know. I know."

"No, really. It is without a doubt the worst French I've heard."

"I get it."

"You know, most people at least . . ."

"I get it. Believe me, I get it."

He continued laughing. "So, you want grapes?" Finally, we were getting somewhere.

"Yes. Preferably village."

"Well, you should really learn French then. You'd have a better chance of someone knowing what you are saying. You know, it really is bad, your French."

"Thanks."

"All right. *Rouge ou les blancs?*"

". . . I . . . don't really know what you just said."

"Red or white, *monsieur*, red or white?"

"Oh. Red."

"I have not any red classed as village."

I really didn't want white grapes. I found reds infinitely more complex, but if I had to start out with some white, it would still be something to celebrate. I quickly thought about the renowned villages that produced heavenly white wines filled with honey and apples—that wouldn't be so bad, right? Chassagne-Montrachet, Puligny-Montrachet . . . Meursault! And what about Saint-Aubin? This really could be exciting!

"Whites then?"

"I'm sorry, I do not have any whites either." *Then why did you even ask?!* I thought.

"OK, please keep my number if you find anything."

"I won't call Australia, monsieur."

"I live in America."

"I won't call there either. You can call me, though."

"OK, when should I call back?"

"Maybe it's best if you don't. Good luck on your experiment."

Against my better judgment I scooted over to Christian and shook her shoulder softly.

"Hey . . . you awake?" I knew the answer, but I couldn't wait until morning.

"What?" She couldn't even open her eyes. "What's that sound, what's with the papers everywhere?"

"I'll explain later. Hey, what do you think about going to France?"

"France. Like, Paris?" Her eyes shot open.

"Mmmm hmm. But also, Burgundy."

"Burgundy?" She saw through me in an instant. "Right. Well, if we go, we have to see Paris too."

"Yeah, Paris, croissants, coffee . . ."

"You hate coffee."

"Well, I'll watch you drink it, whatever you want."

"OK. But let's talk some more in the morning."

"OK, love you, honey." I opened my laptop back up.

"You're not going to sleep?"

"Yeah, I will. I will. I'm just . . . I gotta look at something real quick."

"All right, but don't stay up too late."

As soon as her eyes were all the way shut, I started searching online for anything that might help my cause—sites on how to learn French quickly, cheap deals on airfare to France, and most ambitiously, houses to rent. Soon I had the start of a foolproof plan. I didn't have the middle or ending worked out yet, but I figured that they would come together along the way.

"What did you want to talk about?" Christian asked when she woke up a few hours later. I was still awake, too amped up to fall asleep.

"Well, I think we can do it."

She smiled nervously. ". . . Do what?"

"Get to Burgundy."

Her mouth didn't move. She sat there; the smile on her face had passed, her eyes glazing over. She said a lot of things with her big brown eyes gazing at mine; none of them were things I'd like to repeat.

I assured her that I was only looking to go there temporarily. We'd just visit, get a lay of the land. We finally came to an agreement: I would get to spend some time in Burgundy if we also got to see Paris and Champagne, where Christian had always dreamed of going.

We would have to plan the trip on a shoestring budget. We'd been chipping away at our savings since neither of us had checks coming in. And the money we did have in the account wasn't much to speak of to begin with. But we had eleven thousand dollars, which was plenty to get us to France. It was maybe even enough to enjoy ourselves—so long as we didn't think about how we were using the last of our savings for a trip that may or may not lead to some actual income. But it was enough—perhaps even to start our business if we did manage to find some grapes.

"But won't we need to learn French?" she asked.

I smiled, somehow confident of the journey ahead of us. "Don't worry. I was up all night studying. We'll be fine."

I thought that would be the last of the conversation. I had the green light to go to Burgundy to sniff things out, and Christian and Bella were coming with me.

I RAN THE IDEA BY my parents and my brother, and they were as supportive as they'd been when I first left Merrill. My parents figured as long as you worked hard, you'd get the success you deserved. They'd always been like that. I'd tell them a crazy idea that had zero chance of working and the response was always the same: "You can do it." I couldn't say why that was, but I used it to push myself. If enough people believed it could happen, wouldn't it have to? In my head, our bags were packed, I clutched the tickets in my hand, the smell of fresh and flaky, buttery croissants mere seconds away. But Christian announced she wanted me to write a business plan as a condition to agreeing to our trip.

A business plan? I didn't want to do that. No one thinks about the cost of fuel when fantasizing about driving a sports car around the Nürburgring; they just want to do it! But the woman had a point.

I spent a week on the plan. I couldn't think of anything else. I had to tally up all of our expenses, which would be many. If we stuck to our original plan, we'd be in France for nearly three weeks while still paying rent for the house we had just moved into in Novato. Christian would be missing work, and I'd been without a paycheck for the past few weeks since harvest had officially ended. Then there were the utilities we'd still have to pay while away, airfare, food costs, train fare, incidentals. There, in two little columns on Microsoft Excel, my dream went from feasible to outrageous. Numbers can be heartbreaking, but they don't lie. We didn't have the money.

"Surprise, surprise," said Christian, looking over the long list of expenses from the chair next to me. She was shaking her head, but she didn't look upset. She looked strangely calm.

"I know. I thought it would come together. But maybe it shouldn't happen. It's stupid to even be thinking about wine while we're trying to get our family started. Our backs are already to the wall."

"You're right. We don't have the money to do it if we are trying to be *practical*—"

I cut her off. "I know, I know—you don't have to rub it in. I already feel selfish enough—"

"You didn't let me finish." A coy smile was spreading across her face. "What I was going to say was, while we don't have enough money for this to be entirely logical, that doesn't mean we can't do it."

She looked like my wife, but it didn't make any sense that the words I was hearing were hers. They were far-fetched, unrealistic, and really shortsighted. They sounded like my words. She poked me in my ribs with her index finger, like she always did to cheer me up, and said, "Let's do it. Let's go."

So we did.

CHAPTER NINE

ON THE PLANE I FINALIZED THE LIST OF COURTIERS THAT I wanted to meet with once we landed in Burgundy. I'd called most of them already—some even seemed like they could understand me. My French had come a long way from simply horrible to pretty bad in the six weeks since I first started to make calls. I'd spent hours studying old French films like Jean-Luc Godard's *À bout de souffle*, *Pierrot le Fou,* and *Bande à part* and François Truffaut's *Les Quatre Cents Coups* and mixed in some more recent films like Claude Berri's *Jean de Florette* and *Manon des Sources* and Luc Besson's *Nikita*. I'd watch for three to four hours at a time, pausing, slow-motion playing and rewinding each movie to catch the French dialogue as it lined up with the English subtitles. I also watched English-language movies that I knew well and put on the French subtitles. Christian wasn't immediately convinced it was the most serious training I could be doing, but once she started to catch me talking more in the language, and making some sense, she stopped poking fun about French film school. Bella was usually right next to me on the couch, watching along throughout the day. I'd also stream radio from Dijon and spent hours picking random words in English that I used Google Translate to render the French and vice versa. I made a game out of remembering how to say things, and I wouldn't move on from a word or phrase until I said it perfectly.

A lot had happened since I'd made those first calls. Most important, Christian was on board with the idea of giving Burgundy a chance to work. Plus, now we'd be meeting face-to-face with grape brokers. Anyone could call someone on the phone; I was going to be in their offices, slightly improved French and all—it would have to make a difference. Of course, I didn't yet have any meetings. But I'd find a way to get them and then shake the brokers' hands, look them in the eye, and tell them how much I adore Burgundy. I'd tell them how I wasn't looking for anything special—just village-level grapes that even a rookie couldn't screw up. I didn't even care which village, not that I'd have a choice anyhow. All I would ask was that they be red.

Instead of sleeping on the flight, I reflected on the grapes that I'd spent the past four years reading about, fantasizing about, obsessing over, and drinking whenever the moment presented itself. Gevrey-Chambertin: rich, lush, and brimming with black and red fruits alike, raspberries and blackberries. Then there are the wines of Vosne-Romanée. They have a distinctive spiciness to them, like a dense spice cake. Their perfume smells of warmed cloves, and it only deepens and unfolds the longer it ages. There is a gentleness with a lurking power to these wines that defies logic. A lot of Burgundy wines get better with age, showing layer upon layer of indescribable fruit, meaty, spicy, and herbaceous aromas, and these are no exception. They can challenge their owner to a duel of longevity, breezing through fifty years like it is nothing. But for me, the wines of Chambolle-Musigny were the most thrilling. Burgundy has the reputation for producing sensual wines, wines described with adjectives like *graceful, elegant,* and *poised.* Yet if there is one village that has earned this reputation more than all the others, Chambolle has to be it. The wines from this village tend to smell more like perfume than wine, with a rich fragrance of raspberries, Bing cherries, and rose petals. To enjoy a wine from Chambolle is to see its beautiful ruby color, to smell each of its petals, and to notice each line of its seductive poetry. You don't need to recite each thing you taste, that only ruins it. Think of how much it wishes to please you, and enjoy. Certain phrases, fragrances, even colors can emerge when you're drinking, but getting caught up in those small details is like listening to Beethoven while examining each note on its own, out of the context of the complete work.

In Burgundy, the extreme variations in soil type, depth, and composition as well as rainfall, direction and quantity of wind, distance to the underground water table, topography, microbiology, microclimate, and a multitude of other factors create distinct parcels of land that consistently produce wines of varying quality levels and characteristics. Grapes grown from two parcels located just meters apart can be radically different.

The grapes that provide the most singular expressions over time, wines that are explicit in their message, wines that taste like only a wine of that place can, those are classified as the best of the best. In the middle of the nineteenth century, a landowner, university professor, and writer called these vineyards premier cru, while the most celebrated vineyards at the head of this classification were classified as tête de cuvée. The majority of the vineyards classified today as grands crus, or great growths, were at that time classified as either tête de cuvée or premier cuvée, but a few were ranked as deuxième cuvée, the next level down in potential quality. There are eight white grand cru vineyards and twenty-five devoted to red. The total surface area of Burgundy devoted to grand cru vineyards is around 2 percent. At the premier cru level, the vineyards still have a great individuality to them, but they also share a similarity to the village-level wines that surround them. There are many premier cru vineyards, but they still represent only less than 10 percent of the total surface area of Burgundy. It is important to note that the wines themselves aren't classified; it is only the potential of the vineyard.

The village wines aren't the ones being poetically written about by the likes of famous wine critics or fawned over on wine blogs, but they can be just as magical. They still speak of a place and a moment in time. But because they are ranked third in the Burgundy grape hierarchy—below grand cru and premier cru—I hoped I had a better chance at finding just a few small barrels' worth. Even though they are modest grapes that commonly produce bottles of wine that sell for under thirty dollars, they were still very much in high demand. While grapes of this level don't usually get too complex, they can offer loads of pleasure, especially after a decade in bottle. Far too many of them are consumed too young; not many of them are given the twenty-plus years they are capable of developing through.

I knew the grands crus and premiers crus were the real heroes of Burgundy, the vineyards that had distinct stories to share. But they'd have to wait. Village grapes were proving to be difficult enough.

ARRIVING IN PARIS WAS ANTICLIMACTIC. Coming from the San Francisco Bay Area, being in another big city didn't seem like too much of a change. Everyone was rushing, and no one said hello. Cars honked, cigarette smoke wafted in your face, and everywhere you looked was construction and traffic. After listening to Christian going on about Paris for the past two months, though, I half expected to be visiting the Emerald City. As much as I wanted to be open to the opportunity to get to know a city that I'd heard so much about, all I could find in the sprawling City of Light were countless similarities with San Francisco.

We rented an apartment from a young financial professional in the 18th arrondissement.

"You know, this place isn't too bad," said Christian, taking in our tight quarters.

I was thankful that she still had Paris blinders on. We had a water heater the size of a coffee can, a dishwasher you couldn't open unless all the kitchen drawers were shut, and an electric stove with one burner that couldn't be bothered to get more than warm.

"Sure, if you've ever wondered what it was like to live inside of a mouse trap." I wanted to say it, but I didn't have any right to complain. I figured if nothing else, this would give us a chance to see what living in France was like. We could make our own food—after all, there was a microwave—and walk almost anywhere we needed to. It was a good thing too. Any time I'd use the car to get anywhere I'd need to spend another thirty minutes just to park. And if you left your car on any of those narrow, alley-like streets, you were begging to have your side mirrors yanked off by a Citroën or Vespa passing by at autoroute speeds.

I quickly discovered the perks, though. Every morning I could smell the freshly baked bread climbing up the five flights of spiraling stairs to our apartment. And then there were the pastries. The tarte framboises, tarte au citron, financier, and mille feuilles made me consider how much I actually valued being thin. Turned out I didn't care much since I gorged myself like Paris was going to run out of butter, sugar, vanilla custard, and ruby-like raspberries. I never understood the appeal of the greasy hockey pucks posing as croissants in San Francisco sold at French-inspired bakeries that had nothing French about them besides a name I couldn't pronounce. Here they were flaky, pillow-like, and yet rich with butter. I couldn't think about them without my stomach barking at me through my sweater. Christian would dispense me to buy some in the morning, and I'd grab a few extra just to eat on the way home.

At first I had thought there was no way that French produce could measure up to our California bounty, but the stalls lining the streets were a vision of reds, greens, yellows, and oranges jumping off one of Matisse's canvases. Walking by the produce stands, I could close my eyes and name things they were offering just by their unmistakable smell. Plums and peaches looked ready to burst with sweet liquid, and cherries and wild strawberries were like tiny jewels stacked into neat little pyramids. The tomatoes had just come off the vine and were still warm from the morning's sun. If you stopped to look at anything for more than a second, out would come a paring knife and a vendor would push a slice of his or her ware into your palm. I learned quickly to appreciate the hand attached to the knife just as much as the produce being offered. The guys with dirt-stained, calloused hands were the ones with the best samples. These were the men and women who looked after their crops day after day, nurturing them into their sweetest, ripest destiny.

After two weeks in Paris, we drove two hours northeast to Reims, the capital of Champagne. It was out of the way of

Burgundy, which was pretty much a straight shot south of Paris, but it had been Christian's part of the deal. She loved drinking the sparkling white wine and had always wanted to see the fairy-tale town. I, on the other hand, couldn't stand the stuff. The only time I drank it was to make Christian happy. For me, bubbles take away from the drinking experience. And I couldn't stand all the pomp and circumstance of the culture. The vineyards were way too big to get excited about, and the wineries were such behemoths that it would be impossible to meet the actual winemaker, let alone the owner. More likely, I figured, we'd be stuck with some quasi-executive assistant associate junior marketing intern representative or whatever to show us around. But it was a small price to pay to get to Burgundy.

On the drive down, Christian was still riding the post-Paris high. She chattered on and on about the Eiffel Tower, the old stone buildings, the beautiful bridges, the coffee, the unrelenting pace, and the food (*the food!*). I could agree about the architecture and the food at least. But as the rolling hillside vineyards of Reims came into view, she quieted.

"I know you don't like Champagne," she said while patting my shoulder, "but thank you for taking me here."

I took in the glow of her face. Then I looked down at Bella, who was fast asleep in her arms.

Champagne did produce staggeringly brilliant wines. They weren't my preference, but I wanted to let go of some of the prejudices that I had been holding onto. But what still kept detracting from my experience was that it was so large and so corporate. Yeah, some of the buildings were really old, and the wines bore the names of estates that had been established hundreds of years ago, but I couldn't shake the feeling that I could have just as easily been standing in a cheese factory or lightbulb manufacturing plant. It felt sterile, cold, and distant. I didn't get a sense of who grew these grapes or the work that had gone into making the wine. I couldn't taste the land. I did love the old chalk caves that plunged deep into the earth, but the fact that Champagne wines are blended wines didn't really interest me too much. I decided to focus on what Christian loved about the wines. Our time there would be brief, and soon we'd touch the soil I'd obsessed about for nearly five years.

CHAPTER TEN

THE SNOW HAD BLANKETED EVERYTHING IN SIGHT, TURNING the proud hillside vineyards into sleek slopes that looked better suited to skiing than growing grapes. Below the dustings of snow, the vines were dormant and bare, the branches having been clipped in November, leaving nothing but a stump as a reminder of what spring would bring in a few months' time.

I pictured the breathtaking landscape, taking in each undulation of land, studying each rise and fall of land within a vineyard. The land in Burgundy was alive. Up high on the slopes would be village-level grapes. They'd struggle to get ripe in the chilling winds blowing through the forests above. And the shallower, more limestone-rich soil up there would barely be able to retain enough moisture to help the plants thrive. Conversely, the vines at the foot of each hill, which were also classified as village, often got too much water. While their higher-altitude cousins struggled to sop up every molecule of rainfall, these vines grew in soil rich with moisture-absorbing clay that had settled to the base of the slopes. But absorbent soil combined with water runoff from the higher slopes meant flooding was potentially an issue in wet vintages. In a warm vintage when rainfall was scarce, the vine-yards' ability to hold on to water was precious.

What the monks knew, however, was that the band running through the middle of each rise was usually the sweet spot for growing grapes. There was a more hospitable mix of erodible limestone and spongy clay. The soil got just enough water from what would run down the hill and released what it didn't need. Some of the otherwise better-situated sites had the problem of wind, which could shoot through the gaps in the escarpments. Most of the more renowned vineyards were protected from too much wind and other elements, making them prime real estate for growing fruit to its fullest expression. This was where the grand cru grapes were grown. But all the vineyards were magical. Something that was impossible to quantify and defied logic had allowed each plot of dirt to produce wines for more than a thousand years that were unlike anything else in the world.

Too many times I had thought about what it would mean to be here, to be standing in the very spot that I had read about so many times before. It was humbling imagining my steps crossing over the same steps of the people who'd written important books about Burgundy or had even worked in the vineyards themselves. While drinking in my education back in California, I would hold a bottle of Burgundy and look at the label, thinking about the little piece of land that the wine had come from. But to actually be here, to see the hillsides that had captured the hearts of people like the emperor Napoleon, the noted wine lover Thomas Jefferson, and the great king Charlemagne was almost too much to take in. For my eyes to gaze on what theirs once had was the closest thing I could imagine to time travel.

Unlike in Champagne, there were no large buildings cluttering the countryside. Every now and then we'd drive past small villages, but even these scattered collections of structures were at the foot of the surrounding vines. Smoke curled from the chimneys of stone houses, and our car filled with the smell of baking bread. The few people we passed were bundled up in wool hats and gloves, fetching the morning's baguette. An old man braved the ice and teetered by on his bicycle, his collection of bread rolled up in newspaper and tucked under his folded arm.

After checking into the hotel, we headed out into Beaune, the historical heart of Burgundy. For centuries it had served as the center of the wine trade and provided protection to its inhabitants behind its fortified walls, many of which are still standing. The city seemed to have written the script for storybook cliché. Winding cobblestone streets? Check. Ancient buildings? Check. Giant church in the village square, its bells enthusiastically clanging away? Check. Fromageries, patisseries, and boulangeries at every turn? Check, check, and . . . check. But something was off from the fairy tale. Too much English was being spoken. Many of the old buildings had been converted over to modern boutiques. And the mini tour bus running through the center of town stuffed with tourists snapping pictures of every wall, window, or random handlebar-mustached man made Beaune seem more like a theme park than a historic wine region.

We made our way out of Beaune and toward Chassagne-Montrachet. Driving south gave us a chance to see some of the vineyards and villages known for their white wine. The Côte de Nuits to the north focuses almost exclusively on red wine; nearly all of it is Pinot Noir. To the south, you have the Côte de Beaune, known for its white wines from the Chardonnay grape, but there are also famous villages known for their wonderful reds, such as

Reds

Volnay and Pommard. Today Chassagne-Montrachet is mostly planted with Chardonnay due to the greatness of their white grands crus. The most famous is Le Montrachet, long considered the top white wine vineyard in the world. Though, up until the 1970s, the village was predominantly planted with red grapes! It is one of my favorite villages for red Burgundy, my favorite in the Côte de Beaune. I adore every sip I can find of red from the premier cru vineyards of Clos de la Boudriotte and Clos Saint-Jean. In a rare anomaly, the soil there is more similar to the Côte de Nuits.

We drove down the D974, one of the smaller highways that snakes its way from one end of the Côte d'Or to the other, connecting nearly all of the most celebrated wine-producing villages. Pommard, Volnay, Meursault, Puligny-Montrachet, Chassagne-Montrachet—each village's sign we passed had a name more famous and reputed than the last. At each village we'd turn off the road and drive through the town, comparing, appraising, looking at For Sale signs and fantasizing what it would be like to live there. Every For Sale sign sent us off window shopping. More often than not the only people we'd see were peeping out from behind slightly opened wooden shutters. When someone new was in town, the news wasn't spread so much as it was sensed.

Even though I had long-ago sworn off the boring bread I'd found in California, on this trip I quickly got into the habit of stopping at every boulangerie we'd see in each of the small villages. I figured that I wouldn't be able to get a feel for what each village was like unless I was eating what the people there ate.

"*Vous venez d'où?*" a friendly looking man in the street inquired as we made our way to another bakery.

"Uh . . ." Up until now, no one in France had actually tried to speak to me in French. In Paris it was as though people could smell our American provenance. They weren't fooled by my bag stuffed full of stinky Époisses cheese and hot sliced baguettes. In Champagne, not many people were around, and those who were had been tourists too, so English was the de facto official language. In Beaune, shopkeepers offered up their English once they heard me speaking to Christian. But here in the Burgundy countryside, there was no backup-parachute language to yank me out of an uncomfortable silence. Of course, I remembered quite a bit of French from movies, French Internet news, and from a few French winery websites I'd visited. But hearing it in person left me speechless. I could hear only every third, seventh, and eighth word if I was lucky, and even then I didn't know how to respond.

I tried to let the man know I didn't have a clue what he was saying. "English? *Anglay*?" That made him even more confused. I was struggling to find the words, and he knew it. He smiled. Could this be the part where he steps up and speaks English?

"*Vous venez d'où?*" The wrinkled old man with a knitted hat settled into my uncomfortable moment, entertained by my nervousness.

"I'm sorry, I don't speak French." Just then I remembered the one emergency phrase I'd taught myself back in California. I needed to know it down pat just in case some wise ass wanted to see how serious I was about going to France. "*Je parle un peu de français.*" I speak a little French. It sounded like the words had been yanked off of my tongue.

"*Ah, oui. Vous parlez très bien. Dites moi, vouz êtes* [he pointed at me] *d'où* [he looked into the distance and then shrugged]?" The words whizzed by me as I looked off in the direction he'd pointed and then he wagged his finger at me while making a *tsk tsk tsk* sound. I wasn't getting it, but all I could think of was how cool it was that the guy thought I could speak his language. I tried using my hands to communicate, but no matter how fast I moved them around he didn't know what the hell I was talking about. Those damn movies really made it seem much easier. Instead, he shook my hand, then pulled me in close and smacked me heartily on the back.

"Welcome."

"Oh! You *do* speak English!"

He began gesturing with his hands just as I had done. "*Non, non, non, pas de tout.*" I shook his hand and grabbed his shoulder, he did the same, and Christian and I walked off toward the center of town with Bella in tow.

Christian couldn't wait to laugh at me. The look on her face said it was taking every fiber of restraint for her to not say, "You do realize you're going to have to learn some French, right?" Instead she simply said, "I think we'll do fine so long as people ask us yes or no questions."

The next day we went over to Puligny-Montrachet. We were scouting for a new place to stay, away, we hoped, from the bustling international melting pot that was Beaune. Just like the other towns, we didn't see many people around. The scene was one directly out of the postapocalyptic films in which everyone flees at once, leaving their homes behind. We weren't too confident that we'd find anything promising, but before heading back onto route nationale 74, we saw an old building that had been renovated and turned into a hotel.

No one stopped us at the front door, so we decided to take a peek inside. As we slipped in, we nearly bumped into a tall, robust man with striking silver hair capped by a large leather cowboy hat.

"Are you all lost? I hope not." My chest loosened upon hearing his English, which was quite good.

"No, we're just looking for a hotel."

"Well, you *are* in a hotel. Are you still looking?" He was friendly and charming in a way that melted the defenses we'd put up against the occasional indifferent locals. He saw that Bella was sleeping on my chest in the BabyBjörn, and leaned in and kissed her on her curly head of hair, which draped in front on her face.

He whispered, "I think she would like this place. Would you like to see more of it?"

We didn't know what to expect, but we followed him as he gingerly led us from the front door toward the rooms on the second floor.

The floor was a rich combination of white marble and polished wood. Looking inside the open doors, we saw each guest room had its own crystal chandelier. We passed the hotel's restaurant, where large mahogany tables were set up with twelve wineglasses at each setting, ready for a large wine tasting.

"So, what is the name of this hotel?" I asked.

"It is the Maison Olivier Leflaive," he replied. It finally hit me. I'd seen pictures of Olivier Leflaive when reading about Burgundy. His cowboy hat made me recognize him, and his family was one of the most respected in Burgundy. They had everything from Bourgogne vineyards to several white grands crus. Maybe I'd be able to score some grapes if everything went well.

I pulled at the back of Christian's sweater as we walked back down the stairs and leaned in to whisper.

"What if this place is too expensive? It looks too expensive," I whispered. "We can't afford a place like this."

Christian didn't have an interest in playing shy. "Sir, how much—I'm sorry, what is your name?"

"Oh, I apologize. My name is Olivier Leflaive. This is my hotel."

"Mister Leflaive, we were just curious, how much does it cost to stay here?"

He thought for a moment, taking off his hat, rubbing the edge of it with the flat part of his thumb. "Well, that depends. What is your budget?"

"I'm afraid we don't have much of one."

"Normally, a room during the low season—that is what we are in now—is around three hundred fifty euros a night."

I shook my head, embarrassed. "Yeah . . . that isn't going to work for us."

"But," he continued, paying me no mind, "as you can see, we don't have many visitors right now. In fact, you'd be the only ones. So, what is your budget?"

The last thing I wanted to do was to be specific about just how pathetic our budget really was. But I trusted him and figured he was enough of a good guy to at least wait for us to leave before laughing at us.

"We're looking for something in more of the ninety euros a night range."

"I see. I see. . . ." His expression hadn't changed one bit. He called his daughter over. She was the manager of the hotel, in her early thirties, and while pretty, she looked stern, like she was all business. They spoke together in French off to the corner. I prepared to say our thank-yous and go back to Beaune.

"OK, my father will make you a special price."

"He can do ninety euros a night and you can have our largest room. How long would you like to stay?"

"Do all the rooms look the same?" I thought for sure they'd put us in the one dump of a room that no one else would want—the room that was so embarrassing to stay in that the staff wouldn't be able to look you in the eye. It would probably stink of old cheese as well.

"Yes, you'll like it. Have a look with my father and let us know."

Olivier gestured with a nod to follow him. I tensed up, wondering what kind of a sour bargain I'd talked us into. We went up two flights of stairs before arriving at a large red door, which Olivier proudly opened. The room inside was gorgeous and had much more space than any hotel we had stayed in before. He told us we would be the first guests to stay there since the whole thing had been gutted just a year before. It had the modern polish of the new, with the lavish detail of the old. We were sold.

A few days later I sat in the lobby waiting for Christian to come down from the room with Bella. I had situated myself in one of the perfectly appointed wing-backed chairs in the lounge next to the warm fireplace. There were books and magazines on the vines and wines of Burgundy from all over the world, many of them twenty, thirty years old. In California, I'd spent hours studying the outlines of vineyards on maps spread across my dining room table in Rohnert Park, memorizing the names distinguished by dots and hemmed in by lines. The Burgundy I'd dreamed about had been completely flat, when in fact it is anything but. The patchwork of vineyards unfolds over steep slopes and cliffs and features an endless amount of elevation changes, humps, and dips. Each change in elevation or angle of slope affects the grapes, even if you don't exactly know how. The magic is in knowing there is a difference, even if it is minute. With its undulating dips and peaks, no village or vineyard experiences weather in the same way. The growers planted their rows to best catch the sun and funnel the wind, making the expansive landscape look like a giant maze of a quilt. I had read, questioned, solicited, drank, and read some more to better understand Burgundy. But what I couldn't have understood until I got here was that it has a pulse.

"I'm sorry to disturb you, but are you free to speak with my father?" It was Olivier's daughter.

"Sure." I was puzzled. "Why does he want to speak with me?"

"I don't know. A few days ago you mentioned wine to him, and now he wants to speak. How is today?"

"Of course. When?"

"Ten minutes?"

"OK."

I ran upstairs to the room and grabbed Christian and Bella. We'd been anxious to get some tips on wineries to visit. It would be something to get the advice straight from Olivier.

Olivier tossed down his rain-drenched black leather hat onto the table with a wet thud. It was the same shape and style as the brown one he'd been wearing yesterday, and the tan one the day before that. He greeted me warmly, as usual, and settled into the chair next to mine.

"So, why are you here?" He gave me the look that I imagined he'd give someone asking for his daughter's hand in marriage. I'd expected some small talk, or maybe a suggestion or two about where to go for tastings, so I was caught off guard.

"You asked if we wanted a place to stay, and since we really liked the room—"

He pointed up to the ceiling, not taking his eyes off mine, "No. Not *here*. Why are you *here*?" He jabbed his pointer finger into the table. A slow grin formed on his face.

"Well, we're from California. Actually Christian is from Nicaragua, but she grew up in—"

He shook his head. "No, this is who you are, where you come from. Why are you here?"

"Oh, for the wine."

"See, not so difficult." His smile was back for a second and then gone again. "So, tell me about wine, yes. Don't you have wine in California?"

"Of course. But—" I didn't know exactly how to articulate just how obsessed I had become with Burgundy. What was the best way to explain that the wine here had burrowed under my skin and crept into my veins? That I'd dropped everything in my life—stability for my wife and newborn be damned—just to be here? That is, without sounding like a total psychopath?

"You do like California wine, yes?"

"It's . . . OK. Honestly, nothing against the wines where I'm from, I'm just really only into Burgundy. What I love most about wine is something I have found only in Burgundy." A jumbled mess of words followed—I faintly remember being able to string together my thoughts—about no two places tasting exactly the same, the imprint of the land, the choreography with the elements, the wisdom of the monks. I might have also gone on a tangent about boeuf bourguignon. I probably sounded more like an eager child speaking about a toy he cherished than a Burgundy-obsessed American in France.

"OK, so you will make a big wine tasting here? A wine vacation?"

He couldn't have been more wrong, and somehow he knew it, but this was how he spoke. He enjoyed the sport of watching me squirm a bit.

"Well, actually my plan is—"

"Oh, you have . . . a plan." He wrapped his fingers together and rested his hands on the table between us. He at once looked more serious than before.

"Not exactly . . . the idea is to find a way to buy grapes."

"Ah, yes. So, you are an American winemaker?"

"No. Not at all."

"Forgive me. I don't understand. If you are not a winemaker, what do you do with the grapes after you find them? You will sell the grapes to a famous American winemaker. It's a good plan!"

"Well, I'd ferment the grapes, do whatever was needed."

"Are you an oenologist?" I had only one harvest to my name. I didn't know much besides how to wash barrels, tanks, and wine presses. I hadn't taken a single course in oenology, and if I started right away I would be a lifetime away from having a degree in winemaking.

"No. But I figure it could still work?"

He leaned forward. "What will work? Wine?" He had spit out the last word.

There was a silence. What did he think I meant?

"Well, yeah. What's the worst that could happen?"

He looked at Christian with Bella resting on her lap trying to pull at her earrings. She had been watching the conversation like a tennis match. I knew I was losing. "Wow, I like this guy. You know, you guys could get into a lot of trouble. But you know, I like him." He looked back at me. "I like you all."

"Thanks." . . . *I think.*

"All right. So, I will help you." Christian and I looked at each other excitedly. "I don't have any grapes for you, but I will look around for you. Do you know my wines?"

"We've heard of them, never tried them."

"It's OK. I'll send some to your room. Let's speak about how you are going to get grapes."

My palms were sweating as I held them under the table. I didn't want to have my hands hidden, but I didn't want him to see me nervously tapping my fingers together.

"First of all. You are looking for grapes or wine? Wine is much easier to get a hold of. No one wants to sell grapes."

"Grapes."

"OK, why grapes?"

"I think it would be a bit of a half-assed type of a thing if I came all the way to Burgundy just to put my name on someone else's wine. I want my own."

"And what if it is bad?"

As obvious a question as it was, I hadn't thought about it before. All of a sudden the gravity of actually producing the wine set in. It could most definitely be bad. In fact, the odds favored it.

"I'd like to assume that the wine would be good, at least drinkable," I countered.

"So, your assumption is the best-case scenario?"

"Yes."

He turned to Christian. "This is going to be interesting."

Christian turned to him. "Interesting good? Or—"

"*Bon. Toute façon*, you have the issue of getting grapes, yes?"

"Yes."

"You have other problems, but without grapes, your other problems don't even matter. We will see about those later."

"Wait, what problems?"

"Never mind. So, for example, my family has been here for six generations and it is still difficult for me to buy grapes. I buy wine for my domaine sometimes. Well, I did. Not anymore."

"Why not anymore?"

"Before I thought it made sense to buy wine. I knew how things tasted, and I figured that because people knew my family that no one would try to cheat us. I knew a guy, and he says, 'Olivier, I have wines for you to buy.' *Bon*, I go to his place, I taste maybe fifteen, twenty wines, some the same wine in several barrels. I taste something like thirty barrels. At the end I go"—he motioned with his fingers—"'this one here, that one, these two, and that one.' In total, I took four wines, two of them very expensive grands crus, yes. I know these wines. I was raised in the area and I've tasted these vineyards throughout my life. I've walked through these vineyards since I was a boy, these terroirs are like familiar friends to me. Two weeks later, he brings the barrels by my winery. I taste the wines and they have lost all life to them. They tasted beautiful in his cave, filled with flowers, honey, almonds . . . and then they taste like completely different wines. Something didn't add up. I took the barrels into my winery and tell him that I wanted to buy more wines from him. When we got to his place, I tasted through thirty more barrels, some of them tasted exactly like the wines I said that I wanted to buy before. Each one that I liked he says the same thing: 'This is just a village-level wine, nothing special.' So, you know what I did? I said to him that I would like to buy these village-level wines from him and return the grands crus since they were such a bargain. You should have seen how red his face was."

"Did he sell them to you?"

"Of course. And at the price of village-level wines."

"Do you work with him still?"

"Of course I do. Now that he knows that I am sharp, he will never try to cheat me again."

"But he confessed to it, right?"

"No. We both know. That is all that matters. I don't need to insult him by telling him I know he was a cheat."

"Yeah, but he was a cheat."

"It doesn't mean that he won't do right by me now. And from that day he has. Now I buy just his grapes. But if they try to cheat me, they will try to cheat you too. And this is why you want grapes and why I say you need them."

We talked about the ins and outs of the business and how things worked there. I was still too dumbfounded to be of much use, so luckily Christian asked all the right questions. In Burgundy, he told us, grapes or wines (either before going into barrel or after going into barrel or even in bottle) are usually bought through courtiers, or grape and wine brokers. How much you buy isn't measured in tons like in California, rather in barrels' worth of grapes or liters of wine. It is the accepted rule of thumb that 330 kilograms of grapes is what it takes to fill the standard 228-liter barrel of wine. The smart winemakers then track the vineyards growing their grapes throughout the year to gauge how things are faring, and always—always—pick up their grapes from the vineyards themselves. If not, they run the risk of receiving grapes that come from a completely different vineyard. If the worst happened, how could you prove it without calling the guy a dirty cheat? It doesn't matter even if you are right; you'll have a mark against you with the other growers.

"When did you want to start?"

I shrugged, wearing a sheepish grin. "This year?"

Out came the finger again, this time he jabbed the table with each syllable. "As in 2009 this year?" He waved his hand at me and clicked his tongue. "No, it's finished for 2009."

"How is it finished? It's January!"

"Well, this is going to be an excellent vintage. Everyone knows this so they have held their contracts for the 2009 grapes, many are looking for more but they aren't available."

"Excellent? There's nothing but stumps out there."

"Well, every year that ends with a nine is fantastic—everyone knows this." He had to be joking.

"You can't be serious."

My mind was reeling, looking for a way through the maze of how I was going to put all of it together. I decided I would just focus on step one, which besides seeming nearly impossible, was at least simple to wrap my head around. I needed to get grapes. Over the next few days, we hunted through the region's two largest villages, Beaune and Dijon, looking for a courtier. Olivier had promised to keep an eye out for us, but in the same breath he mentioned that he was on the lookout for grapes as well. We had been in Burgundy for more than a week, but I wasn't one inch closer to finding grapes than I was while stuck on the bed in California making calls in the middle of the night. We still had two more weeks, but I couldn't shake the feeling that time was running out, and something needed to change.

CHAPTER ELEVEN

ONE NIGHT WHILE AT THE HOTEL WE BUMPED INTO ONE OF the sommeliers. He had been in Brazil for the past three weeks and had just popped in to grab some bottles.

"Hey, you're the guy from California, right?"

"Yeah, how'd you know?"

"Seriously? You guys are the only guests." He laughed while scratching at his wild goatee.

"So, what do you do here?"

"I do the wines. Well, basically I show them to the guests, tell them about Burgundy. What do you think about them?"

"I . . . I haven't had many of them. I like them though. Olivier sent six of 'em up to our room. All whites though, no reds."

"What food did you have with them? You know what, never mind. I have an idea. I will cook for you guys at home. You interested?"

"Uh, yeah! That would be amazing. Your place? Where do you live?"

"I live above the village. I don't have heat besides a fireplace and my home is simple, but I have too many wines, good

American and Brazilian records, and I can cook." Before he could finish I was on my way to grab Christian and Bella.

"All right, we're going to dinner. Grab your coat."

"Dinner? Where?"

"With this guy. You wanna go?"

"Wait, what guy?"

"The . . . the sommelier."

"What's his name?"

"I'm not sure, but he offered to cook." She looked shocked, but it didn't slow her down while she grabbed her coat and Bella and darted out of the room.

We met the sommelier downstairs, who we learned was named Guillaume, and then headed out toward Saint-Romain, a small village placed on the steep hillsides high above Saint-Aubin and the rest of what I'd seen of Burgundy. It was dark, and only a few houses in the village had their lights still on. We finally made it to his house, a stone building that was around eight hundred years old. There were wounds in the walls from various wars that had come and gone. I loved it, though it was a bit chilly. But soon we were all having a great time together; even Christian and Bella quickly warmed to the experience.

Christian and I took turns helping in the kitchen, and we ended up staying there for hours, laughing, drinking, and even meeting neighbors of his, a couple from next door. His wife and daughter had just left for Paris. Once Bella dozed off, we carted her off to a little bed not too far from all the action. It was surreal just how casual it all was to pick up and meet new people like that, to be invited into their homes and become friends. Guillaume would soon leave Burgundy to live full-time in Brazil with his family, but he turned out to be a good friend.

We didn't always find people that we instantly clicked with, but little things also happened that endeared us to Burgundy, like the time we pulled to the side of the road while trying to decide where to go to next, and six different people stopped to ask if we were all right and if we needed assistance. I'd never experienced anything like that in California. Another time a stranger offered to escort us to the other side of town to be sure we didn't get lost looking for a butcher known to have the best côte d'agneau. Once we went out to dinner, and the restaurant's proprietor insisted on sending us away with a bottle of wine. For almost ten minutes I tried to press a twenty-euro note into his palm, but he simply refused.

"I have enough in my pockets," he said. "Keep what you have. And take the wine with you."

"I can't take your wine unless I pay for it."

"If you don't take it, I will be insulted. Will you insult an old man?" He pretended to weep, drawing cheers from the staff, who were leaning against the wall by the kitchen.

I still managed to slip the bill into his coat pocket before we left; even Christian hadn't seen it. Once we got back to the hotel, Christian opened up the bag with the wine.

"I've never had someone *pay* me to take free wine." The twenty had found its way back into our bag.

We thought for sure we'd be pushing our luck when we brought Bella into nice restaurants. In California the slightest whimper from your baby is liable to elicit the coldest glare from neighboring tables that says, "How dare you bring such a deranged maniac into this establishment! We're trying to be civilized over here." But in France, parents are encouraged to bring the whole family. People just treated you the way they in turn would hope to be treated. Whenever Bella cried or playfully sent a glass flying off the table to shatter below someone else's table, there was never any fuss, just a knowing look that that's just how babies can be. The chef or owners often asked to hold her, and would kiss her forehead or cheek before giving her back to us.

Driving was different too. In California, once the traffic light flicks from red to green, you'd better already be on the gas because everyone behind you will already be honking and yelling insults out their windows. In Burgundy, you can fall asleep, miss several cycles of the light turning green, and people will literally wait behind you without making a noise or gesture. If they do drive around you, they will most likely stop to make sure everything is all right. The chip on your shoulder that comes from living in a fast-paced city doesn't exist in a place like Burgundy. Instead there is a genuine concern for one another.

Our living situation was turning out to be a different story altogether. After some time in the hotel, we hooked up with a winemaker I'd been in touch with before our trip who had space to rent in his *gîte*, a little house on his property. The winemaker wasn't from Burgundy, and so I thought he might be a good source of information, plus we'd get the experience of really living in Burgundy. We could shop at the markets and cook our own food. Staying at a hotel was making us feel like tourists. It would be a little expensive, but worth it.

We'd been living in the house for nearly a week before I figured out something was seriously wrong with the heating system. During the day there was enough warmth for me to walk around barefoot, as I liked to do in California. But at night, we'd freeze. It would be so cold that Bella would cry for hours, and Christian and I—watching our breath turn to puffs of steam—knew sleep wasn't an option for us either. It didn't make any sense—the heat worked during the day, so why not at night?

When the owner of the house came by to check on his wines as he did every couple of days we asked him about it.

"Hey, what's the deal with the heat?"

"What do you mean?"

"Well, there isn't any. At night, it drops off. We end up staying up through the night since it's too cold for Bella to stay asleep."

"Oh"—he snapped his finger and then pointed at me—"you know what that is?"

I shook my head. "Actually, no." I wasn't in the mood for guessing games.

"I usually come in around eleven at night and turn off all of the heat."

I couldn't believe it. "And . . . why in the world would you do that?"

"Well, you guys should already be asleep by nine or ten, right? You don't need to be that warm when you are sleeping."

"We don't?" I looked at the snow on the ground surrounding the small house.

"Well, gas is expensive. Takes a lot of money to run the machine . . . you know."

"But that is part of the fee in staying here, isn't it?"

"Well, the thing is that usually when people stay here, they use about half the heat that you guys do. That's around six adults taking up less heat than just your family alone."

"We have a baby."

"I saw you the other day wearing sandals. I know you're from California, but you aren't in California, you are in Burgundy, right? That's how things are here. If you were staying at a French family's *gîte*, they'd say the same thing. Why do you really need to be warm just to sleep?"

The next morning, we were packed up and on our way to finishing our time in France back at Olivier's hotel in Puligny. We had only a few more days left and we didn't see the point of wasting any more of our time in a cold house.

We felt like we had experienced France and, more important, Burgundy. But we were coming to terms with the prospect of returning home without making any progress whatsoever in my pursuit of grapes. Not even the list of courtiers had been any help to me. No one wanted to take my call, let alone meet with me. When I did get on the phone with someone, they would stay on only long enough to hang up on me. Worse still, I didn't know what I would do differently if I were given more time. I had used up all of my leads. I was stuck, but at least I'd done all that I could.

Before we left, I had one last thing that I had to do. Roz Seysses, co-owner with her husband Jacques of Domaine Dujac, had given me an open invitation "if we ever made it out to Burgundy." I knew a bit about the domaine and had given her a call, out of the blue, several months earlier, figuring that even though my chances of getting anywhere with the domaine were slim, I might as well take the shot. Roz was a native Californian whose husband, Jacques, was a charming Parisian-turned-vigneron, growing his own grapes and making his own wines. He'd left his family biscuit company and decamped to Burgundy to build his domaine. Shortly after the couple started their winery in 1968, it became one of Burgundy's elite. I'd called Roz before harvest to see if I might be able to intern, and she'd told me that the waiting list was going on three years.

"Three years? Is that a real number?" I'd asked, incredulous.

"Of course it's a real number." She'd giggled just a bit and then stopped herself, and explained that because they were one of the few English-speaking establishments in Burgundy, they got hundreds of calls from people wanting to work for them.

"Honestly," she'd said, "once you consider work visas and everything that goes along with them, it might actually be easier to just start your own winery." Her advice had definitely stuck in my mind.

We showed up at their domaine in Morey-Saint-Denis just two days before going back to California. It hadn't taken much to get an appointment. When I called her, she suggested we come right over. I was surprised she had remembered me, and touched that our forty-minute conversation five months earlier had stuck with her.

We stood outside of their large pale-pink stucco house as bluish-white smoke billowed from the chimney. The estate was actually a small collection of four houses, each of them beautiful two-story residences that had the understated charm that fit their winery perfectly. They were all painted white, and a large stone wall surrounded the main property with an expansive courtyard. Their actual winery was a renovated barn located across the street. It was impressive, but it didn't make a point of shouting out to anyone; it just looked cool.

Roz warmly came out the front door with her arms opened wide. She was in her early fifties, thin, with a short tapered haircut, her straight hair streaked with brilliant silver. "You must be Christian, Bella, and Ray. I am so glad to meet all of you." She kissed all of us on each cheek before inviting us in.

Inside, there was a stylish mix of impressive antiques,

understated wooden furniture, tapestries, and charming family keepsakes collected from cities all over the globe.

"Tea?"

"Sure." We weren't big tea drinkers, but on such a cold day, something to warm our hands was most welcome. Roz explained that she loved to garden and that she had made the tea from the mint in her garden.

Roz got right to the point. "So tell me"—she shot her devilish grin at us—"have we found grapes yet?"

I felt as if I were pleading my case to Mother Burgundy. "The thing is, we can't really figure out how to find them."

"Well, that's the thing, isn't it? You just have to keep looking." She didn't seem to notice how disappointed I must have looked.

"And you are looking for what?"

"Well, grapes."

"Yes, Ray. We can assume this." She winked at Christian. Again, her piercing grin as she playfully squinted at me. "What kind of grapes, Monsieur Walker?" Even when she was playing around, her French sounded melodic, beautiful.

"Oh . . . red. I mean, village."

She nodded slowly, raising her chin as she closed her eyes, again the smile.

"Yes. So"—the chin raised, the eyes closed softly—"why are you looking for only *village*-level grapes?"

"I figured it would be enough."

"Enough?" She spat the word out, disgusted by the taste of each letter. She brought her upper lip toward the bottom of her nose. "Did you come to Burgundy just to have *enough*?"

"Well, I . . . I—"

She cut me off. She didn't care about my response. "Listen. You have a family. You have a wife who is backing you on this." She turned to Christian. "You're backing him on this, right?" Christian nodded. "Well then. You deserve to get more than 'enough,' don't you think?"

"I mean, yeah." I cleared my throat. "Of course. But . . . what do you mean exactly?"

"You need to get at least one premier cru." She leaned in as if she were revealing a secret. She looked both ways to be sure no one was around. We leaned in farther, nearing the large steel and glass coffee table between us. "It wouldn't hurt to think about grands crus as well."

The weight of her words pushed me back into my seat.

"Roz, I appreciate the support. I just can't imagine anything like that happening for us."

She looked surprised. "Well, if you think you can't do it, then it has no chance of working. Look, go home and think about it." It wasn't a suggestion, it was an order. She sat back in her chair and began nodding to herself, and just as quickly she bounced back in a forward lean. "You know . . . things are only possible if you let them be possible."

The ride home felt different from all of the rest we'd taken together. We didn't say much to each other.

"You know," Christian finally said, her hand now resting on the back of mine, "I think she's right. I think if we have the chance, we should go after it."

As much as I was craving to have her be the more enthusiastic one, I hadn't been ready for it to come so quickly. "I think she's right too. Thing is, this is going to be expensive."

"It could be. But only if we get the opportunity."

The rest of the night we talked about how it would feel to get grapes, to have our own wine, and what it would mean for our family. We dreamed aloud about how our wine would taste. I couldn't stop smiling. Not because I thought it could definitely happen, it just felt good to be sharing something like this with Christian. This was something that would be ours.

WE DECIDED TO SPEND OUR last full day in France walking around Beaune. I was able to put the tumult of the past few days out of my mind while Christian and I aimlessly strolled with Bella in tow. We browsed through pottery, fossilized rocks and seashells, and antiques shops—even pawed through the produce stands. We watched a butcher work, then visited the fishmonger down the way. I loved how the small space lined with almost any sea creature imaginable didn't smell fishy, only like fresh, briny sea air. We wandered through the market and envied the women filling their baskets with the day's shopping. They were most likely looking only for tonight's dinner, maybe tomorrow's breakfast or lunch.

In Burgundy, you don't do your shopping on Sunday and hope it stretches until the following weekend. There are no frozen meals, at least not for most of the locals. You buy what is fresh so you can eat it while it is fresh. Besides, what kind of animal would eat a frozen coq au vin? Fish from Brittany, cheese, sausage, local bread made that morning, olives from Provence, peppers from Corsica, lamb, Bresse chicken, mushrooms, wild berries—it is all cultivated with the utmost care in the outlying regions. Each specializes in only one or two things and sends its goods to the market still flecked with dew. You rarely go to one supermarket—that is, of course, if you have any dignity to speak of. No. You go to the artisans whose products hail from a specific place. You go to Alain Hess for your cheese and deli treats, Boucherie Vié for your charcuterie, Virginie Brouant the fish monger for all of your *turbot, dorade, thon, flétan,* and especially *homard.* On Friday mornings, the oyster guy is in Nuits-Saint-Georges with sacks of raw oysters, clams, and scallops from Brittany. The fines de claires from Marennes d'Oléron became my favorite! When that much care is taken in providing the best, it is a sacrilege to not honor it.

We continued around the square at the center of the city, pausing every so often to admire wares in windows. We'd skip the more tourist-oriented storefronts filled with wicker baskets and T-shirts, and I also had no interest in the wine shops. I couldn't think about buying wine; I was consumed by the idea of buying grapes and having my own wine.

"Let's go in." Christian nudged me. "C'mon. We haven't gone into a single wine shop the whole time we've been here. Let's get something. You know you want to."

I had no interest in going in only to browse an overpriced, tourist-oriented selection with fake interest. I wasn't being snobby. OK, maybe just a little. But I just didn't see the point in drinking something that wasn't interesting, something that didn't really have meaning to whoever produced it. The shop was right across from the Hôtel-Dieu—how could it not be touristy? Besides, we'd tasted at a few domaines in Champagne and in Burgundy already. Walking around in an ancient stone-lined cave twenty feet underground with nothing but dim lights, spiderwebs, and a treasure-trove of wines seemed like a much more enjoyable way to spend my time.

"Come on. I'll let you get whatever you want—I won't even give you a hard time."

I smirked at her. "You sure?"

"Let's go! I'm not going to keep asking!"

The shop was covered in polished woods, shiny display racks, and modern halogen lights. It was too bright for a wine shop, and I immediately thought about the wines getting too hot. But when I touched a random bottle of Jacques-Frédéric Mugnier's 2006 Chambolle-Musigny 1er Cru Les Amourouses with the back of my hand, it was fine.

"Sir, I assure you that the bottles are cool and sound."

I turned around to find a short, thin, slightly balding, brown-haired man wearing John Lennon–esque wire-rimmed glasses. He looked to be around forty and spoke excellent English. "You were checking the temperature, weren't you?"

"I was." I was impressed that he had noticed.

"You are . . ."—he looked at my large Nike running shoes—"American." It wasn't a question.

"Yes. And you, you are . . ." I looked him over just as he'd done.

"Yes?" His face tightened, and grew serious.

". . . A Bordeaux drinker."

His face relaxed, and he doubled over at the waist, letting out a snort of a laugh.

"God no! And I'm German."

"So neither of us knows what we are tasting then!" Laughter shot out from him again. He extended his hand. "What's your name?"

"Ray."

"I'm Bernard."

Bernard and I chatted as we made our way around the shop. I'd ask about certain wines, and he would be completely honest about its quality, even calling one "foul." He told us a bit about how he came to Burgundy after knowing nothing about wine and had found the wine shop while looking for a place to eat. What was supposed to be a three-day trip turned into a twenty-year adventure. We spoke a bit about ourselves as well, but not too much about why we were in Burgundy. It didn't matter. I surely didn't want to go around telling people about "the plan" before there really was one. At that point, I figured we had made the official transition to tourists since our grape hunt had come to an unsuccessful close.

We'd stopped in for only a brief look and had managed to hang around for around an hour. It was getting late, so we said our good-byes. As we walked out Christian started nudging me, then pinching me under my ribs, and then actually pushing me.

"Say something to him!" She started to pinch me again.

"We said good-bye, what else should I say?" I kept walking. She stood still in the doorway.

"You know, the courtier thing. Ask him if he knows anyone."

I looked at her. She hadn't done the research. She hadn't made any calls. She didn't know that finding a courtier was a lot tougher than simply asking someone at random. Ridiculous. If it were that easy, everyone would be doing it. She didn't get it.

"Honey." I took my serious tone with her. "You can't just assume someone knows a courtier. This guy sells wine. A courtier is in a completely different business."

She didn't budge. "Just ask him."

I didn't want to. I didn't see the point. But I turned around. I had to. The look on her face told me as much.

"Excuse me, Bernard? I'm sorry, but my wife wanted me to ask you something. I already know the answer, but she still wants me to ask. Do you know any *cortiyays*?"

He hadn't even answered yet and I was raising my hand, ready to wave off the embarrassment of asking such an absurd question.

"Excuse me?" I realized he was thrown off by my still-terrible French accent. "Oh, a *courtier*. Yes, the owner of this store is a courtier."

"Are you serious?"

"Yes, would you like to meet him? I'll give him your details and have him call you tonight."

Point Christian.

As soon as we were back at the hotel I went to the front desk.

"Are there any calls for me?"

"No, sorry."

For the next four hours, I asked again and again, only to be disappointed by the response. We passed the time by getting our luggage ready for the trip back to California the next night.

"Do you think he's gonna call?"

Christian was tired of me asking. She didn't know. No one knew.

Finally the phone rang in our room. It was just after five in the afternoon but the sun had already started to set. "Mister Walker, you have a call downstairs. Can you come down?"

I dropped the receiver, kissed Christian, and took off running out the door. After skipping a few steps along the way, I stumbled a bit as I skidded to a stop at the front desk and grabbed the phone.

"*Allô?*"

"*Oui, Monsieur Walker?*"

"Yes, er, *Oui*."

"Oh, you are American. Should we speak English?"

"Yes! Please! Thank you."

"Mister Walker, Bernard told me a little bit about you, and I am interested in meeting. Can you make it to my shop the day after tomorrow?"

"I'm going to be leaving tomorrow. Can you do anything tonight?"

"I'm sorry, Mister Walker, the shop has just finished."

My heart sank. "Are you sure you can't—"

"Mister Walker, can you be here in twenty minutes? If not, there is nothing I can do until Thursday."

"No, no, no. That's fine. I can be there in twenty minutes." I was about thirty minutes away, but I'd find a way to make it.

"OK, I will see you in twenty minutes or I will see you the next time you are in France."

I passed the phone back to the receptionist and ran upstairs. I ran up to our room, fumbling my keys several times before Christian opened the door.

"I . . . just spoke to him." I was nearly out of breath.

"Who?"

"Him! The guy. The fruit guy, the courtier!"

"OK . . ."

"So, I have to go!" I squeezed into the room past Christian, who was still trying to compute why I was racing around. I grabbed the keys to our rented minivan and bolted toward the door.

"Where are you going?"

I kissed Bella quickly, and then Christian on my way out.

"Beaune! I have to be there in seventeen minutes or he'll be gone!"

"Oh! Go, go!"

"Love you!"

"Love you too! Drive carefully!" She knew I couldn't agree to the second part. Outside of the hotel the snow was everywhere and it was dark, but I had to get there, so I would.

The roads on the way in to Beaune had been cleared earlier that day, but now they had completely iced over. I pushed the minivan to its limits. A sharp turn came up too quickly and I panicked and slammed on the brakes, causing the van to fishtail. The top swayed, threatening to topple over, and I came to a stop a few feet away from a fifteen-foot drop onto an adjacent vineyard near Volnay. My hands were shaking, and I closed my eyes. I was an idiot and I didn't need anyone else there to prove it.

I showed up six minutes late. All of the lights were off at the store.

"Mister Walker." A tall, slender man walked up next to me. He was young, though bald.

"Yes. Are you the courtier?"

"Yes, I'm Thomas. I work with my father; he is the courtier. You know, your accent is very interesting when you say that."

"I've been practicing for the past four months."

"No, it isn't any good. It is just interesting." I laughed. He didn't. "I waited for you. You are late."

"I'm sorry. Can we still meet?" My heart was in my throat, my fate entirely in his hands.

"We can." He let out a slight huff, his eyes pierced through me. "I will just turn everything back on."

I followed him into the shop.

He disappeared behind a corner, turning on the lights. "I will tell you, Mister Walker. I'm not terribly impressed so far."

"Why is that?"

"Well, forget that you were late. But what are you doing here, really? You aren't prepared."

"How should I be prepared?"

"Exactly my point." I scratched my head, leaning on the table by the register. "If you were prepared, you wouldn't need to ask." He grinned a bit, but there was no joy in it. I couldn't tell whether he was joking.

I shook my head. "OK, so I spoke with Bernard—"

"Yes, he told me." He smacked the table with a flat palm. "So, you wish to buy grapes?"

"Yes."

"OK." He pulled out a small notepad and began writing. "OK, Monsieur Ray Walker." He said it in an exaggerated French accent as he wrote down my name. "So tell me."

"I'm looking for village-level grapes."

"OK." He wrote down *village*. "Red or white?"

"Red." He mumbled to himself and continued scribbling on his notepad.

"And tell me. Do you come from wine?"

"What do you mean?"

"Wine. Do your parents make wine, sell wine, anything?"

"No." He scribbled.

"And you, do you have friends here, people you can work with, people that can speak about you? People here like to know the people they work with. You know, someone that is no one makes people nervous."

"Sorry, I don't really know anyone here."

He scribbled, looked at me, and said, "Uh-huh. So, once you have grapes, where do you make your wines?"

"I don't know."

"Let me ask, how many years have you been making wine in United States?"

"I interned for one harvest."

"Intern?"

"I think you call it a *stage*." His eyebrows lowered.

"So, then you make your wine in the U.S. for how long?"

"I didn't, I haven't." Each time he readied his pen in his hand, he showed disappointment before again pressing it to the paper.

"This is an indelicate question, so I am sorry, but do you have any finances for what you want to do?"

"I do." He readied his pencil.

"How much?"

"Six thousand."

He looked at me, his face cold and colorless. "Euros?"

"Dollars." He dropped his pen on his notepad. My budget wasn't worth wasting his ink on.

"Ray, do you even have a wine degree?"

"No. Do I need one?"

"Do I need one?" He repeated my words, but they sounded much worse from his tightened lips, his head tilted, searching for an angle that would make my nonsensical scheme somewhat comprehensible. "And your visa. How long is it good for? Where will you study?"

"Oh, I'm not studying. I was in finance, but I left everything to do this."

"To do . . . this?" His face exploded with an echoing laugh that startled me.

"Yes."

"Do what?"

"What do you mean?"

He grabbed at his notes, and held them up so I could see them. "This is you." He pointed at the page filled with *No* written countless times. "This is how people will see you." He began to laugh again to himself. "Let me ask, do you ever say yes?"

"All the time."

He looked at me again, still laughing. "Look, you're funny. I'm not sure if you are making a very good decision or a very bad one. But I will do my best to help you out."

"How can you help me?"

"There is not much on the market currently. This is not California where you have everyone offering grapes. And village, that will be tough, unless you want white, but you don't. I will keep your information and call you if something comes up."

I knew that line. He'd never call me. I knew I'd messed up yet again. I searched to think of anything I could say that might help my chances but my mind was blank. We stood, shook hands, and parted ways. Getting back to the hotel, I felt defeated, but I tried to hold on to any positivity that I could. I was honest. I was direct about what I wanted and what I could offer. There was nothing left to do.

CHAPTER TWELVE

"Beeeeeeuuuunnnnnnn." "Biun." "Be-ah." "Mer-see bee-ah."
"J-j-j-j-j-j-j-j-j." "Je ma pell Ray." "Sa va?" "S-s-s-s-sa va?"
"Ca-me-own."

I stared at the mirror, practicing. I had so little going for me that I couldn't afford to also sound like an idiot.

Once we got back to California I searched the Internet for tips on how to learn French. I looked up everything from "common mistakes English speakers make speaking French" to "tricks for connecting French to English." What I found were countless words that were practically identical in either English or French.

Exact
Possible
Identity
License
Parking
Usual
Strange

I wrote down all of the words I thought I could use in everyday conversation. I said each word in English and then in a French accent until they felt somewhat comfortable. When I was ready to expand my vocabulary, I started observing which words and phrases I said most often in English, like *how to, when, if, understand, try, drive, I would like*, and *just until*, and then I used them as foundation blocks to build on. I figured I could practice until I had these basics down, add words that sounded close to their English equivalents, and listen hard to the context of a conversation to cheat through it. If I looked confident while mumbling through a word I either didn't know or didn't know how to say, maybe whomever I was speaking to wouldn't notice or at least not have the interest to ask me to repeat myself. If I sold what I knew well enough, the person might even assume I spoke more French than I actually did.

I always had a bunch of words with their French equivalents on a tiny piece of paper that I carried around in my pocket. Whenever I found myself with some spare time, I'd take out the balled-up paper and practice. If there was a mirror around, even better, so I could try moving my mouth more like a French person. When they spoke, I'd noticed they formed the sound in the back of their throats. It was loose, relaxed, and guttural. English required a different movement of the jaws. I tried studying how I was moving my own face, but I ended up only looking ridiculous.

Then I had an idea. I called my cable television provider and asked them to install the French cable channel, TV5Monde. I didn't care what was on—I watched it. Political shows with candidates I hadn't heard of, cheesy soap operas, cooking shows, French history and art—I would watch every frame as if there were going to be a pop quiz.

I'd cross-check words I didn't recognize against my French-English dictionary and add them to my list. I'd hear "*Kellque shows*" and think, *That was with a* k, *right?* No luck. I'd try looking it up under C. Still nothing. Wait. Q? Finally! *Quelque.* It meant "some." All right. What the hell is a *shows*? I'd try S. Nothing. Ch? Then, I'd get it. *Chose*, "thing." "Something!" I'd feel all of the places *quelque chose* moved inside of my mouth. Then I'd say "something." It didn't seem that much more difficult, just—different.

Soon, some French words seemed more natural to speak than the English I had grown up learning. I began to think in French, instead of merely mentally translating. I tried to describe objects in my mind using my new vocabulary. I even began to dream in French.

From the moment Christian left for work in the morning until she came home in the evening, the television was on. I made phone calls, fixed food for Bella, changed diapers, cleaned up the house, took showers when Bella went to sleep—the whole time, French filled the house. And after two weeks, I graduated to classic French cinema.

Bella had graduated too. She was just starting to stand by herself. She no longer needed tables, chairs, and walls to hold onto. I would see an all-too-familiar look of determination cross her face, and with a tiny grunt she'd be on her two feet. I loved being home with her, getting to watch her grow. And she didn't mind having me around either. She never fussed when I switched off her *Dora the Explorer* to watch *À bout de souffle* or *Les Quatre Cents Coups* or *Bande à part*; and she loved when I spoke to her in French. I loved the way she listened as I pointed out objects around the room—*lumière, chaise, tapis, verre*. But her all-time favorite was when I would grab her nose, kiss her eyes, and nibble on her hands—*nez, yeux, mains.* She'd break out into laughter, reaching out to grab hold of my nose or one of my eyebrows. When she would drift off to sleep, I'd pour myself a glass of red wine and engross myself in the films. I loved watching the actors' body language and the crispness of their enunciation. I would copy their hand gestures and the movement of their mouths, pushing through the *p*, forgetting the rough edges of the *r*, seeing the *ce* as a soft *s*, and taking just the tip of the *q*, dropping the rest of the letters in the word. *Pohs-k. Parce que*, "because." Perfect, just like the guy in the movie.

In the time I wasn't watching Bella, studying old French movies, or cleaning up around the house, I worked on my business plan. The disappointment of not finding grapes in France was one thing, but seeing my wife struggle to support our family was another. She loved her work as a probation officer, but recent events in both the city and her department had made the position far more dangerous than either of us would have liked.

Christian's job generally consisted of monitoring and interviewing people on probation for domestic violence, drug abuse, you name it. All of the meetings were conducted in the safety of the probation department, surrounded by armed police officers. I didn't like the idea of her being alone in a room with any of them, as many had long histories with violence. But the new policies would have her riding shotgun with a police officer to someone's home. Many of these visits would be to inform people that their probation was revoked, which meant they'd be cuffed and dragged into the police cruiser. I feared for Christian. She had backbone, sure, and she had received training to deal with people in those situations. But knowing that the training was necessary only made me more concerned. She was even going to have to carry a firearm. I didn't think it made sense for her to stay the course there much longer, and it was the first time my pipedream of working in Burgundy seemed in some way practical. At least she wouldn't be banging down doors in Burgundy; we'd be neck-deep in wine tanks, free to have more time to raise Bella together.

The harvest season had ended months ago, so I could look for positions only in winery tasting rooms. Because those jobs were scarce, I looked for anything else that sounded remotely promising—mortgage consultant, financial adviser, marketing department intern, shoe store clerk, used-car salesman, fast-food restaurant janitor—anything. My CV was loaded with sales experience, accomplishments, licenses, and countless recommendations from every job I'd ever held. But we were neck-deep in a recession, and only the best candidates with degrees and experience got recruited. I managed to get a few interviews, but no one wanted to hire someone with one foot already out the door, and I wasn't exactly skilled at lying about my intentions. I managed to find one job selling double-pane windows door to door, but that ended after a week when my supervisor wanted a full-time commitment from me.

In the meantime, I tried to keep things as upbeat and positive as possible—taking Bella to pick up coffee and pastries in the morning, making sure everything in the house was in good order by the time Christian got home, and she appreciated it. But having only one source of income was wearing thin on both of us.

Working on the business plan felt like a small step in the right direction, but I was still totally adrift. I didn't know which grapes were likely to be on the market or how much they would even cost. I had no idea what rent for a facility would be. And while I did my best to play up my experience, I didn't have much to speak of. The only thing more meager than my hands-on wine work was my capital, six thousand dollars, which looked pathetic next to my estimated twenty-thousand-dollar first-year budget.

I thought about soliciting funds from investors, but I didn't know that many people who would be interested in contributing. I had a lot of wine friends that I'd met through the wine forums, but I didn't feel comfortable bringing it up with most of them directly. And most important, I wasn't keen on giving up any ownership. I'd spread the word on a wine bulletin board that I was looking for capital, and I'd had about twelve people contact me. Their e-mails all had the same concerns:

Are you sure I can't get a majority position for $10,000?

If you don't know where you are getting grapes from at this point, isn't it too late?

If you did have grapes, who would help you make the wine?

You aren't really going to try to make wine with no experience, right?

I didn't have the best of responses to give them. Without much of my own capital in the business, having someone take an interest position based on the total capital invested would leave me with a minuscule ownership percentage. I didn't know if I would be able to find grapes, and I wasn't interested in bringing on someone with more experience to help me run things. Maybe the wines wouldn't be that good, but at least I wouldn't have to stand behind someone else's work. I was going to go for it, if given the chance. Other people had done it. What about all those Burgundy monks? They didn't have degrees or even hundreds of years of experience at that point. It was trial and error until they stumbled on something great, and what they had stumbled on was pretty damn good. All I needed was the chance to stumble.

After two months, I was surprised to have raised around ten thousand dollars from the friends who'd seen my post and from some people I'd met more recently on the wine forums. I struggled to understand the blind faith they had in what I was trying to do, since every time I thought I was close to making something tangible happen, it would inevitably fall through my fingers. But their support humbled me. And I figured if others believed in me, maybe it was for a reason.

WITH HARVEST ARRIVING IN A few short months, I made the decision: If I couldn't get any grapes for 2009, it wouldn't stop me from at least getting to Burgundy. I could lend someone a hand, impress them with my work ethic, and maybe, just maybe, score a fruit referral for 2010's harvest. I pleaded my case to Christian. All I needed to do was go to Burgundy for six weeks, get my foot in the door, then come home and figure things out from there. Olivier Leflaive had said I could potentially help him out for a few days. Who knows, it could even lead to a paying job. Christian gave in, and her mother agreed to come forty minutes from San Francisco to the house we were renting in Rohnert Park to watch Bella while I'd be away and Christian was at work.

"You still going?" Christian asked me the same question every day for a week after we'd talked about it. Each time she'd manage a smile and tell me she was going to miss me. Sometimes she'd lift up Bella and hide behind her playfully, using her arms to gesture, and she'd say, "Finally me and Mommy are going to have girl time. No more stinky Daddy." They would both scream out in laughter, Bella seemingly agreeing with the sentiment. I knew I didn't need Christian's permission, but I wanted her support. And I was asking her for a whole hell of a lot of it.

A FEW WEEKS HAD GONE by since any new potential investors had contacted me, when one evening I checked my e-mail a last time before going to bed. I'd been glued to my laptop for the previous three hours doing free French practice tests. I was doing better, but still nowhere near what anyone would call "good." Since I'd been doing the tests I'd started to get words I was having trouble with stuck in my head. I didn't know how I was going to get to Burgundy or how I'd find grapes, but I wanted to be ready for the unthinkable. So I practiced my vocabulary as if I were cramming for a college exam for a class that I wasn't yet enrolled in. I'd recite words while I was out walking Bella in her stroller, on a covert mission to the ice cream parlor, or during a simple stroll to get her to sleep. I probably started making my neighbors nervous, always babbling on to myself. Especially because I often started laughing, wondering how bad I sounded.

In my inbox that night was a message from a guy named "Steven E." on the wine bulletin board. It looked like most of the other responses I'd had—he was interested in looking at my proposal. It was the first investor nibble I'd had in weeks, so I didn't waste any time sending him a copy. I knew better than to get my hopes up, but it was difficult not to.

Two days went by without a response, until Steve called one day to explain that he personally wasn't interested because he had just started his own project in Napa, but he had a friend who might be. He said he'd run a few things by him and have an answer for me in a couple more days. It sounded flimsy at best, but true to his word, I received a call three days later.

"Ray," a woman's voice said, "I have Steven Eisenhauer and Dave Warco on the line."

"Ray, I'm gonna let Dave and you have a chat. I'll listen in if you don't mind. Dave meet Ray, Ray . . . Dave."

A new voice shot out, "So, Ray. What can you tell me about yourself?"

I cleared my throat. I didn't normally get nervous, but you couldn't have told that to my pounding heart. "Well, I'm basically looking to buy grapes in Burgundy in order to produce my first wines. I don't have much experience, but I believe that I am more than qualified to do a great job because I simply care too much about it to not obsess about any and every detail." I could have rambled on for another ten minutes, but Dave cut me off.

"I see, I see. But I'm asking about *you*. Tell me about yourself, not about what you'd like to do."

I didn't know what to say. I wasn't used to saying much about myself. What else was I but what I wanted in life?

"I'm a father, a husband, a wine geek; I'm an avid reader, collector of old things. I'm persistent, committed, loyal, and trustworthy; and I value the respect of others." I'd never said these things aloud before. But I'd worked hard to earn them, and saying what I knew was true felt good.

There was a pause. I wasn't sure if he had listened to what I said and was thinking about it, or if he had placed me on hold. "OK, and what do you intend to do with the capital?"

"Grapes." That sounded too simple. "That, and materials, rent, whatever the job calls for."

"It sounds like a great plan." It did?

"I also plan to pay back all investments in five years or less."

"I'm not worried about that. Whenever, or if ever, it came back, I'd be fine with it." I couldn't have heard that right. I tried to breathe but couldn't feel any air being taken in.

"Well, believe me, you'll get your money back with interest."

"All right. So, what can you tell me about Burgundy?" This was the question that I had waited a full summer to hear.

"All right, let me tell you," I said, taking a deep breath, preparing the dissertation. "The first thing to know about Burgundy is that it is diverse. Too many people think that Burgundy is a hierarchy based on vineyards that are considered better or worse than each other. One of the most—"

"OK, kid. I'll start you off with twenty. Call me if you need anything else. Hey, Steve, I gotta go; let me know if he needs anything else."

Just like that, he was gone.

"Steven, is this guy for real?"

"That's Dave. I think he liked you."

"We spent less than five minutes on the phone."

"He is about to send you a check for twenty thousand dollars. That might be a good sign."

It didn't make any sense. Everyone else that I spoke with about investing actually knew me, and I still had to answer difficult questions about financial planning to get anywhere with them. But now, after a five-minute conversation with someone that I'd never met, I was in the game.

"Did he even read my plan?"

"He said he didn't have time. He asked me how it was. I said it was decent. That was about it."

"Does he know about the part where I don't want to give up any of the business?"

"Yeah. He doesn't care. I bet you he wouldn't even take the interest. He's just a great guy and loves to help out good people." This had to be a joke, and I didn't want to be around for the punch line. But a few days later, a check arrived with a hand-written note attached:

"Good luck!"

"MONSIEUR WALKER?"

"Yes. *Oui*."

"Do you remember me from Beaune?" It was Thomas, the courtier's son whom I met with on my last day in France.

"Yes . . . yes, I do!"

"Are you still interested in buying your Burgundy grapes this year?"

"I am!" I was half expecting the voice on the other end to fall into laughter, and reveal it was a friend pulling my leg.

"What do you think of Charmes-Chambertin?"

"Charmes?"

"Yes. The grand c—"

I interrupted him. "No, I know it. It is a very interesting vineyard."

"Do you think? What do you know about it?"

"Well, are we speaking about Mazoyères-Chambertin or Charmes-Chambertin proper? The differences are tremendous." I knew that there was a little-known law that permits a practice

THE ROAD TO BURGUNDY • *147*

otherwise forbidden throughout nearly the rest of Burgundy. A wine produced from vines located in the vineyard of Mazoyères-Chambertin can legally be labeled as either Mazoyères-Chambertin or Charmes-Chambertin, but not vice versa. The fact that both vineyards were classified as grand cru makes the leeway given to producers even more alarming since the very concept of a vineyard producing wines of grand cru quality hinges on their ability to produce wines that are unique. How can two unique vineyards have the same exact name?

"I do apologize, but could you please explain to me how an American knows the difference between the two terroirs when we rarely speak of this difference even in Burgundy?"

I laughed a bit. "Some of us Americans have an obsessive interest in Burgundy."

"So, tell me of Charmes and Mazoyères," he said in shorthand. More than 150 years ago, the village of Gevrey and later the grands crus such as Charmes, Mazoyères, Ruchottes, and others affixed "-Chambertin" to their name to reap some of the benefits provided by their proximity to the reputed vineyard of Chambertin.

I went on to tell him that I had read in one of my wine books that in 1855 Jules Lavalle had classified Charmes Hauts, part of Charmes proper among those in the second tier, ranked behind only Chambertin and Clos-de-Bèze. The lower section of Charmes, Charmes Bas is on the other side of a fault line. The soil is completely different from one side to the other. It was classified another tier down, along with all of Mazoyères. Oddly enough, Mazoyères has a worse reputation than Charmes even though it is nearly impossible to know which vineyard you are actually drinking because all but two or three producers call what they have

Charmes-Chambertin and producers usually keep the real source of their wine a secret. Adding to this, many producers blend wines from the two vineyards because they can both be called Charmes-Chambertin grand cru. The two vineyards have completely different personalities and suffer the fate of mediocrity when blended together. This was something I'd learned from reading passages from André Jullien's 1816 book on all of the vineyards in the world. His words were as true then as they are now.

"OK, OK. I get it. You've heard of it." He was laughing; I could tell from his voice that he was finally in a good mood. "So, now the good news. I have both. Will you want the Charmes or the Mazoyères?" For the first time during the entire conversation I was at a loss for words. Not only was I being offered grapes, I was being offered grapes from one of thirty-three grands crus. And I was going to be getting grapes from one of the most interesting parts of the vineyard.

Just to walk in the vineyard would be a teleporting experience for me. To actually buy grapes that I could hold in my hand, that I could help become wine . . . it would be amazing. It was like going from playing fantasy football to actually owning one of the most celebrated and promising teams in the league. Ten minutes ago, either of these choices was beyond anything I had ever hoped.

"Charmes-Chambertin."

"Good. We will see you here before harvest."

"Oh! Wait."

"Yes?" His voice had been trailing as he was putting the phone down.

"How much do the grapes cost?"

"Don't worry, we will speak about this when you meet the owners with me and my father."

"Who are the owners?" I was hoping to do some research about their wines in the meantime.

"I will introduce you once you are here, then you will know each other."

"OK. Can you tell me how many barrels' worth of grapes I'm being offered?"

"I cannot. Sorry. Are you still interested?"

"Yes! Of course I am very interested. I look forward to speaking with you as soon as I am out there in about a month."

"You have a ticket?" He was surprised.

"I do."

"You had the ticket for how long?"

"For the past month."

He laughed again. "You know, you're crazy. Now that I think of it, I could potentially have some Chambertin for you as well." There was no way I had heard him right. Was he offering me another vineyard as well in the village of Gevrey-Chambertin, one of the oldest and highly regarded villages in Burgundy?

"Which vineyard? Mazis-Chambertin, Ruchottes-Chambertin, Griotte-Chambertin . . . ?"

"No, Chambertin. Le Chambertin. You . . . must know it, yes?" It took everything I had to not drop the phone. There were records of Chambertin having already been planted by the thirteenth century, and it has been considered to be one of the top three vineyards in Burgundy for the last seven hundred years. Many of history's most knowledgeable writers have praised it as one of the *world's* top vineyards. It was the favorite of the emperor Napoleon, drank in times of celebration by nobility, a wine with the reputation of being one of the most singular wine experiences in existence. In a culture based on celebrating differences instead of the notion of good, best, and better, Chambertin has proudly worn the king's crown of the region.

"I'll take every berry that you can offer." I didn't even know who was selling these grapes, much less how much they would cost.

As soon as the words lunged from my mouth, he countered. "Mister Walker, I cannot promise this. This is only something I may be able to do. But, you understand, I cannot promise such a thing."

"I understand." The words were a four-inch bandage attempting to close up a gaping wound in my chest where my heart should have been. "But if you can do it, I'd be eternally grateful."

"I will do as I can. I will call you soon to discuss. *On fait comme ça?* Bye-bye."

My mind reeled with what could happen next. There was no way an American with no money, no experience, no connections, no visa, no land, no facilities, no real contacts, and no *French* could have just secured grapes from one of the most sought-after vineyards in the world. If this happened, my name would be added to a very short list of people handling the prestigious grapes. I prepared myself for the inevitable phone call that would follow: "You *stooooop-eed* American. You think you can just come here and have grapes from Charmes-Chambertin, from Chambertin itself?! You are dumber than I thought you were. You are *zeee* dumbest. Stay home, nothing here for you."

I couldn't say anything to any of my friends. They'd never believe me anyhow. Worse still, what if they did believe and then it all fell through? I'd never be able to live it down. But mostly I was too superstitious. I worried that if I told too many people that somehow my good fortune would be scared away.

We hadn't discussed a price, but I knew the grapes would be well beyond the reach of my laughable budget. I started to think it would be too reckless to take Thomas up on his offer anyway. I considered possible responses. "No, thank you" didn't fit. "I would love to [insert casual laugh], but I don't have the money." Too personal. "Chambertin? I was looking for something more modest." I'd be out of my damn mind!

I called Christian, trying to temper the news with the reality of the situation. But with every turn of the conversation that I recounted I couldn't help but get giddy all over again.

"Chambertin, Christian! Shit! Chambertin!"

"Are you joking?" She sounded like she was in tears. "You better not be joking."

She didn't have to say anything else; I could hear the rest in her ragged breath, in her laughs that had turned into sobs of joy. This was happening.

For once I brought up money before she had.

"But I don't even know how much it costs yet."

"Does it really matter? We need to make it happen."

"I know, I thought about that but—"

"Ray, we *need* to make it happen."

"Then I will."

CHAPTER THIRTEEN

"I'M HERE."

"You're where?"

"The train station."

"Now? It's nine thirty at night. Your train was supposed to be here at four in the afternoon. Yesterday!"

"Long story."

"I'll be there soon."

As promised, minutes later, Fabrice picked me up. I didn't know him too well—I'd run into him at the Beaune Chamber of Commerce during my first visit with Christian in January. Overhearing my frustration with the agent assigned to help me with setting up a French business—along with my horrible French and complete miscomprehension of the convoluted bureaucracy—he'd offered to explain how to navigate the system.

In my mind, it was a miracle anyone could start a business in France. You couldn't get to step C without first completing step B, but there was no tackling step B without steps E and F. For example, if you weren't from the European Union or you didn't have a visa to work in France, you weren't eligible to create a business.

To get the visa, you needed to be a student or be employed. I couldn't very well get a visa from an employer because the whole point was to be my own.

Whenever I tried asking for help, everyone at the agency said they could tell me only about their individual department. If I needed instructions on how to fulfill what their department required, they still didn't have any idea how to answer my questions. They'd call their colleagues, their bosses, and I still wouldn't get anywhere. My situation just wasn't in the training books, and no one had seen anything like it on their desks before.

As a higher-up at the Chamber of Commerce, Fabrice had a good understanding about how everything tied together. And if there was something he didn't know how to do, he knew the person to call. Things that had taken me months to untangle in California took him a matter of minutes. I was so grateful for his help that I invited him over to my birthday dinner while we were staying at the *gîte*. We got on so well that he took a personal interest in finding a winery location for me after we left France; and while I scoured the Internet for listings from California, Fabrice sent me leads on eighteen locations for rent. A few of them seemed like they'd work perfectly. He invited me to stay in his house in Chagny if I ever came back, so his was the first number I called when I booked my ticket.

Fabrice was different from most of my other friends. He was in his early forties, and his blond hair was coiffed in what was clearly an expensive haircut. He was vain, spoke English with a surly high street British accent, and lived in a large old house in Chagny, just a few kilometers from the celebrated wine village Chassagne-Montrachet. His house was filled with antiques, old theater playbills, paintings from the eighteenth century, and an eccentric collection of doorknobs and knockers. Eccentric as he was, he was my first French friend and a good one at that.

By the time I got to Burgundy, harvest was only two and a half weeks away. I had no license to buy grapes, no business, and no facility to use to produce wine. For the first couple of days, I'd looked at all of the locations Fabrice had scouted, but to my surprise and disappointment, it turned out that none would work. There was mildew in one place; another had a small cemetery in its backyard. I wasn't so sure that was the type of history I wanted to be surrounded by. There was a ground level space that I'd have to share with a catering business. The most bizarre location was a place owned by a man who wanted to keep his 1984 Citroën next to the wine tanks during the winter along with his collection of vintage tires in the cave year-round.

And then there was the late-eighteenth-century structure that had been built solely for the production and storage of wine. For more than two hundred years it had housed vintage after vintage, with enough room for at least one thousand barrels. I figured I'd have six barrels at the most my first year, then maybe eight the next, but I reasoned that having room to grow wouldn't be such a bad idea. There were two levels to perform the fermentations, an elevator from the main level to the cave, and a loading dock already outfitted with a ramp. It was perfect. The owners were retired and looking for someone to rent the entire building along with the house attached to it. The house didn't have a kitchen or functioning bathrooms. The price was fair at twelve hundred euros a month—I figured I just wouldn't eat in May and August to make things balance out. They were the very first call that Fabrice made on my behalf, but for some reason they stalled long enough that we hadn't made any progress with them even after I'd seen every other property.

Finally Fabrice got them on the phone one day while I sat in his office.

"How many years do you want it?" he jotted down on a notepad, tossing it to me along with a pen.

"As long as I can?" I scribbled back.

He relayed my answer into the phone. He was silent for a few minutes, and I could hear the voice on the other end sending a stream of rapid French in return. He wrote again. "Will you make wine there?"

"Uh, you think?" I tossed the pen and pad back at him.

"*Oui. Il voudrait.*" He stared at his desk and then shook his head. He thumbed the pad of paper, cleaning bits of dust from of it.

"They say no wine and you can have it."

I scribbled on the page in front of him, "What??"

"You rent it if you like to live there."

I would eventually need a place to live, but in a winery where I couldn't make wine? In a house with no bathrooms or a kitchen? I was crushed. I thought for sure by the end of my first week in Beaune I'd have found a place, but now the search was going about as well as setting up my business.

Even with an offer to buy grapes on the table, in the eyes of the French government, I didn't have the *right* to buy them without an established French business. It was looking like my only option was to marry a citizen from an EU country. I decided to not run that possibility by Christian, but who knew how dire things could get? A rental agreement in the name of my business would help me get a license, but I couldn't get that until I had a business set up. I wasn't sure which was worse—proposing to Christian that we live in a house with no bathroom or kitchen, or her finding out that all of this was seemingly impossible.

Fabrice knew that my options were dwindling and quickly, and so after a particularly disappointing day of location scouting, he mentioned that he happened to also be helping another wine start-up. It was two men, and, to use his words, they had done everything right. He beamed with enthusiasm when speaking of how "they simply had it down." They'd gotten their business set up and had already secured their license. Whereas many people established their businesses with the minimum declared capital of a thousand euros, these guys had put up a hundred thousand. They apparently already had a fancy new stainless-steel press, beautiful wooden tanks, barrels, an impressive assortment of tools, and laboratory equipment. He explained that they too were looking for a facility, but because he'd met me first, I'd gotten preference. That said, he suggested that the smart thing to do at this point would be to share a space with them. As he pointed out, I didn't have a fraction of the capital that these guys were coming in with, and most of the locations we'd seen were far too large for my half-baked operation.

Despite all of his logical reasoning, I didn't want to share a space. There were too many variables: What if I didn't like the way they did things? They might want to use chemicals to make their wines and clean their tanks, and if any of that came into contact with my wine, it could be disastrous. If they used commercial yeast, which has a bad habit of completely filling a space with its very distinct-tasting spores, then my wine could taste just like theirs. Barrels contaminated with *Brettanomyces,* or "Brett," a strain of spoilage yeast, make wine taste like burned garbage. But the biggest issue of all was, What if we didn't get along? I felt strangely protective over my not-yet-existent wines for a guy who was coming pretty close to not having any wine at all. And I had a sneaking suspicion that there was something in it for Fabrice if he persuaded me. I was risking too much to get mixed up with the wrong people.

Fabrice's house was always a hub of activity. He was often picking up new friends at the pâtisserie, boulangerie, supermarché, and the tabac, and inviting them back for a glass of amazing wine or dinner. It wasn't unusual for me to get a random text while out running errands that said, "A family from the Rhône is stopping by. Have you tried white Hermitage?" or "My girlfriend and her son are having pizza and want to know if you would like to have a Coke with us in twenty minutes." So I didn't think it was completely strange when I got a message from Fabrice one afternoon that said, "The guys I told you about are coming over. They are bringing dinner." I wasn't sure what to expect, but I was willing to keep an open mind. Fabrice had been so generous— with his friendship, his connections, his time, his home—I could at the very least be cordial.

Xavier and Pierre were both recent graduates from the CFPPA, the famous wine school in Beaune, and shared an intense love of wine. But that's about where their similarities ended. Pierre, who had begun his journey into the industry at fifty-two years old, was in his early sixties, bald and short, and wore thin wire-framed glasses. He didn't speak much English and rarely spoke at all. But when he did, he was insightful and occasionally very funny. Xavier, though, was tall and sharp in every sense of the word. From the Swiss Alps, he spoke angular German-accented English, and a lot of it. Within five minutes of meeting him I was able to gather everything from his philosophy on wine to the brand of socks he preferred.

We spent the night sitting in Fabrice's garden talking about wine, translating, and laughing at one another's bad jokes, eating a rabbit ragout Pierre had prepared, and drinking a few old bottles of red Burgundy starting with a stunning red from Chassagne-Montrachet. We bonded over our harvest plans and setbacks. I told them about what I'd been through to buy grapes, set up a business, and find a location. It just started spilling out—the garbled phone calls I'd made from California to incredulous *négociants*, my dangerously dwindling bank account, the promise of grapes, the letdown of location after location, and how everything seemed so close to falling apart at exactly the wrong moment. I had told myself to stay quiet, but eventually I shared everything with them.

As I rambled, Xavier and Pierre began whispering to each other, exchanging nods. While moments before they'd laughed and shook their heads at my almost comical misfortune, they'd grown serious. Xavier looked worried, Pierre, encouraging. "We would like to help you," Xavier said. He looked hesitant but he nodded as he said it to assure me. And perhaps to assure himself too. "We have a place in Saint-Aubin."

It may sound ungrateful—or just plain dumb—but Saint-Aubin wasn't my first choice for a location. It was at least forty minutes from the closest vineyard I hoped to buy grapes from, which would be inconvenient for checking on the fruit during the growing season, and a major risk when it came to transporting it after harvest. No one in their right mind would want to drive that far with such precious cargo. The grapes could potentially heat up on the drive home, or worse yet, one accident could wipe out a full year's work.

"I appreciate it," I said. "But Saint-Aubin is too far from my grapes."

Pierre spoke up. "Well, how far away is your other winery from your vines?" He had a point.

"OK, I'd love to at least see the space," I said. "It's really nice of you guys to offer. You never know, right?"

Pierre smacked the table with his palm. "Bon. Tomorrow we show to you our place and we will see if it is to your liking."

Xavier sat up in his chair and pointed aggressively at me. "But," he said, "we will not make your wine!"

"He doesn't need us to make his wine, Xavier," Pierre said, the spark of a smile in his eyes, his flat hand raised to wave off Xavier's worry. "He wants to do all of it himself. He is young, capable"—he looked at me, nodded, and turned back to Xavier—"and I bet he can add a good spirit to our place."

Xavier turned to me. "Yes, we would like you to stay, we are . . . I am just explaining that I hope you will be independent. This is what you want anyhow, no?"

"It is. Yes. That is why my preference is to be on my own. But your offer would make things much easier on me."

To solidify our tentative agreement, Pierre picked up the 1979 Rousseau Mazis-Chambertin, poured it generously into everyone's glasses, and declared, "*Santé!*"

I COULDN'T SLEEP THAT NIGHT. This was the step that would unlock so many other things for me. With a place to rent, I could make the business official, buy and ferment my own grapes, and store my wine barrels. Just one dinner after weeks of disappointments and I was back on track. I called Christian to tell her the good news and spoke with Bella, who was now babbling enthusiastically to anyone who would listen. "D-d-d-da, da!" She giggled when she said it. I missed her terribly, my Isabella Ilan. Christian had always wanted a daughter named Isabella, and from the moment we found out we were having a little girl, I could just picture our little Isabella with Christian's beautiful face. It was tough coming up with a middle name that was a worthy addition, but my mind kept coming back to Ilan. There was something about the way the vowels shaped the sound that I just loved. It wasn't a name I'd seen anywhere else; it just formed on my lips as I moved names around in my mouth. I looked it up to see if there were any cultures that had used the name, and the closest was the Hebrew name Elan. It meant "tree." And thinking about how much energy and vibrancy little Isabella had already brought into our lives, it seemed to fit.

After hearing Bella's new chatter, I thought about all of the chocolate and ice cream we'd eat together while Christian was away. I missed hearing her laugh whenever I changed her diaper and kissed her feet and pressed them to my face. I remembered how I'd carry her with her legs wrapped around the back of my neck, her tiny fingers clamping onto my ears, tugging every which way as though trying to steer. Then I pictured what the building would look like, what tools and wine gadgets I'd buy first. I imagined how my barrels would look stacked up in a row. I'd have them branded: "Maison Ilan." It was Bella's birth that had pushed me to do something with my life, so it only made sense to honor her with the very thing she helped create. She was proof of all that was good in the world, that we were already blessed beyond belief. And she was the motivation to keep me moving forward, to keep pushing in the face of everything I stood to lose.

CHAPTER FOURTEEN

P ierre knelt down beside one of the fifty or so boulders on the ground and began running his hands around its base. He grunted and struggled not to topple over, while sweat poured from his brow.

"Success!" He sprang up, jerking a set of keys in his hand. "Today, we hope you will see our place as your place too."

He opened two sets of doors leading into the cinder-block-framed building. The open layout was massive, large enough to house seventy wine tanks. A few old wooden tanks, a couple of barrels, and some clear rubber hoses had been left there, but the rest of the place was empty. There wasn't much to it. The floor was a raw concrete slab, the walls were bare cinderblock. There was no air-conditioning and no cave. It was basically a wine shelter, but damned if it didn't seem like a fine option considering how long I'd looked.

"Are you guys worried about the heat in the summer?"

"No," Xavier said, studying a tiny broken piece of concrete on the floor that anyone else would have just walked by. He held the pebble-size bit and stared at it, nearly touching it to his glasses. "We'll have air-conditioning by then."

"How many barrels do you think you will have this year?" We'd talked only about my plans during dinner, and it occurred to me that I didn't really know much about what they were planning to do themselves.

"Nothing too important." Xavier was only feigning modesty, but he couldn't pull it off. "We are doing maybe one hundred fifty, two hundred barrels."

The ends of his pointed mustache curled up into a sneer. "We may not even notice your six barrels."

His ribbing didn't faze me. Starting that small would mean I'd only have room to grow, and I really had no clue where I'd be until I met with the growers, which I'd been holding off on until I had a production facility. I assumed I'd still be able to get the grapes, and I didn't want to piss anyone off by pestering them either. I needed to look patient and professional, even though that's exactly what I wasn't at the moment.

"Well, Pierre and I are fine that you have your little operation here as long as it is not more than twenty *pièces*."

"I'll be well below that for sure. Don't worry."

"If you had twenty barrels, it would not be me who worries."

Pierre came from the other side of the old wooden tanks. "What Xavier is saying is that we are happy to have you here. And the amount really is no concern. If it is more, it is more." He shot a gently admonishing glance at Xavier. "We figure that since you are just starting out that we should make rent comfortable for you. How is two hundred fifty euros a month?"

I looked at Pierre and his enthusiastic toothy smile forcing his glasses to rise up a bit off of his nose. Xavier was intensely staring at yet another pebble on the floor.

"That would be amazing!" I had painfully budgeted for three times that amount, on paper at least.

"So, you think this can work for you?" Pierre held out his right hand for me to shake.

I took his hand in mine and shook. "Yes! Thank you!"

"Good boy. Today we are three in this place." Xavier finally let the suggestion of a grin surface, but with anything more than that his face might have cracked down the middle.

I was in business. I had a place to keep my tanks, and barrels, my tools—that is, after I bought it all. I pulled out the list I'd sketched out on the plane ride over:

> Press
>
> Barrels
>
> Tanks
>
> Pump
>
> Hoses
>
> Graduated cylinders
>
> Fruit cases
>
> Plastic shovel
>
> Large plastic bins for rejected material
>
> Large garbage bags
>
> Sorting table

Unlike in California, where you could find whatever wine supplies you needed in one afternoon, in Burgundy stock is much more limited. Most people reserve their supplies months in advance. Trying to buy, for example, 150 fruit-picking bins a week before harvest is considered borderline certifiable.

Store after store I heard the same thing: "*Bac vendanges? Quand? Tout de suite? Pourquoi vous n'allez pas plus tôt dans l'année? Ce n'est pas Californie ici.*" In other words, "Fruit cases? When? Why didn't you come earlier in the year? This isn't

California here." I started worrying that I'd have to walk out of the vineyard cupping the grapes in my hands.

A couple of proprietors sensed my desperation and sent me away with whatever they had left. I got fifteen bins from one store and ten from another. I lucked into twenty-three from a place on the other side of Beaune owned by a guy who is never home and just leaves things he doesn't want any more in his front yard with a price tag. Like they say, "Do you want a deal or a receipt?"

After a few days not only had I collected enough bins for harvest but I'd also gotten wine thieves, nice crystal glasses, brooms, a pressure washer, and stainless-steel barrel supports. My little corner in the facility was filling up. So what if I hadn't heard back from the courtier in more than a month? I had my three tanks lined up, and I'd finally found nine barrels that made me happy. Barrels aren't just for holding wine during aging and transport; they are commonly used as important seasoning for a wine. Each forest produces wood that gives particular trademarks to its barrels—and in turn, wines—and the temperature at which the wood is toasted, the length of the toasting, the age of the tree, and the age of the wood all make a difference. Trees have terroir too, of course. Some winemakers think using a particular barrel is what makes a wine even more special or interesting. But I disagreed. A barrel that interferes with a wine's natural flavor fights its inherent characteristics and its origins. For me, the whole point of producing wine in Burgundy was to preserve that incredibly unique sense of place, so why obscure that with some loud-mouthed oak? If I was going to have exceptional fruit from exceptional vineyards, I wanted to make sure I could nurture that wine in a way that allowed it to express its true self. I didn't need to be an artist looking for a creative outlet, I just wanted to be a wine shepherd of sorts.

Finding barrels that wouldn't impart taste or smell on my wine was a challenge. They needed to be well made so they wouldn't warp or crack, and more important, they had to be realistic for my shoestring budget. To find what I was looking for, I visited a winery with a large selection of wines aged in barrels from a diverse collection of barrel makers. I tasted the same wine and vintage from every barrel I could, not just sipping and spitting, but swallowing it to get the full experience, looking for the barrels that consistently showed as little oak flavor as possible. After an hour, one barrel maker stood out to me. Though I tried, I couldn't think about wood when tasting wine from these barrels; I only thought of how well it captured the essence of the vineyard. It's what I wanted desperately.

Just running my fingertips over these barrels that had come fresh from Stéphane Chassin's *tonnellerie,* or barrel maker, in nearby Rully, I could feel the craftsmanship. Every part had been lovingly sanded and molded by attention and detail, unlike the majority of producers who slapped their barrels together with an eye focused on volume, not quality. Those weren't the future homes for special wines; they were a product to toss out the door—a product to mass produce. Cheaper than day-old bread? Sure! But there wasn't any soul in them, only obnoxious oak.

Of course, I'd still have to battle the dreaded oak. Buying new barrels—no matter how well made—meant that there was a chance that the wood could mark my wine with harsh, bitter tannins or, worse, make it taste like a sawdust cocktail. But I'd have as much control as I was ever going to have. My new barrels had the best pedigree possible, and in time their oaky newness would mellow out. And after five or six years, they'd be completely neutral. And they would have been aged with no other wine than my own.

The craftsmanship came at a price, but it didn't matter all that much—I just needed three new barrels, one for each of the three wines. I wanted to eventually have a good amount of used barrels that I originally bought new, but I was worried about having too much new wood influence on the wines, so I decided to keep the new wood to a minimum. The remaining six I bought used from the same producer with the hope that because they originated from the same place, that would eliminate at least one variable between the different wines. It was still a gamble since there was no way of knowing what kind of wines had been made in them before or how well they'd been treated, but I didn't have a lot of other options. There wasn't any logic to buying nine barrels. After all, I barely knew if I had grapes, much less how much wine I'd actually produce. But it sounded like a reasonable number. If I needed more barrels, I could always find more from Chassin. The market for used oak barrels didn't compare to the strengthening demand for new barrels.

The next order of business was finding a truck I could rent for the forecasted harvest dates. The problem was, just as with the rest of the equipment I'd been looking for, it was incredibly last minute. I looked for two days online and took a series of trains to and from Dijon, Beaune, and Chalon-sur-Saône. One day I walked from one end of town to the other going into car dealerships, which wore several holes in the soles of my only decent-looking pair of shoes. I had to keep wearing them. I eventually found a truck to rent after walking into yet another dealership, but I had no such luck getting a new pair of shoes since no stores in the area had size fourteens lying around. The dealership didn't ask me if I had a French driver's license, or even what I was planning to do with the truck. I just told them a date and pointed toward the best-looking new truck with a huge flatbed on the lot and it just happened to be one that they recently put out for rentals.

That just left the sorting table. Of all the tools to have in a winery, this is the most important. Without it, you can't properly sort out the grapes that are ravaged by mildew, mold, *Botrytis*, rot, or suffering from dehydration. If you were cooking sole meunière, you wouldn't toss in the bad fish with the good. All it takes is a small bit of something bad to offset all that makes something great, and for the kind of wine I wanted to produce, I had to have high expectations for every berry that made it into my tanks.

I began to wonder, how do you really know if the grapes are good unless you pick up every single cluster yourself? The conveyor belt–style table we'd used in my very limited experience moved at a constant speed while we—it was hoped—caught any wayward fruit before it was added to the wine pile. Most wineries used a conveyor belt; it was efficient and, for the most part, effective. But if all went to plan, I would be handling some of the most sought-after grapes in the world, and I wasn't going to risk botching it just because I didn't catch a bad one in time. I was putting everything on the line to do the very best that I could. The conveyor belt system left way too much to chance.

People generally agree that the translucent berries, usually the result of a late start in the season, taste watery, bitter, and unpleasant. The opaque berries are the ones you'd like to keep. The problem is translucent clusters of grapes can look awfully opaque if there is another cluster of grapes directly behind them or even if the sun is at your back. No one wants to pull out the pincer bugs, so they are deemed lucky and left in. Spiders share the same fortune—they end it all in a large pool of expensive grape juice. But brown or green leaves, branches, and snails also need to get

tossed out, and sometimes they are buried under the good clusters. Or what you think are good clusters—that is, even the most
perfect-looking bunch with an ideal assortment of tiny and
medium-size berries can have disgusting, fetid undersides that
you wouldn't even want to hold for too long, let alone eat. But
that's *if* you happen to see their bad side. One time back in California I picked up one of the most beautiful clusters we'd seen all
day. I mean, we were *ooh*ing and *aah*ing over it. But the second I
picked it up, a pus-like fluid started leaking out of the enormous
orange and purple fuzzy patch of mildew on the other side.

It made more sense to me to just have a flat piece of wood that
was large enough to spread out a decent amount of grapes on, and
then go through each one by hand. Sure, it would take more
time. One other problem was that having the grapes in my hands
would warm them up, which could encourage them to start prematurely fermenting. But at least I'd know exactly what was going
into my tanks.

I decided the best way to set something like this up was to
place three to four old barrels on their heads and then top them
with a long, two-inch-thick piece of white laminated wood. I
drilled everything into place with four-inch screws. The whole
setup cost less than an order of boeuf bourguignon. It made good
sense to me, but it was an added bonus knowing that I would
have the exact results that I wanted without spending fifteen
thousand euros on a modern machine all the professionals
thought was irreplaceable.

But the closer I got to harvest, the more tempted I was to buy
some of the gadgets I'd seen decorating established wineries—an
electronic gauge that could instantly measure alcohol content just
by pulling a sample of wine through a plastic syringe-like tube, a

machine with a conveyor belt that would take grapes from ground level to the tanks nine feet up, a high-temperature pressure washer. I bought every gadget that I thought a respectable winery would have.

I liked the idea of being "gentle" with my wine. I was still feeling out what that philosophy looked like, but now that the winemaking process was becoming more concrete thanks to my growing collection of gear, I was beginning to get a better idea. I wanted to question how things "had always been done." Take the punch-down tools, for example. Traditionally, winemakers beat the living daylights out of their grapes to break up the fruit and extract even more color, sugar, and tannins. I met some people who did this multiple times a *day*; it was the same back in California, at least once the grapes began to form a thick cap. But it was a lot of work. And not only that, it crushed all those grapes' seeds against the bottom of the tank, which, if you've ever bitten into one of them you already know well enough, are crazy bitter. Why would you want all that released into your wine? I thought there had to be a way to break up the fruit evenly without pulverizing every last bit of it. I asked myself, What would they have done hundreds of years ago? And because I'd spent so much time with my face crammed in those old wine books, I knew just the thing: I'd just hop in the tanks and push down the grapes with my feet, so that I wouldn't break any seeds and the more innate nuances of the juice would be protected.

In terms of how many times I'd actually need to push the growing cap down, I figured that extracting grape skin color and tannin might be similar to extracting tannins and color in a cup of tea. The hotter the water, the more extraction, and the more pressure on the tea bag, the darker, more bitter, and tannic it turns. For tea, this overpowering extraction makes it lose its nuances. Often, the prettiest tea is the lightest in color. I wasn't even much of a tea drinker, but this idea made sense to me, so I planned to keep any punch downs to a minimum. It sounds crazy, and there was nothing to support my philosophy but a hunch, but I felt like I was being consistent. I wasn't looking to be a winemaker so much as I wanted to be a preservationist. I wanted wine that tasted good, sure, but I also wanted there to be clarity of place and most of all, not a single trace of my having touched it.

As I'd accumulated my equipment, I'd basically been shoving it all into a corner because I was waiting for Pierre and Xavier to finish setting up their own space first. I watched their growing collection of tools, and unlike my fairly minimalist assembly, I couldn't make out what a lot of it was. But I could see that if there was a piece of wine equipment to be had, they bought it. Meanwhile, my little piece of the floor grew smaller and smaller, and every time I went to the winery they'd moved something else. But I was still optimistic my setup could work. I had visions of Ed's neatly organized baker's racks and tidy rows of tanks and barrels.

While Pierre and Xavier arranged their work area, I took a couple of days away from the winery. Every second I was gone I had to force myself to relax. I was becoming obsessive, picturing how everything would look, how I'd move my equipment around. But soon it dawned on me that if I got too caught up in the planning, I wouldn't be able to enjoy letting things unfold. So I tried to spend the time enjoying the calm before the madness of harvest: walking by countless vineyards in Gevrey-Chambertin and Chambolle-Musigny and taking pictures of small rows of vines I had only read about before. Finally I got the call from Pierre that everything was ready.

It was late and dark by the time I got to the warehouse, but Xavier and Pierre were waiting for me inside. "So," Pierre said, grinning anxiously, his eyes wide, brimming with a youthful thrill, "what do you think?"

What was once an expansive warehouse now looked like a huddled mess of stainless steel. Every bit of it was taken over by two gigantic pneumatic presses, a stainless vertical basket press, four grape elevators, twelve wooden fermentation tanks, two hundred barrels, a vintage labeling machine, and two pumps. And somewhere in all of this was my little setup, but I couldn't find it until I walked down one of the tiny passageways they'd left between their rows of machines.

My tools were wedged right up against their equipment, and each tank touched the one next to it. The space in between the tanks and the barrels was so tight that I needed to shuffle sideways in order to pass through. Altogether, my work area was less than half the size of a one-car garage. How was I supposed to do anything with such little room? But then again, how could I complain without sounding ungrateful? It was either be cramped or be homeless. Without their space to share, I'd be back at square one, and with harvest days away, I couldn't afford to be too picky.

"It's perfect!" I said.

CHAPTER FIFTEEN

THE WEATHER HAD BEEN ALL OVER THE PLACE THE LAST couple of days. Rain, then hail, followed by intense, dry heat. Though it was starting to get brutally hot, the sun was a welcome change. Without any news yet on my grapes, I decided to take a break from Beaune. The walls in my box of a hotel room were shrinking by the day, and there was no sense in being cooped up inside with nothing to do when there was an entire country to explore. I'd called Thomas about twenty times since I'd arrived in Burgundy, and e-mailed, but no word. I'd even passed by the wine shop a couple of times, but he hadn't been there when I'd stopped in. I vowed to be patient and not let negative thoughts into my head. I trusted him, and there had to be a good reason he wasn't responding. It didn't mean everything couldn't still work out perfectly. I decided to hop a train going south toward Nice. I figured I'd get off in some random place that looked pretty and kill a few hours. I had to do something to take my mind off the fact that I may have done all this work for naught.

I'd run out of boutiques in Beaune and Dijon to stroll through early in my stay, so I'd been spending most of my free

time in antique bookshops. Old things, especially books, fasci-
nated me. There is something powerful in lasting words. Forget
translations or revisions. The words that have the most texture,
that construct new walls of reality, are those that come straight
from the original author's pen, quill, or printing press. I've always
felt that to be in the moment with the author, you need to feel the
breath of the author's words as if he or she were speaking directly
to you. It's how a narrative can truly blend into your own thoughts
and allow you to see the world around you as the author did.

What I had found in those dank and dark bookstores was a
living perspective that made me feel more deeply connected to
Burgundy and its culture, traditions, and wines. It's where I discovered all the celebrated works that modern wine books tip their
hats to: Louis Pasteur's 1866 study on wines that details the process of pasteurization; Jean (Jules) Lavalle's first thorough classification on the vineyards of Burgundy from 1855; Denis Morelot's
1831 dissertation on the idea of terroir, which explains the connection between the geology and terrain of the vineyards in the
Côte d'Or and the resulting characteristics of the wines. André
Jullien's 1816 masterpiece that describes every single wine-
producing region in the world from his personal visits; and Jean-
Antoine Chaptal's 1801 book on how to make wine, including
techniques on chaptalization, a process he popularized that in-
volves adding sugar to grape must to elevate the alcohol content.
These were the true masterpieces on the subject, but up until now
I'd read only interpretations of their teachings. Reading these
masters' books transported me back hundreds of years to a time
that, wine-wise, wasn't all that different from the present and also
provided rich historical context to the dirt beneath my own two
feet. I imagined myself in these authors' shoes as I walked the

same steps that they had once taken while trying to understand Burgundy.

These epic tomes were my education in the history of Burgundy and its wines, not the unsolicited advice from winemakers who were doing things in newer, more modern ways. I loved the idea that I was learning French—although a much more formal, antiquated version that occasionally got a good chuckle from the locals—from someone who had lived nearly two hundred years ago. I'd settle in for a night of reading with my English-French dictionary and completely submit to the centuries-old wisdom. I'd read of harvest dates, wine prices, important transactions, recorded temperatures, soil content, old harvest songs, and detailed vineyard classifications. I'd learn about vineyards I'd never heard of before that once had massive reputations but had now all but disappeared. It was an awakening to learn so much from these original sources and to see Burgundy as many today never get the chance to. I'd be so taken with the author's send-up of the vineyards that I'd put my book down, head to the nearest wine shop, and look for a bottle from that almost mystical patch of land.

When I decided to take a trip south, I grabbed my copy of André Jullien's 1816 *Topographie de tous les vignobles connus* and, once the train started moving, buried my nose in the tissue-thin pages that glowed like autumn leaves. Just as I'd settled in, though, my phone rang.

"Hello?"

"Yes, is this the American without grapes?" The unidentifiable voice on the other end started laughing.

"Who is this?"

"I hope you remember me since I am the one that has grapes for you."

Thomas! He had finally called. "Really glad to hear from you," I said, feigning calm. "You know, I thought you'd finally call me sometime after next year's harvest."

"*Non, non. Pas de soucis.* Are you in Beaune right now?" The smile he no doubt wore was evident in his voice.

"Nah, man, I'm on a train to Nice."

"You are going to Nice?!"

"No. Just figured I'd get on a train heading to Nice and then hop off somewhere interesting."

"I was hoping I could pick you up to meet the vignerons."

"When?"

"I was thinking in maybe twenty minutes."

I looked at the phone, not sure if I was more upset at the courtier for his timing or at myself for doing something as idiotic as leaving when this was *exactly* the way Burgundy business was done—spur of the moment. If I couldn't be there, my chances of getting grapes would quickly deteriorate.

"I can get off at the next stop and catch the next train back to Beaune."

"OK. But we will meet in Nuits-Saint-Georges at the train station, it will be faster."

"Can I have an hour to get there? I'm about fifteen or twenty minutes outside of Beaune."

"I will call and adjust things. Don't worry, we will make a good impression."

We reached the next stop just after I hung up. The train heading back to Beaune was already boarding on the tracks one platform away. I ran as fast as I could down the stairs, underneath the main platforms, and down the concrete hall, the sound of my worn-out dress shoes slapping against the tile walls. As I came running up the stairs, I heard the train starting to move. I pushed myself to run faster, but it felt as if I were moving in slow motion. My eating habits were finally catching up with me. I made it to the top only to see the train pulling away. Doubled over to catch my breath, I didn't notice the train slowing down until I heard the breaks squealing. They were stopping! I got on the train and thanked the agent as many times as I could manage while doing my best to stay upright, as sweat dripped from my brow and stained the underarms of my blue button-up shirt. I didn't look it, but I couldn't have been more ready to make this meeting.

I came out of the front doors of the train station to find Thomas, whom I had met just the one time a few months before, waiting for me. He was with his father, Dominique, a serious-looking man in an old tweed hat with bolts of silver hair peeking out from under it. Though I had discussed the grapes with Thomas, it was Dominique—like every male patriarch in his family for the past six generations—who was the acting courtier in this arrangement and had set up this meeting. His family had an excellent reputation in Burgundy and was known for having relationships with some of the best growers. The courtier's job was to be the middleman, the matchmaker. My appreciation for him went far beyond the 2 percent commission they typically made. Besides connecting buyers and sellers, he ensured that each side reached fair agreements and handled any potential disputes. But if Dominique didn't like what he saw in me, he could cleanly wipe away my plans of getting grapes. If he liked me, he'd vouch for me, and it would most likely be enough for the grape growers to approve me. That is, unless I screwed something up.

I wasn't in the car for ten seconds before Thomas was on my back.

"Whew. You stink, man."

"Thanks, Thomas. Nice to see you as well."

"Really, it is bad. Maybe I should have you just sit in the car during the meeting." He was laughing like a schoolboy. "Once terms are settled, you can wave to them from the car window."

"Really, it's that bad? I had to chase down a train. No way I was going to call you up telling you I missed it."

"No, it's not too bad. You are fine." I was relieved. "But your shirt is ruined. Hopefully they won't notice." I chuckled back, knowing he was joking, at least a bit.

Dominique, clearly the more stoic of the two, had been quiet. He just looked back in the rearview mirror and smiled. He didn't speak much English but he could understand that Thomas was giving me grief.

"*C'est peut-être de grandes choses pour toi.*"

"*Papa*, Ray *ne parle pas français.*" Thomas turned around in his seat. "He says that this could be a big thing for you."

I had actually gotten some of it. "I know. I'm really thankful that you came through on everything."

"*Des Chambertin. Hmph, c'est pas chaque journée,*" Dominique continued. "*Et toi, tu es très jeune. C'est bon de voir des jeunes comme ça.*"

"My father, he's happy for you. Not many young people get—"

His father raised his index finger, shaking it while looking back at me in the mirror, buckled in tightly. I felt almost as if I were about to receive a lecture. "*Mais, c'est cher. C'est bien cher. Mais, bon. C'est un terroir très spécifique.*" He was giving me a heads-up that the price of the fruit was going to be painful—but worth it.

"*Papa*, Ray *sait que c'est spécifique.*" He shook his head. "I'm sorry, he doesn't know that you know a good amount about Burgundy."

We pulled into Gevrey-Chambertin, then into the courtyard in front of the growers' house. It was plain and not particularly large. I had imagined some grand estate or at least a much more substantial operation to explain why selling a few barrels' worth of grapes wasn't too big of a deal for them. The whole family was waiting—two brothers, their wives, mom, dad, grandma, a couple of grandchildren, and the dog—to greet us in the courtyard. They were lined up as though they were about to have their picture taken. It was clear to me right away from how friendly they all looked, they didn't care as much about the money as they did about who would be at their table. I worried that if I made a bad impression or rubbed them the wrong way, my hopes of getting their grapes would go up in smoke. I knew this was, without a doubt, the most important interview of my life.

"*Je vous présente* Ray Walker." Thomas nudged me forward as I walked toward them.

I shook a few of the men's hands before meeting the women of the family. "*Ah, l'américain.*" Arriving at the matriarch, she took a look at my outstretched hand, pushed it away, and gave me a big hug, kissing me once on each cheek. The whole family broke out in laughter. In Burgundy, nothing happens without the approval of the whole family, but the matriarch has the final word. I knew her enthusiasm was a good sign, but we were just getting started. They led us into their dining room, where the adults settled around an old, long wooden table. Once everyone was at the table, we all sat down. Thankfully I had learned this custom while eating dinners with Fabrice. So far, so good.

Of the eleven of us, I was the only one who didn't speak French. My vocabulary had grown considerably since I'd returned to France, but unless I was going to ask one of them for hotel recommendations, where the bathroom was, or what was playing at the movies that night, I still didn't have much way of communicating. For now, I'd stick with *oui* and *non*.

I leaned over to Thomas. "You know I don't speak French, right?"

He smiled and leaned in toward me. "I think everyone in the room knows this. But I don't believe that they care." His face briefly sketched a smirk.

They didn't? I cared. Why wouldn't they? A few of them spoke bits and pieces of English, and it was a good deal smoother than my French, but it still wasn't enough for us to understand one another in one language. It was awkward sitting like a dull mute among people telling jokes, laughing, and bantering. I tried to use a little of my French, but I was still a mess, using unforgivably embarrassing hand gestures. It was like I was playing a failing one-man game of charades.

"*Bon.*" Thomas addressed the table, and everyone quieted down. "Ray *me dit qu'il est désolé qu'il parle pas trop de français. Parce que je parle anglais, mon père a décidé que je prends des dispositions. Je peux traduire si tout le monde est d'accord.*" He had told them that because I didn't speak too much French, that his father, Dominique, had decided to let him handle things, while offering to translate for both of us, as long as everyone agreed.

One by one everyone at the table began to respond. "*D'accord.*" "*Mais oui.*" "*Pourquoi pas.*" "*Allez en anglais, moi je comprends bien l'anglais. Oubliez tout le reste,*" joked the younger brother, Philippe, starting yet another uproar of laughter. Thomas leaned to me, laughing. "He says to continue in English. He understands English well; forget the others."

"*Donc, Ray vient de Californie. Il oeuvrait auparavant dans le*

monde des finances. Il trouve bien de vins et cultures de la Bour-
gogne. Il connaît bien les vins et l'histoire Bourguignon. Il est très
calme, plaisant, et vraiment passionné." Again he leaned over. "I
told them that you are from California, that you did finances but
you find a passion in the culture here, the wines. I said good
things about you too. Thank me later."

The older brother, Jean-Michel, spoke up, "*Et il a déjà trouvé*
d'autres choses?" Thomas translated: "Have you found other
things so far, grapes?" He quickly studied my face and then turned
back to them without waiting for a response. "*Non.*"

Thomas would continue to translate the questions coming at
me from every direction.

"Are you here with family?"

"No, they are back home."

"They will join you?"

"Yes, of course, once things are set up."

"Does your wife approve of your decision?"

I turned to Thomas. "Tell them that I said that my wife is
the boss, and without her blessings, I would still be in finance. The
decision is one that we made together."

Thomas related my answer to the table. I heard the three
women at the table saying things to one another; the men at the
table only nodded with solemn looks on their faces until one of
them made a joke. A mean look from one of the women quickly
stole his smile and the rest of the air from the room.

Even though we didn't speak the same language, they looked
me in the eyes when asking their questions, and I did the same as
I responded.

"They agree that we can speak of grapes now."

"*Tu recherches pour des raisins?*" The father, Paul, leaned in and stared intensely into my eyes. He looked tough, as though he'd weathered many decades of backbreaking work in the vineyards of Gevrey-Chambertin and Morey-Saint-Denis and had seen people come and many more of them go.

Grapes. I got that part, but didn't understand the rest. "Thomas, what did he say?" I smiled back at the guy, not breaking from it until I got the translation.

"He asks if you are looking for grapes."

"He knows I'm looking for grapes. Why else would I be here?"

"This is how it works. He asks, you answer, he proposes, and you accept or decline. This is not Calif—"

"I know. I know." I shook my head and smiled, happily agreeing to play the game. I looked at him. "*Oui, monsieur. Oui.*"

Then Paul looked back at me. "Oh, so you *do* speak French."

The table was quiet.

I raised my open hands, shrugging an embarrassed smile on my face. "Sorry, that was most of my French right there! You speak English?"

His hands went up quickly as he wiped away the thought of it.

We all broke out laughing.

"*Tu bois un coup? Non . . .*" He gestured like he was drinking a shot. His eyebrows came together and he smirked slightly and slowly shook his head side to side. He was egging me on, and I was up to the challenge. His voice was pleasant and light and he had such humorous facial expressions that anything he said made me laugh, even if I didn't understand a lick of it.

"*Vin? Oui.*"

He waved his invisible glass at the younger brother, asking him to grab a bottle of wine.

"*Le mille neuf cents soixante dix-huit.*"

I could hear bottles in the other room being moved around, sliding out of and then back into their slots. "*Un qui?*" Which one? It didn't matter which wine his son brought back. I wanted to have a drink with Paul.

"Charmes-Chambertin." The brother came back to the old table and set the bottle down in front of us, along with a few glasses.

My mouth was damn near watering at the sight of the bottle in front of me, which was in the hands of the man who'd harvested the grapes more than thirty years earlier. It was a 1978 Charmes-Chambertin. There I was, on the other side of the world, away from everything I had known, moments away from getting my first real offer of grapes, and all I could think about was the wine they were about to pour. I was honored he would offer me a glass of one of their most cherished wines. I'd heard of how insular Burgundy producers were, but I couldn't have felt more at home. While they spoke a different language, their emotions, laughter, and friendliness were comfortingly familiar.

The bottle was dusty, so much so that the thick layer of grime didn't budge when Jean-Michel tried to clean it off with his massive shovel-worn hands. Seconds later, a vibrant red stream of everything that I loved about Burgundy poured into my glass. It showed its age in its striking ruby color and the tinges of amber that kissed the inside of the glass's bowl. The nose first smelled of ripe raspberries with a slight hint of chocolate, but then new aromas came to the surface, changed, and then tucked themselves back into its folds. I tipped the glass against my lips and put as much of my face inside of it as I could, forgetting my surroundings and the meeting. I thought about the vineyard that gave birth to such a compelling wine. Each smell, each taste was different, each a new experience I loved. It captured all of my senses. I was completely inside of the glass, taken back to the memory of the first glass of red Burgundy I had fallen so deeply for only four and a half short years earlier.

As the family looked on, waiting for my impressions, I searched my mind for a word that could do the wine justice. With its fine nuances and my pathetically limited French vocabulary, I racked my brain for a word that was similar in French and English. "*Une expérience.*"

My new drinking friend nodded in agreement as he stared me in the eyes, raising his glass to everyone at the table, and in his deep Burgundian voice boomed, "*L'américain a dit la vérité. Mon vin est une expérience. Bon. On commence. Charmes-Chambertin.*" His right palm met the table with a thunderous pound.

"Now we start," said Thomas, as everyone quieted down. "They want to know how many barrels' worth of grapes of Charmes-Chambertin you would like to buy."

"Are they located in Aux Charmes Hauts or Aux Charmes Bas?" Before I gave my answer, I wanted to know where the grapes were situated. While I liked the family, I didn't want to get talked into taking something that I'd be unhappy with. Thomas knew that I was well aware of the dramatic differences between the two sections of the vineyard.

Thomas looked toward Dominique, gesturing like he had hurt his hand as he shook it—the same look when someone is giving someone a hard time or when a strong impression has been made. The rest of the table stayed quiet.

Thomas leaned toward me and whispered, "I think you've just impressed them."

Dominique gave a widening smile. "*C'est Hauts.*" I tried not to flinch or swallow too hard. The temperature in the room shot up about thirty degrees, but no one else seemed to notice.

Thomas added, "It is the higher side, close to Chambertin; it is on this . . . hump that you spoke about on the phone."

"How many am I being offered?"

"They are saying that you get eight. For a barrel, we calculate three hundred and thirty kilograms for the grapes. If you have this weight, you can most likely get one barrel of wine."

Eight! The growing knot in my throat had swelled, and I couldn't swallow. I didn't have much money to my name besides the investment capital that I had recently fallen into. We had a little savings socked away from some of the larger checks I'd received while in real estate, but that was supposed to help us during the eventual period when I wouldn't have any income. I could barely afford four barrels of village, how in the world was I going to buy the equivalent of eight barrels of grand cru? I tried to regain my composure. Maybe I could get out of here with my dignity. Without that, I'd be laughed out of Burgundy. I could see it now: "The kid from California with the grand cru aspirations on nothing but a beer budget."

"Is that eight barrels of Charmes-Chambertin?" My voice cracked. My voice never cracks. I cleared my throat again.

"Yes, of course." Thomas looked calm. It was all imaginary numbers to him—it wasn't his money. We could have just as easily been discussing the cost of a candy bar.

"How much?" My nervous lump was back, and my eyes were going to water. "I mean, what does that work out to?"

I couldn't breathe. I interrupted them; I had to say something, anything to stop the spinning in my head. "Sorry, Thomas, but is there any way that I can get less than eight?" I figured something along the lines of only six times my budget would be much more prudent—still crazy, but a little less crazy.

He laughed as I thought about how much I could get for my left hand on eBay.

"Of course you can." He looked to them. "*Et moins, c'est possible aussi, oui?*" Dominique looked at the old man wearing a slight shrug; Thomas looked back at me. "They don't care. It is up to you. If you like, you can say what you will take tonight and you will shake their hands. And then we can walk the vineyard tomorrow with the owners. Once you say you are happy, you can shake hands again and we are in business."

"Can I do three?"

"*Trois?*" He held up three fingers to the owners, they nodded, and a few of them stood up smiling, ready to shake hands.

An unimaginable weight lifted off of me and the room slowed down to a more manageable fifty-mile-per-hour rotation.

The old man and Dominique were the last ones seated. Dominique slowly placed his right palm on the table. "*Et pour le Chambertin?*"

Did he say *Chambertin?*

My eyes shot over to Thomas. I tried to remain calm. "Am I getting *it?*"

"If you want it. It is up to you." This wasn't happening. I couldn't believe it. Chambertin. I was going to have Chambertin grapes. I didn't have a clue how to treat them. I understood Burgundy a lot more than I had when I had my first sample four years earlier, but I knew there was a crazy amount that I still didn't know. I'd never even tasted a Chambertin before! And yet, here I was, about to get the chance to hold some of the most precious grapes in the world. Forget holding them, they were going to be mine! This was going to happen. We all sat back down.

I leaned in toward Thomas. "You know I would kill for Chambertin. So, how much is three barrels of Charmes and a barrel of Chambertin?"

Thomas looked nervous; he inhaled and rocked in his chair as he looked to Dominique. I must have said something wrong. The old man shook his head and crossed his arms. Thomas grabbed for a nearby piece of scratch paper and began writing as he spoke.

"OK, this won't work. You see, you cannot buy Chambertin unless you buy all of your Charmes-Chambertin."

"Oh, OK. Wait, you mean. . . . the eight barrels? I thought I could buy what I wanted."

"You can. But they will not let you buy Chambertin unless you take their offer for the Charmes. You know, it is a very good piece of land, the Charmes-Chambertin. I promise that you will be happy."

I was looking for any way to get to a smaller grape bill. "Can I do seven barrels of the Charmes and then take the Chambertin?"

Jean-Michel, a brother, spoke up. "Seven is good for us. We can keep the last barrel."

It was a fantasy negotiation about fantasy grapes with fantasy money that I didn't have. But seven made it seem a more realistic possibility than eight. Seven was ridiculous, but eight? Eight was lunacy!

"OK, so what's the total?" I stared at the paper in front of me, on which Thomas was anxiously tapping the tip of his pen. He didn't seem as used to being in these meetings as his father, who was coolly sitting back in his chair. He held up two fingers.

"*Il y a deux.*"

"My father says there are two barrels' worth of Chambertin grapes on the vines for you."

"Oh, that's cool. I'll just take the one. So, how much—"

Thomas brought up his hand pleadingly. "They say that you need to buy both or none of them. You could still have the Charmes though, however many you wanted. But with Chambertin they are . . . you know, specific."

"Why do I need to buy two?"

"Well, the smaller the lots, the less room you have to make a good cuvée. Anything can happen."

Made sense to me, but I was up to the challenge. "I'd be fine with it." He translated as the family members muttered to themselves.

"No, with a wine of this expense, no one would be dumb enough to take the risk. It wouldn't be prudent."

I tried to break the tension. "Well, I'm dumb enough." Thomas quickly translated, someone replied just as quickly, and they all began laughing. One of them came over and sat next to me, pointing to one of the brothers.

"He said *you* may be stupid enough, but how are we going to find someone else that is stupid enough to take this risk?" The room vibrated with our laughter. I poured more wine into Paul's glass as the laughter kept going until the matriarch walked down the stairs again. As soon as the sound of the boards on the stairs began to shift beneath her feet, the room went quiet. She finally came into view, looking at all of us, her face stiff and taut as we sat there, frozen like a group of teenagers caught staying up late playing video games. Her mouth eased into a playful smile as she turned and set about walking back up the stairs.

"OK, I'll take the two. You know, this is going to be a hell of a harvest."

"Yes, and they are now anxious for you to visit the vines tomorrow."

"Can I just ask, do you think they care at *all* that I am an American?"

"No, it might be better for you; you have a clean slate here!" He then quickly pulled out a calculator.

In Burgundy, there are a few ways to arrive at the price of grapes. Growers can set a price based on other transactions made in the area that are kept on record and account for not only the prices of the grapes themselves but also the finished product. They can also set their own prices. But the big problem with that is that in a vintage where the yields are low and producers scramble to get whatever they need, prices can become ridiculously expensive in a hurry, especially for the most sought-after grapes. As an alternative, growers and négociants agree on a set a price, which typically reflects the average of a grape's cost over time. Luckily, the growers I was working with liked to sell at the average price, which sounded much more fair to me—though it certainly wasn't going to make these grapes any cheaper.

"OK, for Charmes-Chambertin, you will have an estimate to base your payments on of eighty-four hundred euros."

"Oh, that's not bad at all." I was thinking it would be a little more than that for everything.

"Yes, multiply this by eight . . ." Oh.

"And then, Cham . . . ber . . . tin." He drew out his sentence as he continued to punch numbers into the calculator. There was a ride at this theme park I used to visit when I was younger. They'd strap you into a chair and pull you up about two hundred and fifty feet. There you would sit for what seemed like half an hour. It would be dead still; the only movement was the wind whipping up your hair and the rhythmic pounding of your heart in your throat. You'd wait, knowing the inevitable was about to happen, but still nothing. And then they'd pull a pin and you would plummet, your knuckles aching from trying to hold yourself in your seat.

"*Twenty-three thousand euros.*" God, help me. "Two barrels, that makes forty-six thousand euros. He looked at my face and repeated it again. It was white noise to me. It didn't matter at that point if it were a hundred thousand euros a barrel. It didn't make a difference if the grapes were ten times or one hundred times my budget. I still didn't have the money.

"How much time do I have to pay again?"

"Well, usually you can pay starting at the end of December after harvest."

Oh, maybe this could work then. It probably wouldn't, but maybe it could.

He went on, "But since this is your first time buying grapes in Burgundy . . . well, actually anywhere, they will need to have a transfer prior to you taking the grapes." OK, this wasn't going to work.

I tried my best to keep my poker face. I was in the wrong room, the wrong league. I could possibly find enough money to do two barrels of the Charmes-Chambertin, but my budget would be shot after that. Starting out with a grand cru was much more than I ever hoped for. I didn't *need* Chambertin. It would have been cool, but it wasn't worth getting sent to debtors' prison for. I didn't know how to begin to put together that kind of money, but maybe something would fall into place. Fall into place? I wasn't thinking straight. They would laugh me out of their house if they found out just how low on capital I truly was. But it *was* Chambertin. It was worth the risk. I didn't know exactly what it would mean if I had the chance to produce my own Chambertin. It was beyond anything that I had the nerve to wish for, and it would be the first time to my knowledge that a non-Frenchman fermented grapes from the most storied vineyard in history.

"OK, I'll take it all."

No one blinked an eye. "The eight Charmes as well?"

"Just the seven."

"Are you sure?" Thomas and everyone else looked me squarely in the eyes. I looked back at Thomas.

"Yeah, I'm sure." I looked at the old man. "*Je suis d'accord.*" I was glad that phrase had come in handy. We came together next to the table and took turns shaking hands. I kept my grip firm to distract myself from the fact that my knees were about to buckle. Dominique and I traded glances, and he had a proud look on his face that I knew would stay with me for a long time.

The ride back to my less than twenty-euro-a-night room in Beaune was a quiet one—at least from my end. Thomas kept telling me how impressed he was with the way things went. He seemed genuinely surprised that the offer for Chambertin was made official. "Of course the grapes are crazy expensive, you know." My head slid down the side of my door's window. "But, you know, this isn't something that happens every day." The buzz was wearing off; I had no idea how I was going to make this work.

They dropped me off at the hotel. I watched as they drove away because it was most likely going to be the last time I saw them or had a shot at those grapes.

I started racking my brain for people who might have that kind of capital just lying around, but my list was a tragically short one, and most of the people on it had already contributed all they had to give. One name kept coming back to me—Dave Warco, my top investor. He *did* say I could call him if I ever needed anything, but I assumed that was just something nice you said to someone who was babysitting twenty thousand dollars of your money. I worried that he'd think I was ungrateful if I got in touch, or maybe just overreaching, and that he'd want his money back. But I knew I hadn't gotten this far by not taking any chances.

"Hello?" Dave sounded like I'd caught him while he was busy.

"It's . . . it's Ray."

"Oh, hey, man. You in Burgundy?" His voice softened.

"Yeah."

"Kinda late over there, right?"

"A little. I just got out of a meeting."

"So, what's going on?"

"Well, I kinda feel selfish bringing this up to you. And I really don't know how to bring it up."

"Just put it out there, no worries."

"Well, I think I can do something cool, something that isn't really supposed to happen."

"That's awesome, man. What's the problem then? That's great news!"

"The problem is money." There was suddenly no sound coming from the other end of the phone.

"Well, that's not *really* a problem." Who was this guy?

"It's a lot."

"How much are we talking about? Can't be that bad."

"I'd need about a hundred thousand more."

"Really?" He sounded relieved. "What is that, euros or dollars?" He said it like we were talking about Monopoly money.

"Euros."

"Oh, that's not a problem. I can send that to you in the morning." The pin released.

CHAPTER SIXTEEN

I HADN'T FELT NERVOUS THE WHOLE TIME THAT I HAD BEEN looking for grapes. They'd come; deep down I knew they would. A place to ferment my grapes into wine? It would come. But *good* grapes, in addition to enough cash to bring them home? That was the most important piece of the puzzle, and I had no way of knowing whether it would ever fall into place. Without that, the other stuff wouldn't matter. I'd have no reason to stay in France, and I'd be one step further from my dream. But now I had both.

The deep sense of relief I felt was quickly eclipsed by anxiety. What if the growers decided I was too unknowledgeable? Too unpolished? Too un-French? What if someone more reputable came along and offered more money? There was no way something this fortuitous, this insanely lucky, could happen without karmic backlash.

Shortly after arriving at my box of a hotel in Beaune, I called Christian to tell her about the meeting I'd just had. She couldn't believe it either; it hadn't seemed real until I told her. We were both stunned by how quickly everything had changed. There wasn't much time to second-guess the opportunity; we both knew what this could mean, so I'd push ahead with even more intensity. To celebrate would be unthinkable. There were too many other boxes that still needed checking, too many things that could go wrong, and far too few safety measures we'd put in place. Backup plans to the tune of a hundred thousand euros simply didn't exist for us.

We talked more a couple days later while I rode on my pitiful excuse for a bike. It wasn't worth its weight in scrap metal, and I was happy for the distraction from the people staring at me—a six-foot American attempting to ride what looked like a centuries-old mini-bike from the train station in Nuits to Morey-Saint-Denis to look at a possible *cuverie* for rent.

After my sudden grape windfall I knew I needed to find a backup to the space I was sharing with Pierre and Xavier. I certainly didn't want my grand cru wines to be jockeying for room with the water heater. I made a few calls and, as luck would have it, I got word of an older gentleman in Morey who was looking to rent out part of his winery.

Upon arriving, I was greeted by the owner, who led me inside his renovated facility. He explained that while he would be using all of the main building, I would be welcome to use the garage. Moving with a strange sort of "squat-walk"—presumably from decades of work in the vineyards—he led me to an old wooden door and into the space. I had to swat away thick swaths of spiderwebs, and when I brought my face to my hand to wipe the sticky mess out of my eyebrows, it met instead with a low beam.

"Remember to always duck in Burgundy," the old man called without looking back.

"I thought that was only in caves."

"Are you in a cave?"

"Uh, no."

"Well, duck in garages too then!" We walked through the large dusty room, feeling along the walls to find our way, laughing and coughing.

We reached the other side of the room as the old man caught his breath from laughter.

"Hold on, let me get the lights."

"The *lights*? You have lights in here and you have us walking around bumping our heads on things?" My sides hurt enough to force me to fold over in laughter, my eyes pinched tight, stopping the tears from coming.

"I didn't bump anything. I'm seventy-two. Besides, at my age I need to entertain myself somehow. I knew you would crack into something." The lights came on, and despite the dusty introduction, the space looked great. But one problem immediately came to mind.

"So, how do you get into this room?"

"We just came through it."

"I'd have to bring my grapes through the rest of the facility to get here?"

"Well, yes. But you see, it is a good space." It was nice, perhaps the best place I'd seen. Tile floors, a drainage strip, two water faucets, decent head room besides four sets of old beams near the only entrance, and it was going to be cheap. It just needed a little soap and water. But as good as it looked, there was no way I'd be able to bring in anything wider than three feet—including tanks and barrels.

"So, how would I get anything in the door?" He stood scratching his head. "I guess you can't. Sorry, didn't occur to me before. Anyhow, interested in a drink? Maybe we can settle on a wall to knock down." We both shook hands as his laughter took away any disappointment I was starting to feel.

"I'll take that drink next time."

"Make sure to come back for it!"

It was disappointing, but I didn't want to dwell on the only hiccup I was dealing with now. I had grand cru grapes! I wanted to share the news with someone else, so as I walked back to my bike I called Gregory, a winemaker I'd met when I'd contacted another winery in California that also owned a winery in Burgundy. The owner wasn't interested in helping me, but one of his assistants connected me with Gregory. Now, he was one of the few people I counted as an actual friend in Burgundy.

"Greg, I just found my grapes! I'm all set for harvest."

"Tell me, what did you find?"

"I found some Charmes-Chambertin."

"*Bah, non!*" He spat out. He usually spoke perfect English with me, but he switched to French whenever he was excited about something.

"Something else too . . . Chambertin."

There was a long pause. "*Non. Mais, Chambertin, Chambertin? Comment? C'est pas vrai.*" He didn't believe it, and when he questioned me I almost forgot it was real too.

"I still can't understand how everything came together."

"But it did. You know. I thought you only wanted village. Now you are just grand cru?"

"Well, I said I'd take village or better. I just hadn't been offered village, so I thought anything else would be impossible."

"You should have told me earlier."

"Why?" I didn't even want to think about what I missed out on.

"You know. Maybe it isn't too late. Where are you?"

"Morey-Saint-Denis."

"OK, meet me back in Nuits in five minutes. See you."

"Wait! I can't do five minutes."

"It only takes five minutes, trust me. I drive this way each day from home."

"Good for you—I'm on a bike!"

I could tell he put down the phone so he could laugh. When he came back on, he could barely get the words out. "All right." He was trying to catch his breath. "I give you ten."

I'd originally purchased my dinky bike thinking it was the perfect way to meander through the vineyards on some of the neatly paved trails or to go short distances. But I was certain that I was going to break it in half while I was racing to meet Gregory. After the life-changing meeting I'd had two days before, I didn't need to risk my life to make it back to Nuits, but something in Gregory's tone told me the trip would be well worth it.

I pedaled as fast as I could as cars zipped by, having to swerve into the neighboring lane because of the narrow roads. No one honked; they just gave me a look that summed up just how big of an idiot I was. The bike groaned under my weight and the seat was shedding a small trail of cotton stuffing with every push of the pedals. The tires were so cracked and brittle that they could barely hold enough air to keep the whole operation moving. Plus, I didn't want to even think about what bad shape my brakes were in as I sped down the sloping hills. At least if things were squeaking, I reasoned, it meant they were in one piece.

By the time I made it to Nuits-Saint-Georges my shirt was drenched with sweat, my pants shredded between the chain and sprocket, and my right ankle torn up by what had felt like a very dull but persistent saw.

"What took you so long?" Gregory said with a smirk.

I made a show of wiping the sweat off my brow and then extended the same hand to shake his. He pulled back.

"All right, all right. So, I didn't want to tell you on the phone, but I may have some grapes for you."

Grapes? I was already set for the year. I had nine barrels to worry about, but part of me was still worried they could fall through at any moment. I trusted the growers, but what if they sensed that I was in way over my head? I couldn't say that I'd blame them. Maybe a little insurance with some extra grapes couldn't hurt? And if things did work out, producing three wines—well, that could start looking less like a hair-brained scheme and more like a real business.

"What village are they in?"

"Morey." Morey is located smack dab in the middle of Gevrey-Chambertin and Chambolle-Musigny, and doesn't have an elite reputation due to its tiny size. The wines are generally darker fruited than the wines of Gevrey, and unlike those wines, Moreys aren't rich and powerful. But to me, they are beautiful, which Gregory knew. I can't pin down what exactly makes them so special to me, but like all wine of Burgundy, there is a unique sense of place that clings to the fruit.

"Wait, I was just in Morey."

"I know, I know. Coincidence, huh? You wanna go?" He looked at the bike.

"Where?"

"To Morey. To see the vines."

He couldn't be serious. "*I was just up there.*" I said it even more slowly, to make sure he understood the inanity of his asking that I come all the way to Nuits.

"I know. Remember, I said it was a coincidence. It is, right?" *Uh, no*, I thought. *That's not a coincidence, that's a situation where you tell your friend on the old rusted-up bike to stay put while you drive over in your car to meet him.*

He stared at me blankly.

"Never mind. What vineyard is it?"

"Chaffots. You know it?"

"Not at all."

"You will like it. So, you will take your bike or should we throw it away?" he joked. I actually thought about just handing the bike to the next person who walked by, but I thought the odds were so slim that anyone would want it that instead, I parked it and gladly hopped into his car.

We drove through Vosne-Romanée on a tiny dirt road surrounded by vineyards. A plume of dust floated up behind us as his car jostled and shuddered over countless bumps along the way. We passed Vougeot and Chambolle-Musigny, and the scenery was breathtaking. My first glimpses of these vineyards had been through an invisible border; now the color of the leaves seemed so much more vibrant, the smell of warm soil and lush vegetation more redolent.

Once in Morey, we drove through the center of town and continued on toward the vine-drenched slopes above the village. Each individual parcel of land had its own unique slope, undulations that you could find nowhere else but at sea. We continued to climb up higher until the vines that we had first driven past looked like tiny rows of green dots.

"This is it." Because the grapes were still available so late in the season—much less available to me—I was preparing myself for the worst. I imagined the vines would be suffering in some way, maybe sick or dehydrated or falling over from negligence. But there was nothing wrong with them; in fact, they were some of the most lush, vibrant, and lively vines that I'd seen in Burgundy. The vines and the view looking across to the famous Mount Blanc was a sight unparalleled by anything in the region.

We walked through eight of the forty or so rows. I studied the vines we passed, making sure nothing looked odd—either diseased or vines known as Pinot Droit, which are thought to be clones more fit for higher yields than for quality grapes, versus Pinot Fin, which produces wines of the highest quality. After the widespread root-destroying insect phylloxera decimated Europe's vines in the 1870s, growers had to graft their European vines to American roots, which were somehow immune to the bugs. The new grafts worked perfectly, but there were some growers who chose poor clones that produced huge berries with little character, merely because of the bigger yield. I was also looking out for vines that were too young. Before the phylloxera outbreak, vines in Burgundy were commonly more than a hundred years old, but now you can find more variation, and it is generally thought that vines less than twenty years old, with their shallower roots, haven't been exposed to the complex geological system below. Wines from younger vines can taste "good," but the full potential of the terroir isn't unlocked until the plants reach deep into the underlying soil.

But none of this tells you the complete story of what would become harvest. You can have the prettiest vineyard and rule out things like poorly tended vines, subpar clones, and young plants, but until you have wine in a barrel, you have no real idea what you are working with. But standing in Les Chaffots, with the majestic view and beautiful vines, I had a good feeling. It was a good sign that a lot of the vines had a mix of tiny and medium-size grapes, which meant the skins would be nice and thick and most likely add a deep intensity and character to the wine. Big, bloated berries would produce more wine, but volume wasn't what I was after. It was the spirit of a place I wanted to capture, and I felt at home.

"Which section is mine?" I asked Gregory.

He looked confused. "This is the vineyard that I said that you have access to. It's yours."

"I get it. I get it. But which section would my grapes come from?" I kicked at a little chunk of limestone before crouching down and grabbing a handful of the soil, squeezing it and then letting it flow out of my palm in the hillside breeze.

"Everywhere."

"So, it is a mix?" We looked at each other, sure of the lunacy of the other.

"No, this complete section is yours. All that they have is yours." He spread his arms out in front of the glorious view.

"This whole place?" I waved my hand over the sea of immaculately manicured vines in front of us.

"Yes, this *whole* place." He was now using a sort-of sign language to further clarify what to him was exceedingly obvious. "Yours," he said while pointing at me.

Just like that, the landscape broke out from the glass wall it was hiding behind. I could touch it, breathe it in, knowing that it was mine to have. I couldn't wait to taste the wine that the grapes promised to create.

"It should make five barrels in a normal year," he continued once he saw that I was grasping the situation. "This year will be around four."

"I don't care how many it is. I've never seen a vineyard like this." I was still taking in the view. "How much will this cost me?"

"It won't be more than three thousand euros per barrel." At this point, the price didn't matter. I told Gregory I'd take it.

Gregory was doing me a big favor by showing me the vineyard rather than his other—most likely wealthier—clients. But, as he explained to me, he was merely sharing his good fortune. The owners of Les Chaffots had historically sold their grapes to a huge winery that produced over a thousand barrels a year and had grapes from all over Burgundy and a few vineyards in California. In Morey, they had both Les Chaffots and Les Monts Luisants, a vineyard just a hundred feet away. This year, though, the executives decided that two Morey premiers crus were too much and ultimately decided to drop Les Chaffots. But as Gregory put it, "I was glad they were making this mistake." He couldn't wait to put this vineyard into more appreciative hands. The secret Gregory knew, and what the giant producers didn't, is that Chaffots is bordered on two sides by the grand cru of Clos-Saint-Denis, and that this little vineyard—despite its premier cru ranking—produces wines that mirror those from the adjoining land. He promised the owners that he would find someone who would treat these vines like the gems they are.

"The wine from here, you will like it—it is nothing ordinary," Gregory said, breaking my bear hug. "Just don't screw it up." Before I could slug him in the shoulder, he added, "You know, now that we've met, you don't seem so stupid after all."

CHAPTER SEVENTEEN

AFTER SEEING ANOTHER ROUND OF BUILDINGS FOR RENT, I settled into the idea of staying in Saint-Aubin. It wasn't my first choice but I was feeling luckier by the minute to have it as an option because in just a few days all of the growers would call with the news that the grapes were ready. I hadn't even met the family that tended the grapes in the Les Chaffots vineyard. The day after we'd visited it, Gregory set up a meeting with the courtier representing it, Jacques Guyard. All it took to make the deal was a handshake. The growers trusted Jacques, and Jacques trusted Gregory because they did a lot of business together through the large winery Gregory worked for. It was too simple, but I wasn't going to start asking more questions days before harvest.

I still had to figure out how exactly all my equipment was going to work together—or whether any of it worked at all. I'd lain in bed with the same thoughts racing through my mind for the past few days. There was so much to worry about, but in a sense, there was also nothing to fear. At this point, I was just in a steady free fall. I didn't know exactly how I'd land; I just needed to prepare as best I could for the impact. One night, I resorted to opening a bottle of 2001 Gevrey-Chambertin to help me relax. I'd picked it up for less than twenty euros a few weeks back. I poured a glass and fell asleep two sips in.

When the phone rang I fumbled to put it on silent but instead accidentally picked up.

"Monsieur Walker, *demain, on va commencer, huit heures. Vous êtes là-bas aussi?*"

It was the vigneron from the Chaffots vineyard. It didn't make much sense though. The call was coming too early. The Morey-Saint-Denis grower had told me three days ago that we were going to be starting at least five days to a week later. I shook the sleep from my eyes and slowly realized what was happening— the harvest had been moved up. I had to be at the winery the next morning at eight, which meant I had about six hours before embarking on what was undoubtedly the craziest thing I'd ever done in my life.

Even though I wasn't completely sure how all my wine gear was going to work in concert, at least I had the foresight to get it all ready. I'd scrubbed out my two stainless-steel tanks and sanitized them with citric acid. The wooden tank had been pressure washed, scrubbed, sanitized, and filled with water to allow the slats to bloat up enough to keep all of the wine in once the tank was filled. I'd built my sorting table—or rather laid a piece of wood on top of four barrels—and I'd picked up my rental truck and filled the bed with neatly stacked rows of freshly cleaned red and gray plastic fruit cases.

By seven A.M. I was driving up route nationale 74 toward Morey-Saint-Denis. I was trying to focus on the road, but all I could think about was how my fruit cases were going to look heaped with fruit. *My* fruit. I wasn't exactly nervous, but I couldn't shake the reality of how delicate the situation still was. At any moment before I took the grapes away, the owners could decide they didn't like me after all and change their minds. I didn't have a plan for that besides praying that it wouldn't happen.

And what was I going to do once I had the grapes back in my truck? I didn't have any degree on the wall saying that I knew much of anything about wine. I had one harvest under my belt. I didn't want to think about all that could go wrong. And the money? As much as I tried to forget the weight of it on my shoulders, it was there. More than one hundred thousand euros could buy you a Lamborghini or, potentially, case upon case of Gevrey-Chambertin vinegar. I'd have better odds driving the exotic sports car at top speed and not wrecking it.

I'd dreamed about this moment for so long it felt foreign to live it as my reality. There was a time I couldn't even picture the process, but now my vision had crystallized. First came the grapes. After being harvested and loaded into the back of my truck I'd take them back to the cuverie to be sorted. No matter how they looked, they had to be looked at again. Then I'd have to decide whether to leave the stems on. As strange as I first thought it was, leaving the stems in can, some argue, be beneficial to a wine. The grapes have a chance to breathe a bit more because the clusters aren't as crammed together, which allows for more airflow. Stems also can impart an interesting fragrance and taste after a wine matures in bottle for several decades. Wine fermented with stems and all, if it is done right, has almost an extra layer of richness, density, silkiness. But the flip side is that the stems can push a wine to taste vegetal if the stems aren't ripe enough. The greener the stems, the more herbaceous the wine. Stems also raise the pH of the wine, which means it can take away from some of the brightness in the fruit. A good comparison is a young red straw-berry just at the point of early ripeness versus a berry at the peak of ripeness before it begins its decline toward rotting. There is no one right point of ripeness, but I found more nuances in fruit picked at an earlier ripening and pH stage.

With all of this in mind, I wanted to destem everything. While I liked wines that had some of the clusters tossed in with the grapes, now that I'd had a choice, I wanted a clean canvas that would high-light the grapes and grapes alone. My philosophy was that wine should be as transparent as possible. I didn't want to hide behind distractions like lots of new oak, stems, or extreme extraction.

Generally speaking, once the grapes were sorted and either tossed in whole or destemmed, they'd go into the tank and get punched down for the first time, just to mix them and any juice that had collected. Then I'd measure the sugar content with a Brix refractometer, which would show how much alcohol the sugar would make. The more sugar, the more food the yeast has, and so the more alcohol it produces as it ferments. In regions where grapes struggle to get ripe or if you want a little more hair on the chest of your wine, you can add more sugar.

I didn't want to go down the path of changing what I got from nature. With every correction, something else would have to shift. Add sugar, and I'd have to keep an eye on how well the yeast was doing at converting all that sugar, because if it was stuck for more than a few days, I might have to add another colony to keep things moving. If that didn't work, then I'd have to mess with the temperature of the tanks and hope that adding a few de-grees to the Jacuzzi would get those little guys eating at a faster pace. Then the fermentation might move too quickly or the tem-perature might spike too aggressively, threatening to kill off a lot of delicate aromas. If I changed one thing, I would throw off the balance nature intended. It struck me that the plants knew more about their internal balance than I ever could. So many aspects of nature were more interesting as something to be marveled at than to be deconstructed. I liked the idea of going as slow with the fermentation stage as possible, as long as the health of the wine wasn't at risk from sitting too stagnant. If it took a week total, fine; two weeks, great; three weeks, there might be a problem.

Along with not adding sugar, I wanted to discover the least amount of punch downs I could get away with without endangering the grapes. I'd done an average of at least twenty punch downs for each wine throughout the harvest while making wine in California. Some winemakers do a lot more, some less, but this is about average. Punch downs are performed regularly—generally once a day—to keep the grapes on the top of the heap inside of the tank moist. If fermentation is in full swing, two punch downs a day is the norm as the cap dries and stiffens up more rapidly. Most people do punch downs with a machine or manually with a punch-down tool, while I, on the other hand, would be doing the honors by foot. What if I did three punch downs in total? Twice? Just once? I wouldn't know if punch downs were actually necessary unless I started this low. I knew I risked ruining the wine, but I felt a persistent urge to follow my instincts, disaster be damned. I didn't care about following in my peers' footsteps; I thought of my decisions in the context of what I'd learned reading books from the early nineteenth century.

After the alcoholic fermentation finished, my grape juice would go from simmering at a yeast-friendly eighty-eight degrees Fahrenheit to a much cooler temperature that would halt the process just where I wanted it. What had once been a smell of decadent sweetness would now be bitter, awkward, and sharp—the distinct aroma of new wine. For as long as the wine was in contact with the grape skins, it would become more extracted and darker, but in my opinion, more powerful, and more one-dimensional as well. I had two options: I could leave this cranky newborn of a wine in the tank with nothing to do but soak even more in a morass of nuance-robbing, mangled grape skins *or* I could move the wine from tank—sans skins and seeds—into barrels. This first bit of wine in suspension is called *free-run*, what used to be called *goutte de mère,* or "mother's milk." It is where the high tones of the wine live, the dainty fingers to the more firm-fisted notes of what remains in the tank. Some people choose to make a separate cuvée with the free-run wine, but to me the power, the mass, and the skeletal system of a wine still lay in the mostly crushed wine-soaked grapes resting in the tank after the more feminine wine is taken out.

After pulling them out by hand in small buckets, the remaining grapes are then passed through a press and added to the neighboring barrels. Producers are usually split on how exactly to do this. Some top off a free-run barrel if there's room and continue to fill the next barrels with press wine. Others blend everything together in one tank before filling the barrels. The advantage of blending it all is that each barrel is similar. But I wanted each piece of the vineyard as it came, and for it to age in succession, the way it had come from the tank. Each barrel would be different, almost like viewing a sphere from different angles with a single light source projected upon it. The shape is the same, but the perspective changes in each moment.

This all sounded good, at least until I remembered that I didn't even know how to operate a wine pump, one of the basic tools in a winery for moving wine to barrel, to tank, to bottle, or wherever else it needs to be. I'd had my shot a few times in California when we'd filled the barrels, but after I sent a few fountains of wine ten feet into the air after overfilling, I found my way back to cleaning the insides of tanks and presses. But no matter, I was pretty sure I was going to try to avoid using a pump anyway if I could. A pump whips a wine up too much, another unnatural state I wanted to avoid.

The only manipulation I planned to use through the process was to keep everything clean, sort and destem my grapes, and chase them in my tanks with some sulfur to kill mold and mildew. I was wary of using too much sulfur because it could kill off some of the good stuff too, so I decided that I'd use just a little. But beyond that, I was going to have to trust that once my wine was in-tank, nature would take care of the rest. Or most of it, anyway. Certainly no one would be able to accuse me of neglect. I was simply too obsessed for that.

But ultimately, the wine would taste however it wanted to taste, and I didn't want to go into my first vintage with too many plans for altering anything. What would be the point in buying grapes from these exalted vineyards known for displaying exacting personalities if I was going to give them a script? It was bad enough that I was going to have some new oak. I wasn't a painter or a musician. I didn't need to indulge myself by making a "Ray Walker Chambertin." That wasn't the tradition that I'd read about and wanted to honor. I wanted a Chambertin that tasted like it could only be Chambertin—to be true to the terroir.

I DROVE UP TO THE dusty dirt road that led to the grower's house. Outside was a group of harvest workers who were already gathered, dressed in rubber boots and plastic aprons. They were standing around a tractor, some with coffee in their hands. Many were from Burgundy or the south of France, but there were also *vendangeurs*, "harvest workers," from places like Japan and East Africa. Everyone was speaking with one another in French. Someone made a joke as I opened the car door, and they all turned to look at me. It must have been a good one—everyone was laughing, some doubled over.

I smiled and crossed my arms in mock anger. "Another American joke? *Pas* cool."

They turned to look at each other; no one said a word at first until someone in the back responded. "Not a joke about you— Antoine had bet you'd be late; the rest of us figured you would be early. You just cost him *porteur* duty."

Being a porteur was one of the toughest jobs during harvest. While the cutters pruned the grapes from the vines with a pair of special scissors, tossing them into small buckets by their sides, porteurs wore a large plastic conical basket with straps like a backpack. They would make seemingly unending trips up and down the rows of vines so the cutters could empty the contents of their buckets, and then deliver the very heavy load to the fruit cases waiting by the truck. I patted Antoine on the shoulder and said sorry. "*Désolé.*" He just shrugged it off as he jumped into the back of the van, which had already started making its way down the dirt driveway, heading toward the vineyards. I stood there watching in amazement as the others followed suit, the doors eventually closing when they came to the road.

I hopped into my rental truck and followed the van at its impressive pace. My blood pressure climbed as I sped toward the vineyards I usually walked by. The vineyard was only five minutes away; we got there in three. An explosion of jokes flew back and forth and laughter burst out with a dozen vineyard hands as the doors sprang open. A few men came over to pull my fruit cases off the truck's bed and ribbed me about how clean they were.

"*Tout neuf, eh?*" one of the guys asked, alluding to the fact that they were brand new, not something they saw a lot of in a place where people's families had been doing this for generations.

I gave my standard shrug of a response. "*Oui.*"

I was the rookie. It didn't matter that these were my grapes that were about to be picked, I was the new guy and everyone knew it. And it was my first time actually being in a vineyard during the harvest, period. It was clear right away that I was being accepted as one of them. If they didn't respect me, they wouldn't have bothered to joke; they would have just ignored me. Thankfully, it also meant that I wasn't going to be receiving any special treatment. These were my grapes, but I didn't want to be looked at as someone with clean hands, so I grabbed a larger stack of fruit cases and followed the guy in front of me, placing twelve cases at the end of the row of vines.

The porteurs put on their backpacks, the cutters readied their scissors, and the tractor started up, heading down the first row of vines. The cutters took off down their respective rows, their targets only the best clusters that they could find. Anything looking unhealthy or oddly colored was left behind. Mold, mildew, or rotted grapes were also not welcome. They crouched to get a better look because the best grapes are only two to three feet off the ground throughout most of Burgundy. Anything higher up on the vine is part of the second crop; they are clusters that had gotten a late start and wouldn't be able to catch up in time. In Burgundy, the trellising is close to the ground to allow the heat of the day to radiate off the vineyard floor and give some warmth during the cold nights. In California, generally the opposite is true. There is plenty of heat, so the vines are positioned to have their fruit zones farther from the ground, so that the grapes have relief in the evening from the heat of the day.

It is deceiving because sometimes the second crop looks identical to their riper neighbors, but they tend to be acidic or watery and don't have nearly as much character or intensity. In some vintages they are collected later in the season by the vigneron to make rosé for his personal enjoyment, but most of the time they are left to dry out and fall to the ground, giving their nutrients back to the soil as they decompose.

The cutters worked quickly, their scissors disappearing into the green mass of leaves in front of them, with their hands later emerging enveloping a cluster. A quick *pop* into their bucket, and then they inched along in a crouch to the next pocket of clusters. The vineyard wasn't that large, but people were spread out enough to allow for several groups to start singing various old Burgundian harvest songs, some going back more than three hundred years. Some of the songs were about taxes, one was about falling asleep in the vineyard from exhaustion, more than a few were about women, and many more were about what winds and weather gave the best wine. The workers sang and laughed, told jokes, and yelled from row to row to check in on one another. I could understand bits and pieces of the songs but more than anything, wished I could sing along with them.

My job was to stand over the fruit cases and guide the porteur's pour with one hand while quickly pulling out debris with the other. If things like dead branches, leaves, or the occasional critter stayed in the case, it meant more work during sorting, and who knows if I'd even see it then. If I tried to dig too far to get them out before sorting, though, I'd risk breaking the fruit's sensitive flesh and spilling its juice into the bottom of the case. I needed to keep from handling the grapes too much because if they got too warm, fermentation could kick-start before they even hit the tank.

One by one, my fruit cases filled up. I couldn't believe just how beautiful the grapes looked. I wasn't hungry but I couldn't stop picking up the fruit—for "quality checks"—and eating entire clusters. I was in a trance, popping grapes in my mouth like I was at a matinée tossing down handfuls of popcorn kernels.

A short older woman gave me the by now all-too-familiar *tsk tsk tsk*. "*Après vous n'avez pas de raisins pour le vin,*" she said, warning me that I wouldn't have any grapes left for my wine. I thought it was kind of sweet until she held out her hand for me to fork over the rest of my half-eaten cluster, gave me a kiss on the cheek, and then tossed the rest into a fruit case. I later found out that she was the grower's mother. Clearly in her mind, the grapes weren't mine until I was driving away with them. Somehow I knew I'd get the same look if I were munching on a croissant in her kitchen before dinner was served.

Thirty minutes later, my truck was packed up with 105 grape-laden bins, but I had forgotten to bring a rope to cinch everything down. Some of the older men started arguing with one another about how stable my cases could be. One guy said I would be an idiot to leave, while another said I needed to hurry up before the sun warmed the grapes too much. Both agreed that I needed to have a rope, though. Eventually the grower's mother came over to settle things. She said that she used to drive without ropes before these men had been born and that her wine was better than anything the two of them had ever made. And so with that, I was sent on my way. Before I left, I shook every one of the harvest worker's hands and thanked him. It might have seemed odd to them, but my gratitude was sincere, and I wanted each and every one of them to know it.

The forty-five-minute drive through twenty-two villages from Morey-Saint-Denis to Saint-Aubin was nerve-racking. I saw two trucks parked in the middle of roundabouts with their fruit cases scattered on the ground, clusters everywhere, their red juice making it look like a gory accident scene. I didn't want to be that guy. I couldn't be that guy.

Thankfully, not a single cluster seemed out of place when I finally started unloading my truck just before noon. Pierre and Xavier weren't around, so I had the whole place to myself. Going two cases at a time, I made neat stacks in my little corner of the warehouse. The towers of premier cru looked like a mirage, with far more grapes than I'd imagined. I hadn't thought to ask for help, and now, looking at this unbelievable bounty, I realized I might have made a mistake. But there was no sense in lamenting that now. The clock was ticking if these grapes were going to be sorted, destemmed, and tucked into a tank before they turned into a soupy mess of prematurely fermenting, extremely expensive grape juice.

I grabbed the first case off the top of the pile and spread it out on my sorting table. The screws groaned a bit, but we were officially in business. I placed six empty fruit cases around the perimeter of the table and started sorting, tossing everything that looked less than perfect into the waiting cases. Everything that looked right got pushed to the opposite side of the table.

After working for a few hours nonstop, the to-sort pile

dwindled. My hands were sticky and stained purple, my shirt was drenched with grape juice, and my stomach was starting to feel the side effects of my all-grape diet. Somewhere in my brain a little voice begged for a nap, but a break wasn't in the cards. Instead, I turned my attention to destemming. While most modern winemakers used destemming machines, which became widely popular only in the twentieth century, I'd decided to do this part by hand. I had heard about the necessity of being gentle on grapes, especially Pinot Noir, and I obsessed about it a little bit when it came to tools. I worried a destemmer would rip the grapes off of the cluster while bouncing them around too much in a tumbler. I didn't want any of that abuse for my grapes. Chambertin deserved better, I thought. As does Charmes-Chambertin. And even my Chaffots. Why should a premier cru be treated any differently?

I cleaned off the sorting table and carried my full grape bins over to the wall by my tanks, arranging them in a semicircle so each was within reach as I sat on an overturned fruit case. I dipped my hand into the first bin and fished out a cluster. Most of the berries fell off with the slightest bit of effort, and the remaining few needed only a little nudge. *This doesn't seem so bad*, I thought. It reminded me of when I was twelve and would be dispatched to clear out the overgrown backyards of my parents' rental properties. I'd take in the magnitude of the project before me, stretch my arms a bit, then put my head down and work while the hours melted away. Complaining about it or lamenting that I could have been hanging out with friends only seemed to make the work more difficult. The less I groaned and the more I worked, the more quickly I knew I could get out of there. I figured this would be no different.

For the next five hours I destemmed the grapes at a steady clip. I worked with machine-like efficiency, my fingers finding a steady rhythm without any input from my brain. Over time I was able to develop a flow that led to a faster pace and fewer grape casualties. Depending on the minute, I was sure that I was either a grape destemming genius or a raving idiot.

But after five hours I was a mess—a great-smelling mess, but a mess. Slumped on my fruit case perch, I was having trouble keeping myself upright. I took inventory of what I had left to do and nearly toppled over when I realized it looked as though I'd barely made a dent. I eyed the concrete floor longingly, thinking, *I'll just lie down for a minute.* Maybe I could close my eyes for a second. The grapes would still be there when I got up. I argued with myself in a one-man conversation in my drained head. At some point I found myself sitting on the floor, my back resting on the fruit case.

But there is this annoying tic I have. Whenever I entertain the idea of taking the easier route, I imagine a drill sergeant standing over me, commanding me to carry on as planned. It's that nagging, overbearing voice that's kept me going for most of my life. And most of the time when I'm picturing that asshole who won't shut up about taking the higher road, it's usually my own damn self. Because I know the right thing is to keep going and just get it done. Now, trying to warm up a patch of the clammy floor for a little rest, I could picture only a wiser, more capable version of myself shaking a very disappointed head at the situation.

I dragged myself up into something resembling an upright position. It wasn't a heroic moment, not like in the movies when just as it seems that all has been lost the protagonist rouses himself with all he has to save the day. This was more like a zombie resurrection, but it would have to do.

To urge myself on I started setting little goals. After five cases of destemmed grapes, I'd take a break to load them into the "giraffe" machine that carried the fruit up and over into the tanks. Unfortunately, soon the giraffe machine stopped working, so I had to start doing that manually too. Scaling a rickety ladder so old it could have easily been used by some of the original Burgundian monks, I'd hoist a load of grapes onto whichever shoulder hurt less and try not to think about all the bones that were likely to break should I very likely fall. Whenever both shoulders were cramping, which was more often than not, I would use both hands to hold the case and walk up the ladder balancing on just my feet, an undertaking advisable only by the overtired and mildly insane. But I didn't fall that night. The grapes in the tank kept piling higher until it looked like the inside of a caviar jar. The reality was tangible: my wine was coming together in front of my eyes.

The hours went by—sixteen since I had first started—and I still had the cuverie to myself. Four A.M. went by, then nine A.M. The rhythm I'd found by hour twelve had long since dissipated. Three of the crates of fruit that once looked so fresh and vibrant were now sitting in a small pool of their own juice in the bin. Now detached from the vines that were giving them life, they were beginning their slow descent to decomposition, and they were crushing themselves under their own weight. It was still cool in the cuverie, so I still had a little time left before the grapes lost any of their quality, but I could tell that this could all change at any point. Weighing what I stood to lose if I didn't pick up the pace, I started manically plowing through the remaining twenty cases of fruit. What had once been tender and gentle was now rushed and callous; I needed to get the fruit into the tanks and drop in some sulfur before they turned. Soon after I started just throwing in whole clusters I heard two familiar voices at the door.

Xavier and Pierre walked over to my tiny alleyway filled with fruit cases. Pierre shook my hand, clearly unnerved by the unhinged man who had taken my place. Xavier walked past me without saying a word and climbed up the ladder to look into my tank.

"This is a big day for you," Pierre said.

"Well, yesterday was." He was confused. "I started on this yesterday. I stayed the whole night."

"When did you go home?"

"I didn't."

Pierre looked at me curiously. "Why? You don't have too much grapes." He gently picked up a cluster in his hand and held it up closely to his eyes. He whispered to himself, "*Oui, très très belle.*" He looked at me proudly. "What is she?"

"Morey-Saint-Denis, premier cru, Les Chaffots."

"These look really nice."

"Would you like to try some?"

He looked shy and then finally took a nibble, and then a large bite. He didn't bother to wipe up the juice that was streaming down his chin onto his shirt. "*Oui!*" He took another bite. "You must be so proud of yourself." He wrapped his arm around my neck, and I bent down a bit to make it easier for him. "I'm very proud of you. You did good." He playfully tapped me on my cheek.

Xavier came down from looking and sniffing above the tank. He looked somewhat unimpressed.

Pierre continued his praise. "Ah, it's beautiful. Smells good too. It will be a fine wine."

"Thanks."

Xavier piped, "But why do you have stems in here? I thought you wanted only berries." Then repeated again, "Yes, you were so interested in your little berries." I blushed sheepishly. I'd delivered a pretty obnoxious dissertation about my no-stem "philosophy" the night we'd all met at Fabrice's.

"Well, I was going to destem only Chambertin and Charmes-Chambertin by hand—"

Xavier cut me off. "But you have no destem machine?"

"No, I don't."

Pierre climbed the ladder and stuck his whole head into the tank, nearly touching the grape juice with this face. "OK, but then why do you have some without stems and some with the stems in here?"

"I started to worry. The grapes were starting to—"

Pierre picked up a tiny berry between his thumb and index finger and popped it into his mouth. "Oh, the grapes will be fine. Besides, they look better than you right now, *non*?"

"I guess."

"Well, I say you do what you like. Your wine. But if you don't want to use your hands anymore and you don't want stems, I don't know why you didn't just use our destemming machine."

Their what?! I didn't even know they had one. Pierre came down from the ladder and gestured to one of the many sheet-covered machines in the warehouse. He patted me on the shoulder and slowly shook his head with a chuckle. "Right here. Beneath your nose, right next to your tanks, Monsieur Ray."

It took me all of ten minutes to get the destemming machine put together and another thirty minutes to finish filling the tank. It had felt good to take such a firm stance against this "modern bastardization of wine production," but at the end of the day, that thing really did make life easier. And for some parts of the process, maybe the most difficult road isn't always the best one. But even after going through grape destemming hell and then using a machine, I didn't intend on removing myself too much from the action. If I could do the work with just my own two hands and without tools, I was going to run with it to preserve my fantasy of doing things as they were done in the past.

Now that my grapes were safely in-tank, I considered the next step. I had been trained in California to start punching the grapes down right away with a flat disk attached to a pole in order to mix the grapes up. But for whatever reason, I hesitated. Why would I go through all of the effort to ensure that the grapes didn't get abused only to bludgeon them once they were finally nestled comfortably in their new home? I knew that they would eventually need tending once fermentation got under way in the next day or so and grapes at the top of the tank started to swell with carbon dioxide. Submerging the bloated floaters back to the bottom where the juice is was called "breaking the cap." Because I'd smelled the funky, nail polish–like aroma that resulted from bacterial spoilage in wines before—a potential pitfall of those grapes not getting dunked back under the fermenting wine—this was a step I respected. But it didn't make sense to touch it earlier than that. I'd just pour a tiny bit of sulfur on top of the fruit to protect the grapes and juice from any potentially dangerous bacteria that might try to grow inside of the tank, and get to punching down whenever it felt right. I wasn't in a rush.

Pierre and Xavier were still in the cuverie when I finished cleaning up, preparing for their first batch of white grapes to come in. Pierre came over to me once more to congratulate me on getting everything into tank for my first cuvée. Xavier hung back as usual, seemingly oblivious to the fact that I was leaving. But just as I turned to walk away from my tanks, Xavier rushed over as though he was coming over to tell me something urgent. As he got closer his emotionless face turned into a scowl. He stopped abruptly, kneeled down, and returned back to eye level holding a single grape between his thumb and index finger.

"What do you think this is?"

It was a grape, a red one. I was the only one among us to have brought in any grapes at that point, so it was clearly mine. I knew what it was; we all knew what it was. It was a grape that I had left on the floor under a small ledge of my steel tank. It was also the only grape on the entire floor after I was done cleaning up. I tried to respond, but he stopped me short, his right hand waving, intercepting my first syllable.

"This"—he stared at it with his face shriveling up as if he were holding a rotting piece of meat—"this is not a grape." It wasn't? "This is a failing to understand the principle of winemaking." I could see Pierre standing a few tanks over, rolling his eyes while simultaneously doing his best to stay out of it. "I need to tell you a story," Xavier continued. I didn't want him to, but I also didn't want to see his bony, slender hand in my face, so I just looked him in the eyes and tried to listen.

"When I first learned to make wine it was in a very large cuverie. We had all of the tools around us to make sure we knew how to do excellent work with our grapes. Before I could touch a single grape I needed to learn how everything in the cuverie worked. Hoses, chemicals, pumps, everything. Before I could have an important role in helping with the wines, I needed to clean up the work of everyone else. It wasn't like you in America. Nothing was handed to *me*. I had to *work*. I hated cleaning all of these things, but you know, I did it! Instead of being able to use the best tools, I first needed to use the old tools. All of the drains were covered to teach me of the importance of preserving water and of being neat. If I was as sloppy as you, I would never have had the chance to help out with everyone else. Leaving a grape on the floor meant you were fired. Because of this I know how to work in small places, to conserve water and to never drop a single grape on the floor. I only wish you Americans received a similar training."

Every movement of his hands sickened me, and made my stomach twist into knots. I hated everything about him in that moment: his snarky grin, the super-thin leather shoelaces he always had in a perfect tiny bow, his hyperstarched button-up collared shirts and his ridiculously artsy eyeglasses. He was like a schoolyard bully who needed to be taken down, but I remembered: This guy, no matter how hateful, was helping me out in a major way.

"Sorry about that." I held my hand open by his and smiled as widely as I could manage. His smug grin melted into a menacing snarl. "Could I have that back? I'm so sorry that you had to pick that up. I'll be more thorough in the future."

He opened his hand revealing the perfect uncrushed berry. I slowly extracted it as if it were the world's smallest explosive, smiling until my cheeks pressed tightly against my lower eyelids. My jaws were clamped together but they let two words pass freely before reclamping again. "Thank you." I walked away, tossed the grape in the garbage, grabbed my things, and left the winery for the first time in thirty hours. The whole time I was walking out, Xavier's eyes were burning a hole in the back of my head.

Two days later, I was near the village of Gevrey-Chambertin, one village away from Morey-Saint-Denis at the Charmes-Chambertin vineyard. I had arrived early. I trusted the growers, but I wanted to see the exact placement of the vines that my grapes would be coming from, and I wanted to watch as each case was filled. There were two guys who were supervising all of the pickers and porteurs. When the bus pulled up with all of the workers from different countries around the globe, the two guys started to call out names at random to tell them if they would be a cutter or porteur. Halfway through assigning the jobs, one of them looked at me and yelled while waving manically toward one of the rows.

"*Porteur, porteur. Allez!! Vite!*"

Was he speaking to me? I looked behind myself and saw nothing but vines.

He began nodding, losing his patience. "*Toi, oui!*"

"I'm buying the grapes."

He gave a sarcastic laugh, placing one hand on his hip to mock me.

"*Oui, c'est quoi, tu achètes?*" "What are you buying?" He began clapping his hands. "*Allez . . . bougs toi!*"

"I don't speak much French."

The supervisor called over his friend. "*Jean-Louis, tu vies! C'est l'américain.*"

"I can help if you want," I told the gentleman, presumably Jean-Louis.

"No, no, no. I'm sorry," he said. "We were expecting an old American. We didn't know a basketball player was going to be buying grapes." The whole time he was whistling and pointing at people as they walked by, showing them which job they had.

"No worries." I guess he had a point. There weren't too many

American winemakers here, let alone anyone else who looked like me. But I wasn't looking to prove any points.

"So, who makes your wines?" Franck asked.

"Well, I'll be doing all the work myself." His head went back, and he turned to his friend, who looked equally terrified. "Will you have a, you know, local helping at all?"

"Nope."

Jean-Louis continued, "You did a lot of wine in California?"

"No." He started to shake his head while lighting a cigarette. "But," I said as he looked at me hoping to hear about some kind of grand experience I had, "I did learn how to wash barrels, tanks, and presses." The two men broke out into laughter.

"*Attends, attends.* You have no experience and you will do Charmes-Chambertin? *Pas d'expérience?*" They couldn't stop laughing.

I added, "And Chambertin."

Jean-Louis continued laughing but Franck tried to quiet him down. "*Attends*, you're buying the Chambertin grapes too?" The laughing stopped. "You know the grapes are looking very good. Well, they usually do. Have you seen them yet?"

"Just a few times, but I've never walked inside the vineyard." Jean-Louis shook his head in amazement.

"Sorry. I mean, I was thinking, you know, you were going to be an old rich guy." He looked down at my shoes and continued. "Someone having a wine made for them. No, it's a good thing to see someone else getting them, you know."

"Thanks." I didn't know what to make of them. It was clear they spoke their minds and didn't care what came of it.

"You know, if you make bad wines with these grapes, then you know that it isn't for you to do. What did you do in Los Angeles, wine?"

"I worked in San Francisco doing finance. I did a harvest but that's it. Hopefully the wine will be good."

"I'm sure it will. Look at the grapes. But if they aren't, you'll know it was you. This is a good opportunity for you to really see. If you have a bad year, there might be excuses. For this year any idiot could make good wines. Hopefully you are up to it."

"Well, I have no idea what I'm doing, but I'm happy to have the chance."

He struck me on my chest. "Then you are one of us then. We don't know either!"

The rest of the harvest went like clockwork. Whenever a load was dropped in by the porteur that wasn't that good, Franck and Jean-Louis, the two leading the group, would make sure to let the porteurs and the cutters know how to do a better job in terms packed with as many curse words and insults as they could muster. The response was always the same, "*Oui, chef!*" Dominique, Thomas's father, showed up near the end of the pick just to make sure everything was moving along properly. He tossed out some bad grapes from the fruit cases that were loaded in the truck and told the grape grower to add ten more cases to make up for any cases that could have more than the expected amount of substandard clusters. I stood there nearly shocked. I hadn't heard him speak much before, but there he was going to bat for me like I was his best client.

After the scene on the way to the winery two days earlier, I'd brought a rope to cinch my cases down. I tossed it over after making the first tie down and went to the other side of the truck where Dominique helped secure it. His disappointed look said it all. I needed to be careful with the grapes, on the road or otherwise. A rope wasn't going to change that.

Nearly an hour later I was back at the cuverie with my

Charmes-Chambertin grapes in tow, my largest cuvée. The fruit had looked beautiful during the end of the growing season as the other two vineyards had, but now I wasn't as happy. I had done my best to keep up with the porteurs, but I couldn't get all of the substandard grapes out, and I thought that the cutters had been inconsistent in deciding what grapes needed to be passed up and left on the vine. There were the pretty grapes, but there was also a good amount of *Botrytis* or mildew-affected grapes that I wouldn't be able to use. I'd have to do a lot more sorting, which if my first go-round was any indication, meant I might as well move into the winery.

But as I started to sort the grapes, I realized some cases were nearly perfect, requiring almost no sorting at all. Still, the percentage of what I was having to throw away was, in some cases, higher than I would have liked.

I'd sorted twenty cases when Dominique called.

"*Ça va?*"

"Yeah . . ."

He could tell there was hesitation in my voice. "*Il y a des problémes?*" There were problems, but nothing big really.

I didn't want to complain, but I felt I needed to tell him about the inconsistent bins. Sure, I was on a good roll at the moment, but I had no idea what was waiting for me in the other bins, and they weren't exactly giving the fruit away, after all. "*Non, mais, la qualité . . . pas . . . très bon comme . . .* others."

"*Attends.*" He started to speak with someone in the background. "*Tu peux venir dans une heure?*" He asked if I could come back to the vineyard within the hour.

I didn't know what to think. But I was on board with whatever Dominique had in mind. I trusted him. If he said to go back to the vineyard, I was going back.

"*Videz votre bacs à vendage et revenez.*" He wanted me to empty the cases and come back.

I showed up at the vineyard in a little under an hour. The owner was there with his wife and two sons, along with Dominique and Thomas. As I looked at them, I thought: This was it. I shouldn't have opened my mouth. They were going to take back the grapes, and that's how this would all end.

Thomas greeted me first, and the rest followed. "So, my father tells me that the sorting didn't go as well as it should have for Charmes."

"Well, I didn't want to complain. I just wanted to be honest. There was a lot of inconsistency in the fruit that they gave me."

"OK, what they are going to do is give you two more at no cost. If the owner was there during the pick, this would not have happened. He is terribly embarrassed."

I figured two more cases of grapes should more than cover what I'd had to toss.

"That's very generous. Two more cases will be a big help."

"*Non, non,*" he said. "Two more *barrels'* worth of grapes."

He looked back at his father and the owner of the vineyard; both nodded.

Astounded, I walked over to both of them and said it was not a problem for me to keep only what I had. But the vineyard owner looked me in the eyes and shook my hand. "*C'est meilleur pour la qualité.*" It is better for the quality.

WORKING MY WAY THROUGH THE Charmes-Chambertin grapes was a breeze—a backbreaking, thirty-hour-long breeze, but certainly easier now that I'd done it once before. The work was straightforward, and I had the destemmer going. But as the towering stacks of cases dwindled, my body, which now subsisted on a diet of pain au chocolat, croissant beurre, tarte framboises, jambon persillé, charcuterie, escargot, and red Burgundy, struggled to keep up. My arms were the first to go, wobbling as I tried to get the forty-five-pound cases high enough to empty them over the rim of the tanks. One more down, but I started with 150 of them.

Thinking about Christian and Bella was what really helped pull me through to the other side. With every case I emptied and sorted through, every tank I filled, I was building the foundation of our futures. I wanted to be able to show them what I'd done with this opportunity and my persistence. Once I was finished, I'd be able to say my own two hands were on each and every grape that made its way into my tanks.

Around midnight I paused to enjoy the stillness of the cuverie. Xavier, Pierre, and their troops had long since cleared out. And once the whir of the destemmer ceased, I could almost make out the sounds of the still night outside. I climbed the ladder one last time to look at the tremendous mound of berries. My favorite Led Zeppelin shirt was soaked, as were my shorts. They'd turned sticky and cold hours earlier. Grape juice had pooled in my work boots and made a *squish* with every step I took. It had been more than thirty hours since I last slept. But I felt incredible. With a piece of chalk I'd bought the day before, I wrote "Charmes-Chambertin" on the tank. Being left-handed, my handwriting was horrible, and most of the label was smudged. But my shortcomings weren't a part of this moment. I placed both of my hands on the tank, feeling it support my full weight. I could have sunk into that moment for eternity.

I called Christian and Bella just as I had done twice a day for the last month I'd been in Burgundy. They were doing well, but they both missed me, and it broke me up knowing it. It was awkward to be enjoying such a special moment without them by my side, almost like it hadn't really happened. And I'd missed some amazing moments while away from my family. Bella had just learned to say *bye, hello,* and *night-night.* I wished I were there to wrap her in my arms and hear her tiny voice in my ears. I longed to hold Christian while resting my head on her shoulder as I always did; I could still feel her curly hair tickling my face like it used to. *Soon enough,* I told myself. I may have left behind something more precious than words in California, but there was something inexplicable developing in Burgundy.

CHAPTER EIGHTEEN

CHAMBERTIN WAS GOING TO BE THE LAST VINEYARD TO BE harvested. Due to the chilly winds that race down the Combe de Grisard through the forest located above the vineyard it's commonly one of the last vineyards picked in the Côte d'Or. It still blew my mind that I'd soon hold Le Chambertin grapes in my hand. I'd never even seen, let alone held, a bottle of it before because it was out of my price range. I could recite its history and explain how its reputation came to pass, but I couldn't say one thing about tasting it myself.

Whenever harvest is near, everyone living in Burgundy is abuzz with news about the growing season: how the vines are doing, when rain is supposed to come, and how the recent weather could affect things. The weather is a force that people regard with the utmost reverence—maybe *fear* is a better word. In just minutes, bad conditions can reduce a flourishing, promising vineyard to a battle-torn wasteland. Too much rain, too much sun, too much wind, a surprise peppering of hail, too early a frost, too late a frost—anything can disrupt the fragile balance that keeps a vineyard's health in check. To have a livelihood that depends on the well-being of a delicate fruit literally hanging in the wind as it rip-ens is a dicey game of roulette. Burgundians know that better than anyone else, and it creates a culture of humility and tradition.

As the end of harvest was becoming a tangible reality, I wanted to treat myself. One afternoon I decided to visit Thomas's wine shop in Beaune, hoping to pick up a bottle of Gevrey-Chambertin village. I hadn't drunk much in the past week besides a few inexpensive bottles from great years—1978, 1985, 1993; a perk of living in the region—but I'd heard 1959 was an excellent vintage. Even though many of the 2009 grapes were still hanging on the vines, comparisons were being made to that storied year.

When I was first learning about wine, I couldn't imagine drinking or eating anything that was more than six months old, let alone over ten *years* old. I figured old wine must taste like mold or rot or that it would be chewy and leathery. Plus, why would you put something you liked so much away for a decade? Why on earth would you not just drink it right away if it was so good? But people described old wines as though they were sheer poetry, and it began to fascinate me that a liquid made from grape juice could be placed into a bottle, closed up with some bark off of a cork tree, left in a cool dark place, and then blossom years or even decades later.

It took only one bottle of 1983 Domaine Bart Bonne Mares from a shop in California to clear it all up for me. The "shop" was more like a temperature-controlled warehouse with stacks upon stacks of wines that I had only dreamed about: Château Latour 1961, 1982, and 1989; Domaine de la Romanée-Conti La Tâche 1978 and 1959; and Jacques-Frédéric Mugnier Musigny 1993, 1999, and 2001. All of those bottles with their old, discolored, sometimes torn and dusty labels had a story to tell. My mind reeled as I thought

232 • RAY WALKER

about how many people had held each bottle and imagined enjoying it. There is a mystery with older wines that a young wine can't begin to compete with.

I couldn't afford to buy any of the bottles I was drooling over, but I scanned to the last page of their list where they listed bottles that are known as bin ends. They are either the last of a case or wines made by unknown producers and are usually good deals.

"This Bonnes-Mares from 1983. Is it really twenty dollars?"

"Whatever it says. It's cheap, but I can't say how it'll taste. Most likely it's priced that way for a reason."

I didn't hesitate in taking it off his hands. I'd never heard of Domaine Bart before, but I had heard of Bonnes-Mares, the grand cru that was mainly situated in Chambolle-Musigny and stretched slightly over to the Morey-Saint-Denis side. I knew how the wines from the vineyard could taste, and one caveat was that they took a long time to mature. Although 1983 wasn't a year that was championed by critics, who cared? I was getting the bottle for the experience and to see if I could stomach drinking something that was bottled when I was only one year old.

As soon as I got home I rushed to the kitchen and figured I'd surprise Christian upstairs with a pour of the wine. I cut off the foil capsule and tried to understand what I was looking at. The top of the cork was green, coated in a thick petroleum jelly–like substance and fuzzy white hairs. It was compressed from being pushed up against the inside of the foil for so long. I thought about tossing it out, but instead I grabbed a wet paper towel and rubbed it over the top of the bottle so I could make out the head of the cork. Turning the corkscrew slowly, I felt the softness of the cork, but it still offered up resistance. Despite my best efforts to be careful as I pulled, the top half of the cork broke off while the other half remained lodged. I blew into the neck of the bottle, sending bits of old cork into my nostrils. To my surprise, there was a hole in the middle of the cork, and I could see the wine below. How was I going to get the damned thing out? I looked through all of the kitchen drawers. A knife, cocktail fork, toothpick? But then I found a small stainless-steel hors d'oeuvres skewer. I carefully inserted it through the hole, pushed up against the wall of the bottle's neck, and then slowly pulled until the cork was out. *This damn thing better taste good*, I thought.

I poured a small glass and gagged from the stench of it. I ventured a sip, and it tasted nearly as bad as it smelled. Twenty dollars? Vile. It must have expired, and I'd wasted my money. I could have bought a great new bottle, but now I had a science experiment gone wrong.

"Did you go and get wine?" Christian had started to come down the stairs to see what I was up to. She only saw the top of the bottle, not the bits and pieces of old cork scattered near the sink and on the floor.

"Uh, yeah. But I'm going to pour it down the drain."

"Why?"

"It's old and—"

"Old wine? Oh, come on up and bring two glasses of it."

"I . . . I don't think you'll like it."

"Just bring it up . . . c'mon."

She was going to think I was a fool once she tasted it. My role as the resident sommelier would be finished.

I met her back in the bedroom and handed her a glass. The amber color that the wine had in the kitchen fifteen minutes ago had turned to more of a light ruby. I sniffed again, expecting the same wet garbage scent, and instead got a hint of a little fruit, along with something else I couldn't describe. There was a savory quality, almost like grilled rabbit or lamb, and a warm, fruity note as well, like sun-ripened figs. The more I smelled it, the more it continued to change. Christian hadn't said anything; she just searched the walls of her glass with her nose.

"Why did you think I wouldn't like *this*?"

"It didn't taste like that in the kitchen. It stunk."

"Well, it kind of does still."

"It doesn't stink like it did then."

"No, it *does* stink," she insisted. "But it's pungent in a good way, like truffles or something like that. It doesn't smell like wine; it smells like food and some kind of fruit mixed together. And something funky."

"So, you like the way it . . . stinks. But it doesn't really stink?"

"Uh huh."

"Got it." We sat on our bed swirling our wines for a minute before I had to go back down to the kitchen to look at the bottle again. I couldn't believe how much it had changed. I stared at it for clues. Nothing.

I finished my glass and then took another small pour.

Black cherries. Huge black cherries and grilled meats. The funkiness had dissolved, leaving a beautiful perfume that was unlike anything I'd ever smelled before. I put my nose in the empty glass just to smell the perfume again; it was stunning.

WITH THE MEMORY OF THAT bottle of Bonnes-Mares from 1983 in my mind, I walked into Thomas's shop with my mouth nearly watering at the thought of finding another complex gem.

"Ray!" Thomas seemed a bit too excited to see me. "We've been trying to reach you today. You need to harvest Chambertin tomorrow."

I knew it was going to happen at some point soon, but the idea that in less than twenty-four hours I would have grapes from one of the most historically important vineyards in the world in my possession completely dwarfed my original mission at the wine store. I was about to start production on the most important part of my venture; it was no time to relax with a drink.

I thanked Thomas for the update and headed straight back to Saint-Aubin. By now, I'd driven countless times down the road, which made its way through the valley sandwiched between Puligny-Montrachet and Chassagne-Montrachet. Beyond those villages, an expansive landscape shaped like a gigantic amphitheater opened up. On a sunny day, the dozens of dramatically steep, vine-covered slopes catch the light from various angles. A luminescent light show reflected from the greens, golds, and reds of the leaves.

No matter how stressful my day had been, I knew once I saw those slopes that I was near my wines and the creases in my forehead would soften. Stepping in the cuverie, I could smell the first signs of fermentation. I dropped my backpack and sat down on the large wooden bench that had been set up for Pierre and Xavier's harvest crew. It finally hit me. I wasn't there just checking in on some side project—I was at work. This warehouse was my office; my T-shirt and shorts were my work clothes. I was living in France. I was speaking more French every day. When did all of this happen? It had been only a year ago that I touched a cluster of grapes for the first time in California, and now I was alone with my very own tanks bubbling away. It was as though I'd closed my eyes and woken up in someone else's life. I'd never been so focused, but somehow I felt less pressured, less rushed.

the best in world

The next morning I packed up my truck with my fruit bins and headed over to Gevrey-Chambertin to harvest the Chambertin grapes. The fog over the sloping land was gently burning off as the sun rose over the majestic hill. When I arrived at the vineyard, Jean-Louis and Franck—who had overseen the harvest workers for my Charmes-Chambertin harvest—were quick to unload all my cases from the truck. Because the two vineyards had the same owner, the same crew would be handling the day's work.

"*Salut!*" We'd seen each other only once before, but now we had a bond. And because these guys worked at the vineyard year-round, I would be seeing a lot of them.

Watching the crew pick was sort of like watching a swarm of bees overtake a serene pasture of flowers. From afar it was beautiful and calm, but the real labor of it came into sharp focus every time the porteur came huffing up to the cases to empty another load.

Once the cases were filled, the owner and his sons came by to check the quality of the grapes. There was cluster upon cluster of the prettiest, tiniest, most consistently beautiful grapes I'd ever seen. I could almost taste the wine that they'd create just by looking at them. I knew that each grape I ate in the vineyard would mean less wine, but I couldn't stop myself. Even as grapes they tasted more complex, more layered than those from either Les Chaffots or Charmes-Chambertin.

It's a moment I'll never forget. I was in Chambertin, a wine geek's dream. But it wasn't the dream I'd had before of visiting. I was there for business, for my grapes. *My Chambertin grapes.* It still sounded odd. All the twists and turns I'd taken along the way now seemed to have worked together to bring me here, to this place, at this time. Every case that was filled made me want to say thank you to someone, anyone. I felt proud, but more than anything else I felt a feeling of respect for what I was being entrusted with.

Just before leaving, I remembered a tradition King Charles Charlemagne had once made popular but that had all but died out in the last several decades. At the harvesting of the last vineyard for the year, the vigneron would gather a few vine clippings along with some wild flowers to take home to his wife to thank her for her support through the growing season. She, in turn, would hang the bouquet over the cuverie or cave as a *bonheur*, or good-luck charm. I didn't have Christian to go home to, and what I called home in Burgundy was just a cheap hotel on the side of the highway, but I wanted to partake in the tradition in some way and, more important, honor Christian.

I cut some vines in Chambertin, and some flowers growing just inside the vineyard. When I couldn't hold the bouquet with one hand any longer, I took a thinner, green branch from the vineyard and wrapped near the base, making a sort of knot. It looked awkward, messy, and haphazardly put together, but imagining Christian holding it warmed my heart.

The drive back to Saint-Aubin was a blur. The last thing I can remember is watching the vineyard shrinking in my rearview. To anyone else, I just had some grapes in the back of the truck. Nothing screamed out where they came from. But one taste of a cluster sitting in the passenger seat was all it took to make my eyes glaze over again.

Back at the winery, I was filled with a surge of energy. I tried to take my time to take it all in, but the fruit looked perfect so the work went by quickly, and by now the process had ingrained itself into my very DNA. I was more confident than ever that I'd found the right path and the right thing to do in life with my hands. Every soft *plunk* of the clusters in my cases during the morning's harvest sounded like *Chambertin, Chambertin, Chambertin*— and I kept hearing the mantra as I tenderly transferred every last grape into the tank. Even Pierre, who was busy with his own grapes, had to stop and acknowledge the moment. "*Le Roi Chambertin est arrivé!*" King Chambertin has arrived. It almost didn't seem real until I heard him say it.

In less than an hour, I was done. Just a handful of clusters weren't good enough to make the cut, but they were still too good to throw away, so I cradled them in my arms, eating handfuls of berries at a time as I admired my three full tanks. I cleaned up my work area, mopped myself up as best I could, and had started to leave when Xavier stopped me.

"Do you have the papers?"

"Which papers?"

"For your grapes. The ones that say you have paid for your grapes."

We had initially agreed to a plan Xavier came up with that allowed me to buy my grapes with the help of their business name. Everything was handled legitimately and legally, but Xavier had recently been on edge about documents that no one else seemed to be too concerned about. The customs office as well as the other various governing agencies had helped us piece together the agreement, and we'd followed each detail of their strict rules.

"If you don't have your papers, they can seize your wine!"

"They?"

"The douanes, the customs agents." They had supreme power

in Burgundy. They did audits and location searches and even pulled people over on the side of the road to see if the driver had documents supporting whatever was being transported. He didn't know that I had just been in their office in Dijon the day before to make sure everything was running smoothly. My accountant was handling the process just fine, which was the way things were done in Burgundy. He knew that just as well as I did.

"I will not have your wine jeopardize what we have built," he continued. "If you don't have the documents by tomorrow, I will remove your wine from the cuverie myself."

The honeymoon was officially over. Pierre saw the look on my face and rushed over, trying to sort everything out.

"Xavier, there is no problem. His wine is safe with us here."

But Xavier couldn't be reasoned with. "It is only safe once I know the wine is paid for."

Pierre looked at Xavier's eyes, unsure of his intentions. "Why does he need to show this to you? The douanes do not care. And if they do care, he has paid—he said so himself!"

Xavier finally broke eye contact with me and walked away, bumping into Pierre. "That is fine, but if he has not paid, he and his wines are out of here." There weren't any papers confirming I'd paid for the grapes, but I had an invoice that had been paid in full. All of the legal documents had been accepted by the douanes. Xavier knew that already. He should have been fine with the plan—he'd drawn it up himself. But he wanted me out of his cuverie, and it was clear that he would simply wait for another opportunity to pounce.

CHAPTER NINETEEN

CHRISTIAN AND I WERE ON OUR WAY DOWN TO MARSEILLE for a weekend trip to celebrate her thirtieth birthday. It had been two months since I had seen her or Bella, but it seemed like years. I'd been through so much in that time—found grapes, set up my cuverie, and was neck-deep in the production phase, all the while inching along the process of making my business official. I'd finished doing the punch downs, settling on three for the Morey, two for the Charmes-Chambertin, and only one for the Chambertin. Xavier thought I was crazy and let me know as much, but I had a gut feeling that I was honoring these grapes by doing only the steps that were necessary for their healthy advancement.

"You'll make rosé. Is that what you came here to do? You cannot treat Chambertin without two punch downs a day, at least twenty in a season. Just one time? You are going to ruin it within the week."

Xavier had taken to looking over my shoulder as I tended to my wine. It didn't bother me; it was his space too, and if he was waiting for me to slip up, I simply wasn't going to give him that satisfaction. I worked cleanly, efficiently, and as smartly as I knew I could.

And as for his ribbing about the rosé, that was just a common misconception that "modern" winemakers had—that not punching down your grapes would mean producing a less-saturated, less-expressive wine because the skins hadn't released all of their ruby dye or, by the same token, harsh tannins. But I'd tasted countless Burgundies without deep color that were still exploding with life and character. I knew I was on the right track; I could feel it.

I bit my tongue when Xavier mocked me, but I thought to myself, *How would you know what to do? You've never touched grapes above village level.* Then again, I wasn't exactly in any position to gloat because I didn't really know how my wine would turn out in the end. The best thing I could do would be to keep my mouth shut, so I did.

I'd spent nearly every day in the winery just listening to the tanks bubble and periodically tasting the fermenting juice. It still tasted like a carbonated, slightly more complex grape juice. Yet each day I could taste something different, and it thrilled me to see the changes, however small they were.

I'd made it a habit of offering samples to Pierre and Xavier, but Xavier usually ignored the offer. One day, after I'd dropped yet another sample on his desk, he came over to the wooden bench where I was eating my jambon beurre.

"They smell wonderful; you have done well," he said unexpectedly. Before I could process such a shocking compliment he followed quickly with, "But you know they are rosé, so of course they smell nice."

I'd spent so much time there that soon I felt as though a little time away would probably do me and the wine some good. I still had work to do, but nothing needed to be done right away. The winery was cold, so the fermentations were moving slowly and steadily. It was perfect. When the fermentations were finished in a few days, I'd need to transfer the wine from its tank to the barrels. Then I planned to get into the tanks with a couple of buckets so that I could scoop out any whole grapes that were still kicking around. Each load would be heavy, slippery, and unwieldy, but it was worth it for the extra yield and backbone it would give the wines.

I'd met some locals that offered to rent me their press whenever I needed it, even saying they'd show me how to use it, which I suspected was largely so the newbie didn't completely mangle their equipment. Pressing and moving to barrels were the finish line for the harvest season. I still wouldn't know how much wine I'd eventually have, but it would be safely resting for at least the next eighteen months, working quietly away to create its own distinct nuances.

So when Christian and Bella came to visit, it couldn't have been better timing. We visited the cuverie so Christian could taste the wine, and she too was surprised at how good they tasted so early in the process. I held a glass of the Chambertin up to Bella's nose so she could breathe it in, and she tried to take a lick of the fermenting juice.

"I could never have done this without you," I told her.

She waved her hand, as if to say, "It was nothing" or "You don't have to thank me."

I didn't force her to accept my gratitude; I just added it to the seemingly countless blessings that I attributed to being a part of her life.

OUR PLAN WAS TO TAKE a quick trip to the south of France because it was one of the regions we didn't get a chance to see during our first visit, and the warm weather would be a nice change from the numbing cold of Saint-Aubin. Based on the amount of heat and bubbling the wines were putting off and the firmness of the cap—or fruit collecting at the top of the tank—I figured I had at least four days before the first fermentation would be complete.

Getting down there, we figured, would be the hard part. Bella had just turned one, and her schedule wasn't exactly conducive to travel. She also wasn't used to traveling on trains, so the four-hour-long ride was punctuated by her screaming fits. Thankfully people that we encountered along the way were sympathetic. Each time Bella would yell, we braced for sighs or grumbling only to have people come up to her to stroke her hand or kiss her head. One elderly woman lulled her into a deep sleep with a soothing French song, giving us about an hour of peace before we reached Marseille. We were relieved to finally get to the hotel, but just as we got our luggage up to the room and I had finally flopped onto the bed, my phone rang.

"Where are you?" It was Fabrice, my friend from the Chamber of Commerce in Beaune.

"In the south, why?" My eyes were closed; it was the middle of the afternoon but all I could think of was how soft the pillow under me was.

"South where? Puligny-Montrachet?" It was strange how he was asking. We hadn't spoken in weeks, and in my mind, we'd put business aside leaving just our friendship.

"I'm in Marseille." I heard him relaying my response to someone else in the room.

"Why aren't you here with your wines?" There was an angry undercurrent to his questioning. "This isn't professional."

"Wait, what?" I looked at the phone, puzzled by why Fabrice

would take such a brittle tone with me. And why was it any of his business what I did in my own free time?

"You *need* to be here with your wines. These are very expensive grapes and *we* are worried." What was he talking about? Nearly every day since I'd brought the grapes in, I'd driven twenty minutes from Beaune to Saint-Aubin just to be close to the tanks while I ate my lunch. I'd open one of my old books and read about the terroirs my wines had come from. When I didn't have a book, I'd work on painting the metal bands around my barrels red, just to have a reason to be near them.

"We are in your cuverie." My face flushed with heat.

"You are *where*?" My grip tightened on the phone.

"Xavier invited all of us here to see how you work. He is concerned and said we needed to see your work space."

"And why did he want you to see my work space?" I tapped the phone with my index finger as I anxiously awaited his response. No matter what he said, I knew it was only going to upset me even more.

"Well." He paused. "He says that you leave grapes on the ground and that you really don't treat your wines right."

"I don't treat my wines right?" Where in the hell did this guy get off telling people that I wasn't treating my wines right? "Fabrice, who is with you?"

"Everyone."

"Who? Tell me who they are."

"I am here with your grape growers, your accountant, and your courtiers." I was speechless. What was Xavier trying to prove? "And he is worried about your bills."

I didn't know what to do. I felt cornered, helpless, and angry. But I was hours away from them and my wines. My face started to wash over in heat, my ears began to burn.

"Fabrice, put me on speaker phone, please."

"Why?"

"Please just help me and translate for everyone."

There was another pause. "OK. We are listening." His voice echoed off the walls of the warehouse.

"Hello, everyone. I don't know exactly why you all have been invited here, but I must admit that it is more than a small shock."

Fabrice translated on the other end.

"I was speaking with Fabrice and he says that my cleanliness and practices are being questioned."

"Yes, well, we are here and there are things everywhere," Fabrice responded. "Grapes, stems, a filthy wine press."

"Wait, where are you right now?"

"We are by the rolling door, by the wine press." I laughed to myself.

"You are by Xavier and Pierre's section. Mine is the little alley by the machines with white tarps on them."

"Hold on." I heard the echo of footsteps on the other end and French chatter. "OK, we are here."

"Now, what do you see?" A grin started to cover the whole of my face.

"I see . . . nothing. Well, one wood tank and two steel tanks."

"Anything on the floor?"

"No."

"Those are my tanks. You are in my workplace. Please let everyone else know that." He translated.

"Yes, but what about your practice on your wines?" He didn't seem to care that my area was clean.

"I just don't like heavy extraction."

"Xavier says you need extraction to be high on these types of wines."

246 • RAY WALKER

"Fabrice, why do I need to listen to someone else about how to treat *my* own wines?"

"He is just concerned." He lowered his voice to a whisper. "And do not forget that unlike you, he has a wine degree. So, he knows things you do not. You should appreciate his concern in calling us."

"I'm not going to get into this with you. I appreciate people looking out for me, but this is something different."

"Well, I have your accountant here as well and he is now losing confidence in you and your project succeeding. He is questioning if he has wasted his time with you. Are your bills paid?"

"Yes."

"No, they are not. You could not have paid for your fruit already."

"I had to pay for my fruit up-front. My courtiers are right there; ask them. And let my accountant know that I can show him proof of the payments when I return."

"They have now left. But they do wish to have a meeting with all of us together when you return to your wines. When will you be back?"

I couldn't believe it. I wanted to strangle Xavier. What was his problem?

"I will be back in a few days." I wanted to leave that minute, but nothing back in Burgundy was worth more than celebrating Christian's birthday as we had planned.

Two days later, Christian and Bella were heading home to California after an all-too-brief reunion, and I was sitting in Thierry's, my accountant's, conference room with Gregory; Dominique; Thomas; Jacques (the other courtier) and his assistant, Jerome; Fabrice; Xavier; and Pierre. Laid out on the table in front of us were my bank statements, financial correspondence, and bills. Xavier had called my finances into question, so I asked Thierry to pull my online checking account up on a PowerPoint presentation projector for everyone to see. I logged into my bank account and walked them through each of my investor deposits, including those from Dave, which understandably raised a few red flags. They had a hard time believing that I was all paid up on the expenses I'd accrued during harvest, especially without having taken out any loans. Instead, I explained, I was living modestly and paid for everything—tanks, barrels, fruit, etc.—upon receipt.

"Where are all the laboratory analysis tools? You haven't even mentioned a pump in your list of purchased equipment. How much did your pump cost? And what about a destemmer, or a wine press?" they asked. But because I would need only simple analyses run on my wines, like alcohol percentage, sulfur levels, pH, and malic/lactic numbers, I didn't need my own analysis tools. I could just pay ten euros each time I needed a wine to be checked. I didn't need a pump because I planned to use buckets to move my wines the full two feet from my tank to my barrels. I had used Xavier and Pierre's destemmer. I was borrowing a press. As I explained my process, Xavier and Pierre bickered among themselves in French about my practices and philosophy, while Fabrice refereed. I watched them lob their opinions back and forth like a tennis match as the squabbling reached a crescendo. Finally, Jerome, Jacques's assistant, addressed the room in English, presumably for my benefit.

"I don't believe it is necessary to go to school to have good wine. He has good grapes; therefore, he should have good wines. Simple. He has paid for his grapes. What he does with them next is only for him to decide." I couldn't have said it better myself.

But the damage of Xavier's distrust had already been done. Before leaving that day, Xavier, Pierre, and I agreed that I had three months to move my wine out of their facility. It was going to be just enough time to establish my own business, though if I could have, I would have moved that afternoon.

The biggest step was still setting up my visa, which would give me the right to live and work in Burgundy. The catch was, I could get it only if I had a business in France. I had a visitor's visa, which had to be reissued every ninety days.

I was running from office building to office building, creating several bank accounts to verify my funds and meeting at the customs office almost daily. I had to file documents promising to pay any debts in France that I might acquire, furnish background check clearances, and show that I was financially solvent before anyone would even look at my files. Whenever I did manage to get someone to start clearing my applications for a new business or visa, I was always told to come back with yet another document. Sometimes I'd scramble to complete what I was told was the necessary next step only to be informed that it was, in fact, unnecessary. And inevitably the employee who had helped me last was transferred to another department when I returned, or their name rang no bell with the man or woman currently sitting in the window. God forbid someone decide to take a vacation for, say, the month of August—the entire department would close. But the biggest obstacle was that the system is set up for French and EU citizens. It isn't common for an American to come looking to start a business. Even the most experienced manager or department head wouldn't know exactly what to do with me. The only advice I got was, "If you were an EU citizen, this wouldn't be a problem."

I knew that there were three other American wine producers who had set up shop in Burgundy before me. One had his father set up the business years before the wall of regulations went up, while the other two had European citizenship cards. I wasn't so lucky.

One morning I was walking the usual two miles to Thierry's office, when the perfect solution came to me. I picked up the pace, looking particularly crazed with my arms full of the loose papers that I'd collected over the past few months. Thierry had relentlessly scoured the system for any breaks in the red tape, hoping as much as I did that we could find a way in. Like me, he'd finally make progress with someone, wait a few days for a reply, and then call back only to hear that the person no longer worked in that department. Time after time we'd start over, filling out requested documents only to reach dead end after dead end. I could tell his confidence in the business progressing had started to fade. He didn't joke anymore, didn't smile, and spoke tensely.

Walking in, I spotted Thierry going into one of the conference rooms with some other clients. I was the only one in the office not wearing a suit. A secretary looked like the CEO next to my ensemble of roughed-up jeans and a wrinkled sweater. My bike had long since given out, and after the brisk half-hour walk, I wasn't exactly fresh. But still, I confidently barged into the conference room. Thierry gave me a quick once-over and offered me a tight smile.

I looked at his clients. "*Bonjour.*"

They were seemingly unbothered by my appearance—or the fact that I was interrupting their meeting—and gave me a hearty, courteous bonjour in return.

"Thierry, I have an idea."

"At least one of us does. I've looked in each corner and have found nothing."

I leaned in, knowing I had come up with something good. "So we keep hearing the same thing over and over. If I were a citizen of France—"

He cut in, "Or the European Union at all."

"Right, at all," I continued, "that things would be much smoother."

"Well, most of all, we keep hearing them say no."

"Well . . . yeah. There is that too."

"There is. And believe me, I've heard more of them than you."

"OK, that's not important though." I continued while Thierry squinted at me and pushed his fancy square-shaped eyeglasses farther up the bridge of his nose. "Why can't we have someone with citizenship here start the business for me?"

His glasses slid down again; they always did when he was thinking. "You know, we could have you as the business owner and just have a European Union citizen be your *gérant*." He had a devilish grin on his face. "This could actually work, you know. *Holly sheet!*"

I smiled wide, having to hold myself back from giving him a lame, but perfectly appropriate high five. "Wait, did you say *holly* . . . shit?"

The smiles left, in came confusion. "Yes, holly. What?" He started to laugh.

I cackled helplessly, probably scaring a few people down the quiet hall. "Never mind. So this could work?"

"Yeah, it will have to. We've no other ideas."

"But it *should* work?"

"It will work. Instead of the list I gave you with all those things to turn in—"

"The thirty-two." Yes, I had counted them.

"With this *gérant*, a business manager, you would have two, maybe three steps in creating your business and getting licensing."

I was floored! "That's it?"

"Yeah, pretty much."

I wanted to shake him. "Why in God's name didn't you mention this before, man?"

"It didn't occur to me. Sometimes the best path comes from stepping in *sheet* a few times."

"And we did."

"Yes, we did."

But the problem was I didn't have many friends from the EU whom I knew well enough or trusted to have access to all of my business's money and account information, and share any potential risk. I wasn't about to take a chance on someone who would create more issues than I'd managed to create myself, but I also knew there was a lot at stake if I didn't find a partner soon.

That night, I was on a UK-based online wine bulletin board writing updates on how things were progressing. Minutes later, I received a private message from a guy who had been one of the eight people who had looked at my original business plan as a potential investor. His name was Filippo, and he was from Italy but went to school in California and now worked in finance in the UK. At the time we hadn't been able to agree on terms, and I hadn't heard from him since. But his message said that he applauded my efforts and that if I ever needed anything, I shouldn't hesitate to ask. He said that he could only imagine how tough it would be to sort out the regulations in France because I didn't speak the language.

I normally wouldn't have dared asking a stranger for this kind of help, but he seemed sincere, and my desperation had made me bold.

"Hey, thanks for your e-mail," I replied. "I appreciate the support. Can I ask, are you an EU citizen? If you are, I was curious if I could ask you for a favor—it's a big one!"

His reply came less than two minutes later. "Yes. Whatever you need, just say it!"

I poured my heart out in a lengthy e-mail, describing my incredible investors, the miraculous fruit I bought, how the harvest went, how promising my wines were looking, and what the situation was with Xavier and my paperwork. I told him in no uncertain terms that while this business had all the makings for success, I didn't see a way it could work without his help.

I hit "send" and sat at the computer hitting the refresh button, sweating over his possible responses. "Sorry, not your guy" seemed likely, or maybe he'd keep it simple with "Get lost." But not more than two minutes later a message notification popped up on my screen:

"We need to get your wines out of there. Just let me know what you want me to do, and I'll do it!" Even though we'd never even met before, I trusted him. Desperation may have played a part, but he was also known in the wine community, and he appeared to be genuine and only looking to help out. Plus, he had a lot to lose by placing his name on my business because he didn't know how well I'd run it or how the product would turn out. If something went wrong, I could potentially try to make him responsible too. There was an immediate mutual trust, but I stood to gain everything out of the arrangement while he was simply being incredibly generous and asking for nothing in return.

Thierry made quick work of the process after that. With

Filippo on board, we sailed through the obstacles that had once threatened to derail my dream.

Going back to the winery felt odd after all that had happened. It had been two days since the meeting, but my anger toward Xavier was still fresh and cooled only by my knowing that it would all be over once the paperwork was finalized. I'd still need a place to move my barrels once they were filled, and the important thing was to get them out of there quickly, and at all costs.

I laughed a bit seeing Xavier's workplace, which was littered with old, dried-up grapes someone hadn't bothered to clean up. Even though everything had worked out for the best and I'd never have to see him again, I still couldn't believe someone could be so conniving. I was thankful my wines had no way of knowing about the negativity surrounding them. In fact, they tasted even better than they ever had. The warm gassiness of fermentation was subsiding, the bitter notes had rounded out, and the sugary taste of grape juice was replaced with an unoaked wine profile that had somehow crystallized what I tasted when eating the grapes at harvest.

I finished my last rounds of punch downs on the Les Chaffots and Charmes-Chambertin, leaving the Chambertin alone since I'd done the only punch down a week ago. It was already sealed off in its steel tank. The fermentations were moving even slower than I had planned. It didn't bother me; the longer they took, the more time I figured the delicate expressions of the wines would have to come together. All I had to do now was wait for the bubbling to stop and for the temperatures to drop, which would signal the end of fermentation. It would be any day now, and then the source of all my elation, joy, heartache, pride, and anxiety could rest safely in barrels.

TWO DAYS LATER, THE LAST tank, Chambertin, finished its alcoholic fermentation. Some guys who'd offered their six-foot-tall wooden vertical press came over and gave me a hand emptying the tanks into the barrels and with the pressing process. As much as I took pride in doing things myself, it was a welcome change of pace having people around laughing, cracking jokes, and working hard for a shared outcome. After the wines were in barrel, my active work as a Burgundy cellar rat would taper to a standstill. Short of the remaining administrative work to finish up my licenses, there wasn't much left to do. I took advantage of the new-found quiet and planned a much-needed trip home.

Even though I'd spent almost my entire life in Northern California, on that trip it suddenly seemed like a foreign place. The angry drivers, the homeless men and women begging for change, the odd look I got when I said hello upon entering a business—it didn't quite feel like home anymore. The foods that I used to love gorging on now seemed so sugary and artificial tasting. And the portions were so huge! Bottles of juice, sandwiches, steaks—a single-portion size in America would feed at least two or three people in France. I was used to eating the freshest butter, cheese, bread, chocolates, meats, wines, seafood, cream, fruit, and herbs from villages and regions that specialize in just a few commodities. I didn't eat cheese in France, I ate Époisses—because that's where it was from. I couldn't go back to eating processed food produced in the middle of nowhere. All I wanted was some fresh jambon on a freshly baked baguette with butter from the Loire Valley oozing out the sides.

I'd seen what life could offer all of us, and I was having

trouble forcing myself to ignore it. Christian tired quickly of my constant comparison of California to France. While I enjoyed being back in the Bay Area with my family, I couldn't help but feel that France would be a better home for us. I understood the people in Burgundy. Maybe not their language, but their way of life. But I didn't want to pressure Christian; she had already granted me everything that I had asked for. To push for anything more would be greedy.

I did my best to focus on my life in California, but Xavier was doing everything in his power to derail my resolution. He had taken to calling and harassing me at all hours.

"Ray?"

"Yeah, man. It's three in the morning. You woke up my daughter."

"Well, your barrels are keeping me up as well. Where are your papers for your business?" He was frantic, manic even.

"Xavier, I told you just yesterday that the business will be set up in a week or two." I didn't want to upset him, even though I was starting to get upset myself. "So you understand that I'm really trying to get out of your hair. Really, I am." I was trying to move as quickly as I could. It had been only two months since we'd agreed I'd be gone in three months, and I still needed a little more time.

There was a pause and then he continued, his voice calm, but almost bizarrely so. Like someone had switched a dial on his back from angry to psychopath.

"You have two days, Monsieur Walker. After two days, your wine is on the street."

My eyes went wide and my jaw clenched. The threat wasn't serious; it couldn't be. Not two weeks ago he had said that he would be patient and that I didn't need to rush. We had shaken hands, looked each other in the eyes, and I had left for California confident that we'd be able to move toward a transition on good terms. There wasn't any way I could have seen this bomb coming.

"You know I am in California, in another country. How can I get things finished from here in two days?"

"It was your decision to see your family, not mine. You wanted to come to Burgundy, and there are sacrifices for this."

I called Pierre after we hung up. He sounded concerned, but he didn't feel there was much need to worry.

"I think that he is just going through a difficult time."

"OK, but his hard time is now threatening my wines!"

"He wouldn't do anything to your wines. He loves wine. As a winemaker it would make him sick to hurt someone's wines. Just do what you can. I will watch Xavier for you."

I felt a little better, but I still didn't know what Xavier was capable of.

I spent the next hour telling Christian everything about Xavier, which I'd mostly kept hidden so that I wouldn't worry her unnecessarily. When I told her about Xavier's threat, her mouth hung open. I'd never seen her so concerned before.

"Well, what are you going to do?"

"I can't do anything."

"No one can help us speed things up?"

"No one." We both sat there speechless, taking turns shaking our heads in disbelief.

I called Thierry relentlessly, badgering him about where things stood. He was almost as helpless as I was, completely at the whims of the licensing offices and their notoriously slow bureaucracy.

The next day, Thierry called to say all we were waiting for was a caution, which was the last step in creating the business. We just needed my bank to confirm that they would pay the two hundred euros in taxes for wines that were sold in France should I default on the payment. It would be only a matter of days before things were official.

I braced myself and dialed Xavier's number. It had been three days since we had last spoken.

"Hello, Monsieur Walker. Have you news for me?" He spoke through his teeth.

I relayed the updates from Thierry to him.

"I am hanging up," he replied. "You should really think of your wines, Monsieur Walker. I have. I may not throw them out in the street, but something may be added to a barrel or two if the wines are here for too long." The phone went dead before I could decide how to respond.

Christian had heard the whole exchange. "We have to get our wines out of there."

"But where?"

"We need to find our own place." She hesitated before sighing. "You may have to find a place for us to stay out there as well."

I loved the idea, but we had talked ourselves in circles about this very topic countless times before. She wanted to have a place to live in Burgundy *and* San Francisco. I didn't see how we could do it with no financial income besides what the winery made, when and if it ever did.

"I just don't think we can support rent for two homes."

"No. We wouldn't need to."

"Flying back and forth would kill us too." We had already spent thousands of dollars in transportation costs over the past two months.

258 • RAY WALKER

"We can't keep risking our wines being alone. Anything could happen to them." Everything she said was true, which didn't help too much with my stress. But we finally had a logical, practical reason to do something completely crazy and unexpected: We'd leave California to live in Burgundy. There wasn't any need to discuss it further. We were moving to Burgundy just as soon as we found a place for us and our wines to live.

CHAPTER TWENTY

THREE WEEKS LATER AND I WAS STILL ON THE HUNT. AFTER lurking through village after village after village between Gevrey-Chambertin and Chassagne-Montrachet, my confidence in finding a place was running on fumes. I'd decided to take the day off from looking and went to Nuits for a thick slice of jambon persillé, a traditional Burgundian terrine with baked ham and parsley. It was considered one of the best simple pleasures in Burgundy. And I happened to know that the butcher in Nuits was the best in the region. They had won all types of awards, but all I needed was to taste their version myself to know that it was extraordinary.

I walked slowly and aimlessly around the village, eating my jambon straight from the butcher paper.

"*Bon appétit!*" said a local passing by, wishing me a good meal. It was one of the many charms of living in Burgundy—people did nice things without giving it a second thought. Why? Because it made their day better too.

Just then, I passed by the window of yet another real estate office. Because it was easier to stop to eat than to keep walking in circles, I looked over the listings—assuming they'd be the same

I'd seen just fifteen minutes earlier in another office window nearby. There were a couple new ones that didn't look completely futile, so on a whim I went inside.

"Bonjour, do you have anything that isn't on that same list I've seen in everyone else's window?"

"For rent?"

"Yes, for rent." The twenty-something real estate agent probably assumed that I wasn't in a position to buy based on the fact that I was wearing a T-shirt, one of my only good ones, that I'd spilled wine on.

"Your budget?" She looked at the stain.

"I'm open."

"Shall we say three thousand then?"

I wasn't *that* open. "How about one thousand two hundred?"

"As you wish."

"There is one house that is going to be on the market in two months. It is right up the street."

"I forgot to mention—I need a cave." I'd been to countless real estate offices and had been shown dozens of pictures of beautiful, affordable homes before specifying that I needed a cave. It was always the deal breaker since it was a rarity for anyone with a cave large enough to store much more than a few dozen bottles to be listing their place for rent. If they did have the space, they likely didn't want anyone to actually use it for storing barrels, and risk being connected with a commercial lease. Who would want to take that gamble?

"Oh, it has a cave. I believe a large cave."

"But would I be able to store barrels there?"

"Do you have barrels?" She looked down at the wine stain again.

"I do." Was she going to ask me if I had wine in them, or only ketchup?

"Well, I don't see why you couldn't. You would be renting the space. It would be for you to decide what you store there, wouldn't it?"

"Uh, I guess." There was no way that this was going to work. Somehow it was falling into place too easily.

"Here, take the keys. Go take a look at it yourself. It's up the street."

"Do I need to sign anything?"

"No, they are keys. Put them into—"

"I mean for taking the keys."

She looked at me, shocked that I'd ask her such a stupid question.

"I gave you the keys. You take them and open the door. Simple."

"Oh, and my name is Ray Walker. I figured since I have the keys—"

"OK," she said with a smile that made it clear she didn't have the slightest concern about who I was. She trusted me on sight alone, stained shirt and all.

I got lost a few times before finally finding the address. The huge house couldn't possibly have been the right one—it was the size of the other four-room apartment buildings in the area, and yet priced far below at under a thousand euros a month. I walked back to the office to ask if the agent could help me find the right place, and a few minutes later we were standing in front of the same house. It had stucco plastered on the walls that made it seem almost modern, but just like the other houses in the neighborhood, it must have been at least three hundred years old.

262 • RAY WALKER

"This is it?"

"Yes. Why?"

"I thought it would be smaller based on the price."

"Should we raise it?" She smirked, then opened up the front door.

I followed her in, fearing the worst. I would have slept on a dirt floor if it meant my wines would be safe, but by the looks of the space, such measures wouldn't be necessary. Not even close. It was spacious and bright. The downstairs floors were covered in beautiful tile, except for the living room, which was a rich dark wood. The kitchen was small but filled with fresh air and light from all the windows that looked out on a patio. The bedrooms would fit good-size beds, and the ceilings were high enough so I wouldn't bump my head, something I took for granted until I got to Beaune. I walked from room to room, able to picture where our furniture would go. I thought about how comfortable and happy Isabella and Christian would be here.

When I finished my tour I stepped out on the patio, which flanked a courtyard we'd have all to ourselves. From the backyard I could see into some of the other yards because the houses were huddled so closely together. Suddenly it hit me—this wasn't the suburbs or the city or even a small town. This was a *village*. And not only that, one with more than two thousand years of history. I wasn't just on vacation, either. This would be our life. We could walk down the street for fresh croissants and pain au chocolat. There was a market that sold all the bounty of the region just minutes away. There would be a real sense of community. It was the one place in the world where I wanted to be.

"Should we see the garage?" I didn't know it had one.

She led me just outside the back of the house to a set of red double doors that opened to a room just smaller than a one-car garage. I held my arm up toward the ceiling, checking the height. I had about two feet of clearance. The walls looked good, and the floors were clean, no motor oil anywhere. Best of all, it didn't smell like anything.

"You know, I could put some tanks in here."

"Tanks?"

"For wine."

"Oh." She smiled politely. "Do you buy a lot of wine?"

"No, I buy grapes for wine."

"Oh, you are a"—she searched for the word—"winemaker?"

"Not really. I just do the basics, not the complicated stuff."

"Well, do you need to do the complicated things? It's just wine."

What were the odds that I would meet up with a real estate agent in Burgundy who could so adeptly distill one of the most fundamental principles about wine? She studied the width of the room, pacing from one side to the other. "Tanks? I think it could work."

"Can we see the cave?"

"There it is." She pointed to a steel door in the ground next to the house. It looked more like a storm shelter than the entrance to a cave.

"How old is this house again?"

"There are records from over four hundred years ago." After living in the United States, this was impossible to digest. Two hundred and fifty years ago the Declaration of Independence hadn't even been signed!

She stayed back while I figured out how to open the large metal doors of the cave. Once I pried them open, I started down the flight of stairs slowly. Burgundians from a few hundred years ago were generally much shorter than we are today, so I made sure to duck my head on my way in. I kept low and felt along the sides of the wall for a light switch. I could feel cool brick covered in the woolly gauze of ancient spiderwebs. As I moved deeper into the cave, the light from the outside could barely penetrate the darkness inside. I imagined thousands of little spider eyes watching me.

"I got the lights!" The agent called from above as the lights went on, revealing the pointy ends of a grappling hook next to my head. These hooks had been used as far back as three hundred years for tethering rope while one raised or lowered full barrels into the cave. There was an identical hook on the other side of the cave, across from the stairs. Ropes were run from either side of the cave and wrapped around the four-hundred-pound barrels to help support their weight. The pulley system made it possible for about six men, typically three on each side, to guide the barrels up and out or into the cave. I'd read about them in one of my books, and was elated to see one in person so I could now understand the mechanics.

The rest of the vaulted stone-lined cave was just as amazing. There were two sections, and the larger of the two—the *chai*— was big enough to hold around seventy barrels. The smaller had eight alcoves for storing bottles, and there were about thirty sitting there now. Some still had labels intact, which revealed a now-defunct domaine or wine region I'd never heard of. But most were anonymous, the only identifying characteristic their burgundy-colored capsule that suggested they were from Domaine Dujac, one of my early favorites of the region. Whoever owned the bottles must have had them for a long time.

It wasn't the deepest cave in Burgundy, but it would certainly work. I would barely fill a fraction of the chai with my barrels, and I'd have room to grow. The alcoves were ideal for storing wine after bottling, since the temperature would be consistent and cold, which is crucial for ensuring the wine's temperature wouldn't fluctuate too much or, worse, get too hot. The place would need a good scrubbing—there were spiderwebs lining almost the entire cave—but it was perfect. The agent told me that it had been more than seventy years since the space had been used for wine production.

I walked back up to the courtyard, grinning like I'd found gold hidden in one of the cave's corners.

"Can I make a quick call?"

"Of course, go ahead."

I paced around the courtyard as the phone rang.

"Christian?" It was four in the morning in California. She *did* say to call if anything urgent came up. This counted.

"Hey, honey." She sounded happy to hear me, if groggy.

"I found it!"

"Oh great! Good job. Call me in a few hours, OK? I love you." She began to hang up the phone.

"Wait. I didn't tell you want I found."

"Oh, that's nice." She was still half asleep. I figured it was as good a time as any to get her permission to sign for the house.

"I found a house, for rent." I went in for the kill. "Should I . . . sign for it?"

"Sign for it? I haven't even seen it!" Guess she wasn't as asleep as I thought she was.

"What does it look like?"

"Uh, big."

"What does it look like though? The shape, the floors, you know. . . . does it have a nice bathroom?"

I didn't have the heart to tell her about the one downside of the entire place—the phone booth–size shower stall. My wife didn't require luxury, but I knew she wouldn't consider being able to extend her arms in the shower an extravagance.

"It does have a bathroom. Yup. Bathroom—check. It has nice floors, high ceil—"

"Is the bathroom nice? Can I at least take a decent shower there?"

I bit my bottom lip. There wasn't any way to sugarcoat it. "No, it's not really nice. No."

She didn't say anything. Her silence said it all. Well, that was it. I started to walk back over to the agent. She could tell by the look on my face that it was a no. She closed her binder, closed any chance of my search being over.

Christian finally spoke. "Well, do you think the rest of the house looks good though? How's the cave?"

"The cave is beautiful."

"Is it big?"

"Uh, no. But it has character, it'll work."

"And you think that we will be comfortable there?"

"Well, yeah." I looked over at the entrance to the cave. "We should have enough room to get us through the next couple of vintages. We'll be able to fit maybe seventy barrels down there."

Again silence. "No. I mean *us*. Will our family be comfortable? Is there central heating? Is it clean? Is the neighborhood—"

"They have radiators."

"Do they work?"

"I think so."

"OK, please check to see if they work."

I ran over to the agent and asked about the heat.

"Oui, le chauffage marche très bien!"

"Honey, the heat works just fine. She's actually showing me a huge water heater right now that is about the same size as a Dumpster. And the floors are nice, wood. Some parts are tile. Ceilings are nice."

"And it's clean?"

"The house is very clean."

I heard her inhaling. "OK, then grab it!"

The only thing that still didn't add up was the price. The agent mentioned that the family had set the price fifteen years ago and didn't see any reason in changing it. I was sold! Just like that, we were going to be living in Nuits-Saint-Georges.

Back at the real estate office, I anxiously rocked in a little plastic chair as I waited for the owner to arrive to approve the rental. When he arrived, he introduced himself as Christian Gouges. We shook hands. Gouges. Sounded familiar. But I couldn't put my finger on it.

The agent had a smile plastered from each ear. I wondered what she was so excited about.

She began to explain to Mr. Gouges, "*Donc*, Monsieur Walker is very interested in renting the house." He nodded. "He is in agreement with everything. But he asks if you would mind if he used the cave."

He looked over at me and shrugged his shoulders. "Of course he can. He is renting it all."

I wanted to make sure that he knew exactly what my plans were. "Would it be all right if I put some barrels in the cave?"

"Barrels." He looked at my shoes and then smiled. "You make wine?"

"I don't make anything, but I help the grapes while they become wines."

His smile grew. "Yes, that would be a pleasure."

The agent leaned over her table toward me. "Ray, do you know what Christian does for a living?"

I looked back at him blankly. Then Christian waved his index finger and gestured toward his worn brown boots. They had even more old mud on them than mine did.

"He is from the Gouges family," the agent said. "He makes the wine. You know about wines? They are very well-known."

"If you do take the house," Christian interjected, "it would be a pleasure for you to make wine. It has been some time since anyone has done this in the old house. How much wine will you make? How many barrels?"

"I just started this last harvest. I have around ten and a half barrels."

"*Pas mal*, not bad. And you wish to stay at this level or will you grow like Mondavi?"

"At this point, I don't even know what will happen tomorrow, let alone ten years from now. But I love Burgundy, and something tells me that staying small would be the best for us. If we stay that way, I can still do the work myself."

"You know, the best is to do the least possible. I think an old Burgundian said it first?" He chuckled.

"So, there are no machines that you'll come with? No chemicals?"

"None, besides some sulfur."

"Good. *À l'ancienne*, eh, old school. That's all you need. I'll need to taste your wine once you are there. I'll finally see how an American does it." Was that all he was going to ask? There had to be a catch.

"So, how to progress? What do I need to do in order to complete the application?"

The agent and Mr. Gouges looked at each other, neither understanding what I was speaking about. He turned to me and held out his hand.

"*This* is the application. Do you accept?" Was he serious? It couldn't be this easy. I shook his hand firmly, my eyes directly on his, both of us nodding.

He rested his left hand on mine, and held eye contact.

"It excites me to know I am a part of what you are doing. And to have you continue in the house where my father once made wine brings a new life to it. I wish you success."

"Honey, can you blow up the couch when you get a second? It's gone flat again."

We were home. Well, we were in our house, and we were slowly making it our home. I could tell that Christian was a bit taken aback by the house when we walked through the door. Apparently I'd taken some great photos, so the reality was a bit too sobering. She quickly put things in perspective. It wasn't a brand-new house like we'd bought near Napa when we got married, with custom countertops and doorknobs. This was a house that had seen history, and most likely been a part of it. Now it was going to provide shelter for our family.

The last tenant had moved out of the Nuits house in late December, and by mid-January 2010, just weeks after I'd found it, Christian and I had come over together to move the barrels in from Saint-Aubin. The wines had been in barrel for just under four months. Isabella stayed in California with Christian's mother, since the last thing we wanted was to have her suffering through a cold, snowy winter. Besides, we had a lot of work to do.

We were thankful that the electricity and water services were still active when we arrived in snow-coated Nuits-Saint-Georges, and the heat worked better than expected. There was snow on the ground, but half the time it was hot enough that we had to walk around the house half naked. But the rest of the time it was shut completely off, making us wish, as we watched our breath vaporize into the air, that it would go back to the fever-like conditions.

To make what we had assumed would be a short trip more comfortable we had bought some blankets, towels, coffee mugs, plates, and steel utensils. Until our furniture was shipped from California, we were making do with a blow-up mattress and matching blow-up sofa that had a bad habit of deflating when you sat on them.

It was supposed to be simple. We'd camp out in the house while the rest of the documents were approved and I could officially pick up my barrels from Pierre and Xavier's. Things were close to being finished up; Fabrice and I spoke almost every day making sure the douanes, the bank, and my accountant had everything that they needed. Documents were delivered overnight by FedEx from Beaune to London several times over to ensure the application was approved as quick as possible. For most Burgundy winemakers, getting this last piece of the puzzle, the bank caution, resolved itself in a matter of weeks, or at most, a month. But for me it had taken four long months. With the clock ticking until our flight back to San Francisco, we spent two more weeks feverishly calling the bank and pleading with anyone who would listen. Meanwhile Thierry was looking for ways to help, but to no successful end. Then one day Roz, from Domaine Dujac, pulled a few strings to hurry things along. The good news was that I'd get the papers I needed in three days. The bad news was that we were supposed to leave in two. I so badly wanted Christian to stay and help me move the barrels. It was a big job, yes, but also such a huge moment for us. But I also knew one of us needed to go home to be with Bella, so Christian suggested that we work together to get our cave ready before she'd have to leave.

It was a pretty day, but cold. It had snowed the night before, though by the late morning most of it was gone, except for a few stray tufts that dotted our stone-tiled courtyard. This would be the first time she'd been inside the cave.

"All right," she said, nodding. She was almost as impressed with the space as she was with how much we'd have to clean. "Where do we start?"

"I guess we'll get rid of some of the spiders."

"Some?" She already had some webs in her hair, but I didn't dare say a word. She'd run out and never come back in.

"Well, I don't want to get rid of all of them. It would feel too new down here. I need *some* spiders." Whenever I walked into a winery and it was completely clean and sterile, it seemed phony. I wanted this cave to reflect its history.

"So, what else?"

"I dunno."

"Where are you going to put the barrels?"

I knew the answer to that one. "On top of some concrete runners."

"What runners?"

"Well, I have to buy them."

"So, the runners will go on top of the dirt?"

"No, I'll put down some gravel."

She continued studying the floor, the walls, and where my imaginary concrete runners were. The subtext of her silence was clear: *When the hell were you planning on doing all this?!*

"I'll be right back!" I said. I gave her a kiss and darted out.

In the car, my heart was racing. It hadn't dawned on me before how much I had to actually do before moving my barrels. The first challenge was getting to the hardware store before it closed for lunch at noon. Like most stores in France, if I showed up after lunch, my order wouldn't be submitted until the next day. And if the paperwork came through earlier than we'd anticipated—which, shockingly, was now a possibility—I couldn't risk not being able to act on a moment's notice.

I pulled into the parking lot just as they were closing the doors and begged the owner to let me in. I ordered my gravel and concrete runners, and left with the reassurance that it would all be delivered the next morning from the local quarry in Comblanchien, the next village over.

As promised, the next day a huge pile of gravel, which I'd planned to transport with only two little buckets, was dumped into the courtyard. But my concrete runners weren't there.

"*Uh, monsieur, les supports fûts? Sont où?*"

"*Au magasin. Sont prêt.*" Apparently they were at the store, and I needed to pick them up myself. Six-foot-long slabs of concrete. I eyed my rental car, which could barely fit four adults. I drove to the store, and the manager agreed to deliver the supports, laughing when he saw my pitiful vehicle—but it would take a week, which wouldn't work. I thanked him and headed back to my car. But another guy who worked at the store, Habib, who had always been friendly when I picked up odds and ends for the house, saw and stopped me.

"You aren't taking your supports?" he asked.

"I can't fit them."

"Where's your car?" I pointed to the tiny hatchback we were standing in front of.

He pulled open the hatch and thought a minute. "It'll work." He started back to the store, then turned around and yelled to me as he disappeared. "I'll be back in a second."

A minute later, he came around the corner with my stack of supports. We loaded everything in, trying not to break the car in half as we did. The headliner got torn, a bit of the plastic on the backs of the chairs got scratched, but hell, they were in. Sort of. The passenger side front seat had three barrel supports laying on top of it, and the other two were under my arm, leaving me just enough room to shift into first and second gear. They sat just inches below the windshield, and about a foot and a half stuck out of the hatch. It was a very real possibility that the concrete would push through the windshield or slide out the rear of the car while I was on the road.

When I got home, Christian started shoveling the gravel into the two buckets, which I'd then transport down the stairs and into the cave. And after nearly a hundred trips up and down that tiny stairwell, the massive pile of gravel in the courtyard was gone. Christian and I sat in the entrance and took in the work we'd done. The even white gravel looked beautiful. I wanted to close my eyes and fall asleep on those stones. We sat in silence, too tired to move, and admired our wine's new home.

There was a knock on our courtyard doors. It was eight at night, and we didn't know of anyone who knew we lived here. But when I answered the door, I found Habib standing there with a friend.

"Are you finished?" he asked. "We thought you might need help. I hope you don't mind; I got your info off the delivery slip."

Once again, by the grace of the universe, help arrived to dig me out of yet another sticky situation, because even after carting gravel for hours, I still had to get the runners into the cave. I showed Habib the way to the stack of concrete, and seeing that I could barely keep my eyes open, he patted me on the back and called his friend over to help him with one of the supports. I insisted we take turns, and we worked silently and smoothly until all the runners were in place. As Habib and his friend headed toward the door to go home, I jogged over to stop them. I pulled out a twenty-euro bill and tried handing it to Habib, insisting that he take it as a gesture of my gratitude.

He pulled his hands back. "A friend doesn't have to pay for help."

"Are you sure?"

He looked over to his friend. "Maybe he will take it." His friend shook his head, waving his hands. "I can't take it. It was a favor for a friend."

We shook hands, and they left. It was the sort of kindness that I never experienced in California but formed the very foundation of the community here in Burgundy. And now, of my cave.

Christian left the next morning for California. I was sad to lose my only source of company for a while and also because I knew she would be able to hold Isabella soon, without me. I was going to miss out on the kisses, joking, laughter, and special moments that neither pictures nor phone calls can quite capture. But I was nearing the finish line now; all I had to do was dig deep and finish strong for my family.

CHAPTER TWENTY-ONE

THE LAST OF MY BARRELS WERE LOADED UP AND OUT OF Pierre and Xavier's warehouse. I had thirteen in total, ten of them full, sealed with wooden transport bungs. In the passenger seat was an envelope with the douanes dispense de caution document granting my barrels their long-awaited freedom. All of my experiences of the last year fit all too neatly into the back of a rented pickup truck. Seeing the barrels together, they didn't look like much. They were wine barrels, no different from any other in the world, and what was inside would simply look like red wine to anyone else. But it wasn't just anybody's red wine, it was *my* red Burgundy. I had poured myself into those barrels too.

With my precious charges riding behind me, I drove home. I passed the rolling hillsides filled with bare vines. They still looked gorgeous even without a leaf in sight. Though I had once driven past these vineyards without knowing what they were called, now they were landmarks I used to get my bearings, and each village recalled a memory of tasting wine. Montrachet from Chassagne-Montrachet, Clos des Chênes in Volnay, Clos des Épenots in Pommard, and Les Saint-Georges in Nuits-Saint-Georges. This panoramic spread from a high-gloss wine magazine was my neighborhood.

It was a snowy January, and the wine had been alive for just four months. But they would now have someplace to rest until they were ready to be placed into bottles, clothed in labels, packaged, and sent off to destinations around the world. That is, once I sold them.

I still didn't know who would buy my wine. I didn't care. My job was to watch over them, protecting them from the elements, and be patient. And if they didn't sell out that was fine. They were mine until they were handed to someone else, and if all else failed, I'd just drink them myself. It didn't seem too unlikely.

It was easy to feel that way, to be proud before I even knew what the results of it all would be. My body ached, my mind filled with snapshots of the vineyards; I prayed I hadn't screwed up anything. No matter what, the wines were mine. But I wasn't rich, and I had no backup plan; sooner or later they'd have to be sold to finance the next vintage. How could I sell them, though? The wine was just as likely to be horrible as it was to be drinkable.

A few groups of people from a US-based wine community had come by to taste at the warehouse winery while I was back in Saint-Aubin just a few short months after my first harvest. The first to visit weren't in the area to visit me; they came for the annual Vente des Vins in Beaune, when the Hospices de Beaune auctions off wines made from vineyards that were donated for charity. It's an event that has gone on for 150 years. The tasting had gone well enough to give me some early confidence, but who knew if they weren't all just being nice.

"Are you sure you made these?"

"Well, I didn't *make* them—"

"These are impressive! Bet *yer* glad you didn't screw 'em up!"

I didn't say as much, but there was still plenty of time for me to make a complete mess. The wines were still young; they hadn't even gone through their second fermentation yet. But who was I to turn away potential buyers?

"Well, I'd be on board to buy some. How much are they?" I had no clue what I was going to sell them for. The thought never crossed my mind that someone would be asking about buying some so early on.

"Can I get back to you?"

"Sure, but put me on your mailing list. Here's my card." Cards came in from everyone in the group. I didn't even have a wallet to put them in, let alone a card of my own. And mailing list? What made them think I had one? Just something else I'd have to figure out on the fly.

BACK AT THE HOUSE WITH the barrels still in the bed of the truck, I realized I'd arrived at yet another step in this process without a plan for how to move forward. I'd known I was going to have a problem getting my barrels into the cave since I first saw its layout. I'd spent the last three months trying to figure out a way to do it, working every angle in my head, jotting down plans, speaking with friends, and still there I was, standing in the court-yard with a truck full of wine and nothing more than a blank sheet to work from.

The sheer weight of the full barrels made it impossible to simply carry them down the stairs. Rolling them would work, but the problem would be to stop their momentum before they crashed against one of the cave walls and exploded. Using the pulley system could work, as it had for the last several hundreds of years. But there was one huge difference between then and now: Those guys knew what they were doing. I was figuring it out for myself, and if one barrel slipped, rope popped, or pulley ripped out of the stone wall, not only would someone get hurt, but the wine would surely be destroyed. I couldn't risk it. Adding to all of this pressure, I was supposed to be on a plane from Paris to San Francisco in less than eighteen hours.

After spending an hour trying to think of the best way to get the barrels into the cave, it became apparent that my ideas were getting worse as the time slipped away. Draining the barrels before moving them down by hand was my best bet. An empty barrel weighed only 120 pounds, versus more than 600 full. I could position them exactly as I wanted, then funnel the wine back in. Even though I was in pretty lousy shape, I could manage to get the barrels down the stairs. The complicated part would be transferring the wine. Too much exposure to the air and the wine would age prematurely, limiting any chance of it gradually maturing for decades, as other red Burgundies do. I sat on the stairs to consider my options. Sitting there I spotted a water hose next to a forklift that Monsieur Gouges let me borrow to take the full barrels out of the truck. It gave me an idea.

I hopped in my car, sped over to the winery supply shop, and grabbed twelve meters of food-grade silicon tubing, about the size of a quarter in diameter. I moved one of my three empty barrels into the cave and placed a full barrel right at the entrance above. Then I put one end of the tube into the full barrel and started suctioning the wine out the other end. It was slow going, but it worked.

I got a bit too proud of my neat siphoning setup and too

confident about how much time I had left on the clock. It looked like I was going to make it. I pulled myself up into the squeaky seat of the forklift, and made my way back to the truck to pick up another load. To line up with the side of the truck properly, I extended my approach angle, not paying much attention to the ground beneath me.

Then I realized: I was stuck.

One of the driving wheels in the rear was caught in the mud. I jumped down and threw some boards under the tire to give it traction, then feathered the gas. The tire finally caught traction, only to toss the board a good ten feet and take off a good piece of an old stone wall nearby. Now the tire was dug in even farther, and part of the forklift's frame was touching the ground. The other rear wheel was a couple feet in the air. I tried everything I could to get the wheel down. I even talked three guys who were passing by into yanking on one side of it while I gave it gas, but it was no use. Meanwhile, the buried tire just spun against the mud and rocks I'd tossed in for traction until an enormous white cloud choked the whole backyard. That was it. It was up to me to finish it all and I blew it.

Then I had another idea. I could call Habib! He had a truck. He could nudge the forklift out of the hole.

"*Salut, Habib. Ça va?*" It was always best when you called your friends, even in emergencies, to ask them how they were doing first.

"*Oui, merci. Et toi, ça va?*" Things were in the shit for me, but I didn't yet know how to say that in French.

"*Oui, ça va.* Well, actually, I'm in a pinch. Are you free?"

"Of course. I'll be right over."

"Could you bring the truck?"

"I'll be there in five minutes." And he was.

He showed up smiling, as usual. He rubbed his beard as he surveyed the forklift situation, then dropped to a crouch and cringed. He rubbed his beard some more, then the top of his head.

"We need to pull it."

"Exactly. Wait, what? You mean *push* it, right?"

"No, pull." He mimed the motion. Had I been in a better mood, it would have been hilarious, but I was just confused.

"Why not push it?"

"Well, I have this rope. This way is much more fun."

"But it's also a whole lot more dangerous, right?"

Shrugging his shoulders, he started tying a rope to the rear bumper of his truck. I didn't argue with his logic—or lack thereof—and tied the other end of the rope to the top of the fork-lift's cage. I had to laugh to myself. It might not work, but something sure as hell was going to happen!

He leaped into his truck, I into the forklift. His arm came out the window with one finger raised. Wait, is he counting? We never said what number we'd go on so I waited for three. His third finger went up and I pushed the thin pedal down. It hit the rubber floorboard with a pathetic thud. My wheels were spinning. But Habib's hand was still out the window. Four? Five fingers? What the? Who goes on five?

He gave it a little gas at first, jerking the forklift up a few inches from the hole while taking out all of the slack of the braided nylon rope. He gave it more gas as my tires squealed and kicked rocks into the wall behind me. The truck started to sway left as it searched for traction, and smoke billowed off the back tires. I could just make out Habib moving the front tires, and then *POPPPPP*! The yellow rope exploded in the middle, the forklift dropped back down, and Habib slammed on the brakes, halting his truck just inches from the retaining wall fifteen feet from where he started.

We both got out and looked at the rope, laughing uncontrollably, buzzed from having barely escaped injury.

He looked serious for a moment. "We should try the new rope this time."

"New rope?"

"Well, I wanted to try the old rope first. The other one hasn't been used yet. I've been waiting for the yellow one to break." What could I say? He was crazy, but his idea was still the best we had.

We tied the rope and tried again, and this time successfully yanked the forklift out of the mud and back onto the cobblestones. I was back in action! Though I was at least an hour behind schedule. Habib offered to stay and help.

As I showed him my process, Habib shook his head at how slowly the barrel was filling up and showed me how to secure the tube more tightly in the barrel with a cloth. His trick made it run about three times more quickly.

We went through four more barrels before he had to get home to his family, and I continued on alone, working into the night. The temperature dropped below freezing, turning the water at the top of the staircase from when I washed the barrels into ice. Even though I wasn't done, I had to wrap things up. The taxi pickup I'd arranged to take me to the train station was scheduled for four thirty A.M, and it would be here any minute.

I took one of the last two barrels down and tried siphoning it, but it didn't work. How had Habib done it before? I started to panic. Should I just start dumping out wine into fruit cases and carrying it down? But I knew rushing that way would screw it up. If I had to change my flight again at least I could do it taking my time. I picked up my phone and started dialing, but then hung up. Christian and Bella were expecting me home, and I couldn't bear the thought of disappointing them. After twenty minutes of tying, I was able to get the wine moving in the hose at a slow but consistent rate. I closed the barrel with a silicon bung and ran upstairs, scrambling to get the last barrel over to the cave from in front of the garage.

Hoooooonk hoooonk honk honk hooonk!

The taxi was here, and five minutes late. *Shit.* I was screwed. What was I going to do with one of my barrels outside?

I didn't like it, but I knew what I had to do. I ran out to the taxi and said I needed a minute, tossing my bag in before he could protest. Then I inched the barrel into the garage instead of toward the cave. I closed the doors and stood there hoping I'd done the right thing.

Hooooooooonnnnkkkkkk!!!!!

The taxi driver was standing by the car with my bag in his hand.

"Are we going to the train station or not?"

"Please, let's go."

"You're going to Paris?"

"Yes, to Charles de Gaulle Airport."

"You aren't going to make it. The train leaves Nuits-Saint-Georges in two minutes. But let's see what we can do."

Three minutes later we were at the station. All the lights were off. No one was standing outside. I had missed it.

But I heard a train coming.

"Is this the train with the connection to Paris, Charles de Gaulle?" I asked the train employee when it stopped.

"*Bien sûr, on est en retard.*" It was my train after all! It had just been delayed.

I shook his hand and found a seat inside the car, freezing and sweating at the same time. The image of the cave filled with my barrels, their vineyard names written with chalk in awkward left-handed cursive, burned into my memory. It was an image I was going to preserve for the rest of my life.

But I still had the problem of the barrel in the garage. I sank deeply into my seat and closed my eyes, hoping a solution would come to me by the time I woke.

Rrriiinnnnggggg. . . . rrrriiinnnngggg!!!!!!!

Whose damned phone is that? I opened my eyes to see that I was the only one in the train car. It was six o'clock, and the morning light was nothing more than a faint blue. It was pretty, but the sun coming into view drove nails into my sleep-deprived eyes.

"*Allô?*"

"*Oui*, Ray?"

"*Uh, bonjour.* Who is this?"

"It's me, Sasha. We met at the winery in Beaune." I had to plumb the depths of my memory to conjure up who he was. Then I remembered—we'd talked at length about our work in wine, and I'd told him the entire saga about how I'd needed to move my barrels. But when we parted ways we'd done nothing but exchange contact info, his business card, my chicken scratch on a piece of scrap paper. "Have you moved your barrels to Vosne-Romanée?"

"Nuits-Saint-Georges."

"Oh. Yes, Nuits. Are they safe?"

"Not all of them." I spoke through my yawn.

"You just waking up?"

"No, I'm just going to sleep."

"So, your barrels. Are they good? You said you were leaving tomorrow. Do you need any help? I'm just out at the vines. We are going home early today."

"I'm leaving today. Well, now. I'm already on the train. And the barrels are fine, but one is still in the garage."

"This isn't a good place for a barrel, you know. You don't have a cave?"

"I have a cave. I just ran out of time."

"I can help."

"It's too much work."

"How many barrels?"

"Just the one. But it's complicated."

"Tell me."

"Well, you'd have to siphon the wine out and into the last empty barrel already in the cave."

"What is the complicated part?"

He was up for it. I guess it was a good thing I got business cards after all.

I explained that he'd need to go over to the Gouges family's domaine to get the keys to my house, which was just around the corner. I gave him the rundown of the system I'd used and asked that once the wine was transferred into the cave he mark it as "Morey-Saint-Denis 1er Cru Les Chaffots."

"That's it?" he said.

"That's it. You are doing me a huge favor." I had gone nearly the whole harvest priding myself on doing every last detail myself, but at that moment I realized just how many people there were who I couldn't have done it without.

"Ray, we'll call you when we're done."

I dozed off after thanking him again.

The phone started ringing again less than an hour later.

"We're done."

"How did you finish so quickly? Did the siphoning go OK?"

"No, that wasn't going to work. We just picked it up and carried it down. More simple that way." I could barely hold on to the phone.

"You *carried* a full barrel down?"

"There were five of us, so we figured it would be better. I hope that was OK."

Why hadn't I thought of that?

"What's your address? I'd like to pay you for your help."

"*Non, c'est normal.* It's nothing. Have a good trip home. The keys are already back with the *famille* Gouges. Hey, gotta run. *Salut!*"

Just then, the loud speaker came on: "*Paris! Paris! Paris! Bienvenue à la Gare de Lyon!!!*" Well, that was about right. Who needed sleep anyway? I was too busy living my dream.

CHAPTER TWENTY-TWO

"*Une autre tarte framboises?*" The owner of the pastry shop looked worried for me. Every two days I'd come looking to buy three large tarts—one for me, another for Christian and Bella, and the third for whoever got there first. "*Ce n'est pas bon pour la santé.*" She waved her powder-coated finger at me. "I don't want to see you fat because of me." I didn't see what she was fussing about; it was just a handful of raspberries, though encased in sugar, layers of luscious butter, and heavenly cream. But shamed like a French schoolboy I crept out with just one lonely tart. It was all right; I'd be back the next day.

After two months at home in Novato, we packed up our belongings, gave the keys back to the landlord, and officially relocated our little family to Nuits. I knew Christian was going to miss home more than I was. Most of her family from Nicaragua lived nearby in San Francisco, whereas my family was much more spread out between Sacramento, Stockton, Richmond, and Oakland, and I didn't see them too often. I figured moving to France might even encourage more visits. It was difficult leaving behind the only part of the world we knew so intimately. We were taking the leap into uncertainty together, unsure of exactly where we would land. Though as long as we had each other, we knew that we would have everything that really mattered to us.

Now it was spring, and we were settled into our new home. We felt like we belonged here, but it was still a fairy tale. Of course there were the hillside vineyards with more than a thousand years of history that we could see out of our living room window, and the boulangeries, bouchers charcuterie, chocolatière, pâtisseries, and marchés brimming with some of the most beautiful food I'd ever seen. It inspired me to try to cook some of the dishes I'd seen at the local restaurants, and I soon became that guy walking around the market with a wicker basket filled with local fruit, fish, and meats, Christian and Bella at my side.

But France is more than a pretty place with amazing food and wine. We learned people take their time and enjoy speaking with one another. They look forward to visiting the butcher because she always has a bit of insight about the growing season or local politics, or the fishmonger for her cutting humor. They ask how someone is doing and mean it, then listen patiently to their response. They check on neighbors because they haven't seen them in a while. It isn't going through the motions of life just to get to the next day, the next paycheck. It's living, enjoying time, and letting it slowly slip by, knowing that you can't possibly be happier in any other place than the one where you already are. There is enjoyment to be found in time passing by if it is filled with as many moments with meaning and pleasure as possible.

I wanted to slow down and enjoy the lifestyle, especially now that my wines were in-barrel, but I had been pushing myself at a breakneck speed for a year and didn't know how to turn that mechanism off. Every day I'd go into the cave and just stare at the barrels. Even though I'd vowed to let the earth and the magic of time give my wine its personality, it felt strange to have nothing left to do but wait.

While I was struggling with doing nothing, the wines were busier than ever. Every few days I'd draw out a pipette of each cuvée, amazed to taste the changes. They once tasted similar to one another, but with time, their individual voices became clearer. Their aromas, flavors, textures, and intensities were unmistakably their own. The Les Chaffots was forward, lush, powerful, and intense, with wild fruit. The Charmes-Chambertin was the most aggressive of the bunch, with incredibly up-front aromas and flavors of ripe blackberries. The texture was far silkier than that of the Les Chaffots and the flavors notably more complex. Each time I took a drink, there was even more depth and detail that demanded attention. The Chambertin tasted as if it had come from a different type of grape, it was so distinct from the other two. There is no way to accurately describe the nature of the Chambertin. It was delicate in one moment, powerful in the next, focused as specific flavors rose, but then beautifully inexplicable. While my Chaffots and Charmes had layers, the Chambertin was spherical—harder to pin down, and rotating constantly. But each sniff or taste was a full, even transcendental experience. What I was most proud of in breathing in and tasting my wines was that I was instantly taken back to the land, being able to connect the history that I'd read so much about along with the feeling I had while walking through those very vineyards. That connection was something at once magical while being just as real as anything else in the world around me.

Once in a while I'd have a visitor come by for a tasting. I never advertised; people would somehow just find their way to our front door after reading something about me on the Internet or in an article in *Bloomberg*, *Wine Spectator*, or *The New York Times*. It didn't matter to me; if they loved wine, we were going to get along just fine. I didn't have a hook to describe the wines. They were changing so quickly that just as soon as I thought I'd gotten to know them, they'd take on a completely different expression. In one minute they would be shy, not showing much, the next they'd have their beauty on full display. I was so close to them that I had no way of objectively judging them. I thought my wines were good, sometimes great, but mostly they just tasted like my wines.

There was a local guy who always poked his head in through my courtyard doors whenever they were open, so one day I had him over for a tasting. Neither of us said much through the proceedings, which was pretty normal in my cave. He asked the occasional question about where the vineyards were located, but offered no notes on the wines. But when I offered a taste from the final barrel of 2009 Chambertin, he performed an elaborate ritual closing his eyes, sniffing for what seemed like five minutes, tasting and letting the wine slowly reveal itself, then finally swallowing. Smiling, he said, "Pure. All of them . . . pure."

Soon wine lovers who had visited started buzzing on wine forums about what I was doing, and even more people began to show up. It was a shock to me that anyone would want to come all the way to Burgundy from places like Manhattan, Chicago, San Francisco, Tokyo, and Ontario to spend time learning about what I had in my ten barrels. I still had a hard time hyping my wine, so I focused on showing people my one-car garage winery and talking about the history of the region, the concept of terroir, and how things used to be done. I would tell them about the small amount of oak I'd used and why in the first vintage, how I'd foregone the typical rigorous punching down, all of the additives I'd chosen not to add, and how exactly these barrels came to rest in that very spot—forklift accident and all. They enjoyed hearing the stories and adventures I'd had, and learning how I'd ended up in Burgundy, with my family along for the ride.

Not three years ago, I had spent months worrying about whether I'd ever find buyers, but through word of mouth on the Internet and after a few articles were published about our wines and story, we were able to sell out all of our wine from the first vintage in a matter of weeks, only a year after harvesting the grapes. Our mailing list ballooned from eighty people to a little more than a thousand before I picked my grapes for the second harvest.

I never expected my wines to be something people would actually look for. I assumed I'd have to sell them a bottle at a time by going to trade tastings or public wine events. Even though I didn't know of any other producers in Burgundy doing it, I wanted to be able to establish direct relationships with our customers. I didn't want someone to learn about my wines from a restaurant menu, some stale importer literature, or a generic blurb on a wine shop's website. I wanted to see faces at the winery of those that would someday enjoy the product I'd worked to create. I needed that connection and to share a piece of myself with people who would appreciate it most. It meant everything to me. The experience of those who supported us, and our relationship, mattered most.

For our first two vintages, the critics had praised our wines with colorful commentary and scored them high, putting them shoulder to shoulder with some of the most revered names in the world of wine. But though the attention was overwhelmingly positive, it made me uncomfortable. Wine doesn't care what people say. It doesn't improve or decline based on a number. To me, the one thing the scores change is the experience of the taster.

Suddenly someone isn't drinking a Morey-Saint-Denis premier cru from 2010; he's drinking a ninety-one-point wine. The points and descriptions put a living thing into a rigid framework. It's like relying on CliffsNotes. Gone are the taster's first impressions, the guesswork of discovering a wine and learning about it firsthand.

Finally, I decided to do something drastic that would make most winemakers—if they didn't already—think I had completely lost my mind: I publicly asked the professional wine critics to not review them again. The critics were welcome to taste, and I personally invited them to do so, but I didn't want their subjective stamp of approval or disapproval. I know it sounds like I may have been playing it safe in case my wines weren't good enough. But I knew that wasn't the case. It was written all over the face of everyone who tasted them. Ratings devalued what I believed made wine—especially Burgundy wine—so special.

Such a large part of what makes wine special is that no two people will ever see the exact same thing inside a bottle. The memories and experiences they've lived through, the things they've seen, smelled, and tasted—all of that informs a person's connection. It is a pure and entirely personal discovery, and I didn't want that tainted by another point of view, mine included. Even when someone came for a visit and asked me to describe the sensory experience of our wine, I didn't dare say a word. I felt strongly that my impressions shouldn't matter.

It was a big risk to lose the ratings. I knew people were already wary of my being such a small producer, and damn near a rookie at that. But I couldn't see doing it any other way. I'm thankful that none of the critics who had previously reviewed my wines made a fuss. Instead, they asked about coming for tastings off the clock.

We're now at full capacity, expecting forty barrels' worth of grapes in a full vintage. Still, there never seems to be enough for us to hold on to much wine for Christian and myself, let alone for the girls and the families they'll one day have.

WE'VE BEEN IN FRANCE FOR three years now. These days, we are all speaking a great deal more French. I'm still scouring my old books, looking for once-cherished but recently forgotten vineyards. Christian goes to school in Dijon to study French, has taken an interest in learning to cook traditional French food, and keeps busy with me during harvest. She gave birth to our second daughter, Siena Jesline, in Dijon after our third harvest. She's still a city girl, and her heart still lies in San Francisco, but she always finds something new to love in Burgundy. Isabella Ilan has now lived a majority of her life here in the Côte d'Or. After going to school in Nuits for the past two years, she now has enough language skills to switch back and forth fluently, and she likes to teach me new words and songs.

The people we have met along the way have made for unforgettable memories, filled with laughs, frustration, celebrations, doubts, determination, and triumphs. I consistently wonder what else but wine could have brought so much needed passion into our lives. I rarely look back on how things used to be, and when I do I never second-guess the decisions that I've made. There's barely a day that goes by when I don't recognize with awe just how potent our fantasies can be. I wouldn't dare call any of this fate. I worked too damn hard for that. But what I do believe is that where there's a dream, there's a way to make it a reality. And if you're brave enough to dream it, everything you need is already inside of you.

ACKNOWLEDGMENTS

Mom and Dad, it has always been a gift to have your love and support.

Richard, thank you for being such a loving and caring brother.

Thank you to everyone who looked me in the eyes and supported me regardless of the odds in front of me.

For your timeless guidance:

André Jullien
Topographie de tous les vignobles connus (1816)

Dr. Denis Morelot
Statistique de la vigne dans le département de la Cote-d'Or (1831)

Dr. Jean "Jules" Lavalle
Histoire et statistique de la vigne des grands vins de la Cote d'Or (1855)